Following God

Leader's Guide

Leader's Guide

for the Bible Study Series by

Wayne Barber

Eddie Rasnake

Richard Shepherd

AMG
PUBLISHERS
Chattanooga, TN 37422

Following God
LEADER'S GUIDE

© 2000 by Eddie Rasnake and Richard L. Shepherd

Published by AMG Publishers
All Rights Reserved.

ISBN: 0-89957-306-1

Printed in the United States of America
05 04 03 02 01 00 –RO– 6 5 4 3 2 1

Preface

A Leader's Guide is for leaders. What does it mean to be a leader? The apostle Paul stands as one of the most noteworthy leaders in all of human history. In 1 Corinthians 3:10, Paul states, *"According to the grace of God which was given to me, as a wise master builder I laid a foundation, and another is building upon it. But let each man be careful how he builds upon it."* Upon close examination, that verse speaks volumes about leadership. As a small group leader you are building on a foundation laid by someone before you. What is the counsel of the Holy Spirit to us through the apostle Paul? What was he saying to the Corinthians that applies to us today?

First, Paul speaks of being a wise master builder. The Greek word he uses for master builder, *architekton*, is where we get our word, "architect." But *architekton* pictures more than simply the act of designing a building. It comes from two root words: *arche,* meaning "beginning," "origin," or "the person that begins something" and *tekton,* which means "bringing forth," "begetting," or "giving birth." *Architekton* carries the idea of one who leads forth, who goes first, who is the first to bring something to light. As a small group leader, you have the opportunity to guide people in the discovery of what it means to follow God. As you discuss each of the lessons and the people you will meet in those lessons, you and your group will learn some eternal truths about what it means to follow Jesus day by day.

Paul speaks of another aspect of being a Spirit-filled leader, and it is the essential work of *"the grace of God."* All Paul did, all he taught, every spiritual truth he helped others to see, was by the grace of God. It should be the same for you. You must depend on the Lord to be the Teacher for these lessons. By His Spirit, He will guide you in understanding His Word and His ways with His children. He will open the pages of Scripture. He alone knows the heart of each group member, and He alone has the wisdom you and your group need to walk through these lessons and to make the applications to daily life.

In 1 Corinthians 3:10, the Greek word for *"building"* refers to continuous, ongoing building, and pictures placing brick upon brick, stone upon stone. We are building day by day as we spend time with the Lord in His Word and obey what He is teaching us. As you walk through each lesson week after week, another stone can be added to the life of each group member, another truth can be built into each life, and another set of truths can be added to what God is doing in you as a group. Each group will be unique. Each week will be unique. The creativity and work of the Spirit of God will ebb and flow in different ways in each heart and in the group as a whole. You as a leader have the opportunity to encourage your group to be watching for the building work of the Spirit of God. Some insights will come when each is alone with the Lord. Other insights will not be seen until you come together as a group. The Spirit of God uses both means. It is a continuous adventure of discovering more about Him, His ways, and what it means to follow Him.

With this Leader's Guide, we want to come alongside and help you lead your small group in **following God** more closely and more consistently. Be a focused, attentive leader/builder. Paul said *"let **each** man be careful how he builds."* That means each of us. No one is exempt. As a small group facilitator, you will have the opportunity to lead others and experience one of the greatest times of building lives. Let us lead as *"careful"* builders depending on the grace and the wisdom of God.

Following His Leadership,

Wayne A. Barber

Eddie Rasnake

Richard L. Shepherd

V

Table of Contents

How to Lead a
Small Group Bible Study 1

Life Principles from the Old Testament
Adam, Noah, Job, Abraham, Lot, Jacob,
Joseph, Moses, Caleb, Joshua, Gideon, Samson 17

Life Principles from
the Kings of the Old Testament
Saul, David, Solomon, Jeroboam I, Asa, Ahab, Jehoshaphat,
Hezekiah, Josiah, Zerubbabel and Ezra,
Nehemiah, The True King 57

Life Principles from the Prophets
of the Old Testament
Samuel, Elijah, Elisha, Jonah, Hosea, Isaiah, Micah, Jeremiah,
Habakkuk, Daniel, Haggai, Christ the Prophet 97

Life Principles from the
Women of the Bible
Eve, Sarah, Miriam, Rahab, Deborah, Ruth, Hannah,
Esther, The Virtuous Woman, Mary and Martha,
Mary Mother of Jesus, The Bride of Christ 137

Life Principles from the
New Testament Men of Faith
John the Baptist, Peter, John, Thomas, James, Barnabas,
Paul, Paul's Companions, Timothy, The Son of Man 177

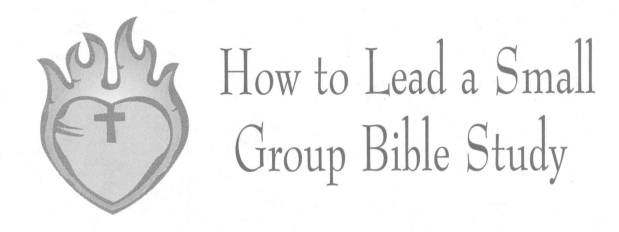

How to Lead a Small Group Bible Study

Causes of a Poor Study Group 3

Helpful Hints 5

Evaluation: Becoming
a Better Discussion Leader 11

Getting Started: The First Meeting
of Your Bible Study Group 13

Causes of a Poor Study Group

The best way to become a better discussion leader is to regularly evaluate your group discussion sessions. The most effective leaders are those who consistently look for ways to improve.

But before you start preparing for your first group session, you need to know the problem areas that will most likely weaken the effectiveness of your study group. Commit now to have the best Bible study group that you can possibly have. Ask the Lord to motivate you as a group leader and to steer you away from bad habits.

How to Guarantee a Poor Discussion Group:

1. Prepare inadequately.
2. Show improper attitude toward people in the group (lack of acceptance).
3. Fail to create an atmosphere of freedom and ease.
4. Allow the discussion to wander aimlessly.
5. Dominate the discussion yourself.
6. Let a small minority dominate the discussion.
7. Leave the discussion "in the air," so to speak, without presenting any concluding statements or some type of closure.
8. Ask too many "telling" or "trying" questions. (Don't ask individuals in your group pointed or threatening questions that might bring embarrassment to them or make them feel uncomfortable.)
9. End the discussion without adequate application points.
10. Do the same thing every time.
11. Become resentful and angry when people disagree with you. After all, you did prepare. You are the leader!
12. End the discussion with an argument.
13. Never spend any time with the members of your group other than the designated discussion meeting time.

Helpful Hints

One of the best ways to learn to be an effective Bible discussion leader is to sit under a good model. If you have had the chance to be in a group with an effective facilitator, think about the things that made him or her effective. Though you can learn much and shape many convictions from those good models, you can also glean some valuable lessons on what not to do from those who didn't do such a good job. Bill Donahue has done a good job of categorizing the leader's role in facilitating dynamic discussion into four key actions. They are easy to remember as he links them to the acrostic ACTS:

*A leader ACTS to facilitate discussions by:

Acknowledging everyone who speaks during a discussion.

Clarifying what is being said and felt.

Taking it to the group as a means of generating discussion.

Summarizing what has been said.

*Taken from *Leading Life-Changing Small Groups* ©1996 by the Willow Creek Association. Used by permission of Zondervan Publishing House.

Make a point to give each group member ample opportunity to speak. Pay close attention to any nonverbal communication (i.e. facial expressions, body language, etc.) that group members may use, showing their desire to speak. The four actions in Bill Donahue's acrostic will guarantee to increase your effectiveness, which will translate into your group getting more out of the Bible study. After all, isn't that your biggest goal?

Dealing with Talkative Timothy

Throughout your experiences of leading small Bible study groups, you will learn that there will be several stereotypes who will follow you wherever you go. One of them is **"Talkative Timothy."** He will show up in virtually every small group you will ever lead. (Sometimes this stereotype group member shows up as "Talkative Tammy.") "Talkative Timothy" talks too much, dominates the discussion time, and gives less opportunity for others to share. What do you do with a group member who talks too much? Below you will find some helpful ideas on managing the "Talkative Timothy's" in your group.

The best defense is a good offense. To deal with "Talkative Timothy" before he becomes a problem, one thing you can do is establish as a ground rule that no one can talk twice until everyone who wants to talk has spoken at least once. Another important ground rule is "no interrupting." Still another solution is to go systematically around the group, directing questions to people by name. When all else fails, you can resort to a very practical approach of sitting beside "Talkative Timothy." When you make it harder for him (or her) to make eye contact with you, you will create less chances for him to talk.

After taking one or more of these combative measures, you may find that "Timothy" is still a problem. You may need to meet with him (or her) privately. Assure him that you value his input, but remind him that you want to hear the comments of others as well. One way to diplomatically approach "Timothy" is to privately ask him to help you draw the less talkative members into the discussion. Approaching "Timothy" in this fashion may turn your dilemma into an asset. Most importantly, remember to love "Talkative Timothy."

Silent Sally

Another person who inevitably shows up is **"Silent Sally."** She doesn't readily speak up. Sometimes her silence is because she doesn't yet feel comfortable enough with the group to share her thoughts. Sometimes it is simply because she fears being rejected. Often her silence is because she is too polite to interrupt and thus is headed off at the pass each time she wants to speak by more aggressive (and less sensitive) members of the group. It is not uncommon in a mixed group to find that "Silent Sally" is married to "Talkative Timothy." (Seriously!) Don't mistakenly interpret her silence as meaning that she has nothing to contribute. Often those who are slowest to speak will offer the most meaningful contributions to the group. You can help "Silent Sally" make those significant contributions. Below are some ideas.

Make sure, first of all, that you are creating an environment that makes people comfortable. In a tactful way, direct specific questions to the less talkative in the group. Be careful though, not to put them on the spot with the more difficult or controversial questions. Become their biggest fan—make sure you cheer them on when they do share. Give them a healthy dose of affirmation. Compliment them afterward for any insightful contributions they make. You may want to sit across from them in the group so that it is easier to notice any non-verbal cues they give you when they want to speak. You should also come to their defense if another group member responds to them in a negative, stifling way. As you pray for each group member, ask that the Lord would help the quiet ones in your group to feel more at ease during the discussion time. Most of all, love "Silent Sally," and accept her as she is—even when she is silent!

Tangent Tom

We have already looked at "Talkative Timothy" and "Silent Sally." Now let's look at another of those stereotypes who always show up. Let's call this person, **"Tangent Tom."** He is the kind of guy who loves to talk even when he has nothing to say. "Tangent Tom" loves to chase rabbits regardless of where they go. When he gets the floor, you never know where the discussion will lead. You need to understand that not all tangents are bad, for sometimes much can be gained from discussion that is a little "off the beaten path." But diversions must be balanced against the purpose of the group. What is fruitful for one member may be fruitless for everyone else. Below are some ideas to help you deal with "Tangent Tom."

Evaluating Tangents

Ask yourself, "How will this tangent affect my group's chances of finishing the lesson?" Another way to measure the value of a tangent is by asking, "Is this something that will benefit all or most of the group?" You also need to determine whether there is a practical, spiritual benefit to this tangent. Paul advised Timothy to refuse foolish and ignorant speculations, knowing that they produce quarrels. (See 2 Timothy 2:23.)

Addressing Tangents:

1) Keep pace of your time, and use the time factor as your ally when addressing "Tangent Tom." Tactfully respond, "That is an interesting subject, but since our lesson is on _____, we'd better get back to our lesson if we are going to finish."

2) If the tangent is beneficial to one but fruitless to the rest of the group, offer to address that subject after class.

3) If the tangent is something that will benefit the group, you may want to say, "I'd like to talk about that more. Let's come back to that topic at the end of today's discussion, if we have time."

4) Be sure you understand what "Tangent Tom" is trying to say. It may be that he has a good and valid point, but has trouble expressing it or needs help in being more direct. Be careful not to quench someone whose heart is right, even if his methods aren't perfect. (See Proverbs 18:23.)

5) One suggestion for diffusing a strife-producing tangent is to point an imaginary shotgun at a spot outside the group and act like you are firing a shot. Then say, "That rabbit is dead. Now, where were we?"

6) If it is a continual problem, you may need to address it with this person privately.

7) Most of all, be patient with "Tangent Tom." God will use him in the group in ways that will surprise you!

Know-It-All Ned

The Scriptures are full of characters who struggled with the problem of pride. Unfortunately, pride isn't a problem reserved for the history books. It shows up today just as it did in the days the Scriptures were written. Pride is sometimes the root-problem of a know-it-all group member. **"Know-It-All Ned"** may have shown up in your group by this point. He may be an intellectual giant, or only a legend in his own mind. He can be very prideful and argumentative. "Ned" often wants his point chosen as the choice point, and he may be intolerant of any opposing views—sometimes to the point of making his displeasure known in very inappropriate ways. A discussion point tainted with the stench of pride is uninviting—no matter how well spoken! No one else in the group will want anything to do with this kind of attitude. How do you manage the "Know-It-All Ned's" who show up from time to time?

Evaluation

To deal with "Know-It-All Ned," you need to understand him. Sometimes the same type of action can be rooted in very different causes. You must ask yourself, "Why does 'Ned' come across as a know-it-all?" It may be that "Ned" has a vast reservoir of knowledge but hasn't matured in how he communicates it. Or perhaps "Ned" really doesn't know it all, but he tries to come across that way to hide his insecurities and feelings of inadequacy. Quite possibly, "Ned" is prideful and arrogant, and knows little of the Lord's ways in spite of the information and facts he has accumulated. Still another possibility is that Ned is a good man with a good heart who has a blind spot in the area of pride.

Application

"Know-It-All Ned" may be the most difficult person to deal with in your group, but God will use him in ways that will surprise you. Often it is the "Ned's" of the church that teach each of us what it means to love the unlovely in Gods strength, not our own. In 1 Thessalonians 5:14, the apostle Paul states, *"And we urge you, brethren, admonish the unruly, encourage the fainthearted, help the weak, be patient with all men."* In dealing with the "Ned's" you come across, start by assuming they are weak and need help until they give you reason to believe otherwise. Don't embarrass them by confronting them in public. Go to them in private if need be. Speak the truth in love. You may need to remind them of 1 Corinthians 13, that if we have all knowledge, but have not love, we are just making noise. First Corinthians is also where we are told, *"knowledge makes arrogant, but love edifies"* (8:1). Obviously there were some "Ned's" in the church at Corinth. If you sense that "Ned" is not weak or faint-hearted, but in fact is unruly, you will need to admonish him. Make sure you do so in private, but make sure you do it all the same. Proverbs 27:56 tells us, *"Better is open rebuke than love that is concealed. Faithful are the wounds of a friend, but deceitful are the kisses of an enemy."* Remember the last statement in 1 Thessalonians 5:14, *"be patient with all men."*

Agenda Alice

The last person we would like to introduce to you who will probably show up sooner or later is one we like to call **"Agenda Alice."** All of us from time to time can be sidetracked by our own agenda. Often the very thing we are most passionate about can be the thing that distracts us from our highest passion: Christ. Agendas often are not unbiblical, but imbalanced. At their root is usually tunnel-vision mixed with a desire for control. The small group, since it allows everyone to contribute to the discussion, affords "Agenda Alice" a platform to promote what she thinks is most important. This doesn't mean that she is wrong to avoid driving at night because opossums are being killed, but she is wrong to expect everyone to have the exact same conviction and calling that she does in the gray areas of Scripture. If not managed properly, she will either sidetrack the group from its main study objective or create a hostile environment in the group if she fails to bring people to her way of thinking. "Agenda Alice" can often be recognized by introductory catch phrases such as "Yes, but . . ." and "Well, I think. . . ." She is often critical of the group process and may become vocally critical of you. Here are some ideas on dealing with this type of person:

1) **Reaffirm** the group covenant.

At the formation of your group you should have taken time to define some ground rules for the group. Once is not enough to discuss these matters of group etiquette. Periodically remind everyone of their mutual commitment to one another.

2) **Remember** that the best defense is a good offense.

Don't wait until it is a problem to address a mutual vision for how the group will function.

3) **Refocus** on the task at hand.

The clearer you explain the objective of each session, the easier it is to stick to that objective and the harder you make it for people to redirect attention toward their own agenda. Enlist the whole group in bringing the discussion back to the topic at hand. Ask questions like, "What do the rest of you think about this passage?"

4) **Remind** the group, "Remember, this week's lesson is about _____."

5) **Reprove** those who are disruptive.

Confront the person in private to see if you can reach an understanding. Suggest another arena for the issue to be addressed such as an optional meeting for those in the group who would like to discuss the issue.

Remember the words of St. Augustine: "In essentials unity, in non-essentials liberty, in all things charity."

Adding Spice and Creativity

One of the issues you will eventually have to combat in any group Bible study is the enemy of boredom. This enemy raises its ugly head from time to time, but it shouldn't. It is wrong to bore people with the Word of God! Often boredom results when leaders allow their processes to become too predictable. As small group leaders, we tend to do the same thing in the same way every single time. Yet God the Creator, who spoke everything into existence is infinitely creative! Think about it. He is the one who not only created animals in different shapes and sizes, but different colors as well. When He created food, He didn't make it all taste or feel the same. This God of creativity lives in us. We can trust Him to give us creative ideas that will keep our group times from becoming tired and mundane. Here are some ideas:

When you think of what you can change in your Bible study, think of the five senses: (sight, sound, smell, taste, and feel).

SIGHT:

One idea would be to have a theme night with decorations. Perhaps you know someone with dramatic instincts who could dress up in costume and deliver a message from the person you are studying that week. Draw some cartoons on a marker board or handout.

SOUND:

Play some background music before your group begins. Sing a hymn together that relates to the lesson. If you know of a song that really hits the main point of the lesson, play it at the beginning or end.

SMELL:

This may be the hardest sense to involve in your Bible study, but if you think of a creative way to incorporate this sense into the lesson, you can rest assured it will be memorable for your group.

TASTE:

Some lessons will have issues that can be related to taste (e.g. unleavened bread for the Passover, etc.). What about making things less formal by having snacks while you study? Have refreshments around a theme such as "Chili Night" or "Favorite Fruits."

FEEL:

Any way you can incorporate the sense of feel into a lesson will certainly make the content more invigorating. If weather permits, add variety by moving your group outside. Whatever you do, be sure that you don't allow your Bible study to become boring!

Handling an Obviously Wrong Comment

From time to time, each of us can say stupid things. Some of us, however, are better at it than others. The apostle Peter had his share of embarrassing moments. One minute, he was on the pinnacle of success, saying, *"Thou art the Christ, the Son of the Living God"* (Matthew 16:16), and the next minute, he was putting his foot in his mouth, trying to talk Jesus out of going to the cross. Proverbs 10:19 states, *"When there are many words, transgression is unavoidable. . . ."* What do you do when someone in the group says something that is obviously wrong? First of all, remember that how you deal with a situation like this not only affects the present, but the future. Here are some ideas:

1) Let the whole group tackle it and play referee/peacemaker. Say something like, "That is an interesting thought, what do the rest of you think?"

2) Empathize. ("I've thought that before too, but the Bible says. . . .")

3) Clarify to see if what they said is what they meant. ("What I think you are saying is. . . .")

4) Ask the question again, focusing on what the Bible passage actually says.

5) Give credit for the part of the answer that is right and affirm that before dealing with what is wrong.

6) If it is a non-essential, disagree agreeably. ("I respect your opinion, but I see it differently.")
   Let it go —some things aren't important enough to make a big deal about them.

7) Love and affirm the person, even if you reject the answer.

Transitioning to the Next Study

For those of you who have completed leading a **Following God** Group Bible Study, congratulations! You have successfully navigated the waters of small group discussion. You have utilized one of the most effective tools of ministry—one that was so much a priority with Jesus, He spent most of His time there with His small group of twelve. Hopefully yours has been a very positive and rewarding experience. At this stage you may be looking forward to a break. It is not too early however, to be thinking and planning for what you will do next. Hopefully you have seen God use this study and this process for growth in the lives of those who have participated with you. As God has worked in the group, members should be motivated to ask the question, "What next?" As they do, you need to be prepared to give an answer. Realize that you have built a certain amount of momentum with your present study that will make it easier to do another. You want to take advantage of that momentum. The following suggestions may be helpful as you transition your people toward further study of God's Word.

❑ Challenge your group members to share with others what they have learned, and to encourage them to participate next time.

❑ If what to study is a group choice rather than a church-wide or ministry-wide decision made by others, you will want to allow some time for input from the group members in deciding what to do next. The more they have ownership of the study, the more they will commit to it.

❑ It is important to have some kind of a break so that everyone doesn't become study weary. At our church, we always look for natural times to start and end a study. We take the summer off as well as Christmas, and we have found that having a break brings people back with renewed vigor. Even if you don't take a break from meeting, you might take a breather from homework—or even get together just for fellowship.

❑ If you are able to end this study knowing what you will study next, some of your group members may want to get a head start on the next study. Be prepared to put books in their hands early.

❑ Make sure you end your study with a vision for more. Take some time to remind your group of the importance of the Word of God. As D. L. Moody used to say, "The only way to keep a broken vessel full is to keep the faucet running."

Evaluation
Becoming a Better Discussion Leader

The questions listed below are tools to assist you in assessing your discussion group. From time to time in the Leader's Guide, you will be advised to read through this list of evaluation questions in order to help you decide what areas need improvement in your role as group leader. Each time you read through this list, something different may catch your attention, giving you tips on how to become the best group leader that you can possibly be.

Read through these questions with an open mind, asking the Lord to prick your heart with anything specific He would want you to apply.

1. Are the group discussion sessions beginning and ending on time?
2. Am I allowing the freedom of the Holy Spirit as I lead the group in the discussion?
3. Do I hold the group accountable for doing their homework?
4. Do we always begin our sessions with prayer?
5. Is the room arranged properly (seating in a circle or semicircle, proper ventilation, adequate teaching aids)?
6. Is each individual allowed equal opportunity in the discussion?
7. Do I successfully bridle the talkative ones?
8. Am I successfully encouraging the hesitant ones to participate in the discussion?
9. Do I redirect comments and questions to involve more people in the interaction, or do I always dominate the discussion?
10. Are the discussions flowing naturally, or do they take too many "side roads" (diversions)?
11. Do I show acceptance to those who convey ideas with which I do not agree?
12. Are my questions specific, brief and clear?
13. Do my questions provoke thought, or do they only require pat answers?
14. Does each group member feel free to contribute or question, or is there a threatening or unnecessarily tense atmosphere?
15. Am I allowing time for silence and thought without making everyone feel uneasy?
16. Am I allowing the group to correct any obviously wrong conclusions that are made by others, or by myself (either intentionally to capture the group's attention or unintentionally)?
17. Do I stifle thought and discussion by assigning a question to someone before the subject of that question has even been discussed? (It will often be productive to assign a question to a specific person, but if you call on one person before you throw out a question, everyone else takes a mental vacation!)
18. Do I summarize when brevity is of the essence?
19. Can I refrain from expressing an opinion or comment that someone else in the group could just as adequately express?

20. Do I occasionally vary in my methods of conducting the discussion?

21. Am I keeping the group properly motivated?

22. Am I occasionally rotating the leadership to help others develop leadership?

23. Am I leading the group to specifically apply the truths that are learned?

24. Do I follow through by asking the group how they have applied the truths that they have learned from previous lessons?

25. Am I praying for each group member?

26. Is there a growing openness and honesty among my group members?

27. Are the group study sessions enriching the lives of my group members?

28. Have I been adequately prepared?

29. How may I be better prepared for the next lesson's group discussion?

30. Do I reach the objective set for each discussion? If not, why not? What can I do to improve?

31. Am I allowing the discussion to bog down on one point at the expense of the rest of the lesson?

32. Are the members of the group individually reaching the conclusions that I want them to reach without my having to give them the conclusions?

33. Do I encourage the group members to share what they have learned?

34. Do I encourage them to share the applications they have discovered?

35. Do I whet their appetites for next week's lesson discussion?

Getting Started
The First Meeting of Your Bible Study Group

Main Objectives of the first meeting: The first meeting is devoted to establishing your group and setting the course that you will follow through the study. Your primary goals for this session should be to . . .

- ❏ Establish a sense of group identity by starting to get to know one another.
- ❏ Define some ground rules to help make the group time as effective as possible.
- ❏ Get the study materials into the hands of your group members.
- ❏ Create a sense of excitement and motivation for the study.
- ❏ Give assignments for next week.

BEFORE THE SESSION

You will be most comfortable in leading this introductory session if you are prepared as much as possible for what to expect. This means becoming familiar with the place you will meet, and the content you will cover, as well as understanding any time constraints you will have.

Location—Be sure that you not only know how to find the place where you will be meeting, but also have time to examine the setup and make any adjustments to the physical arrangements. You never get a second chance to make a first impression.

Curriculum—You will want to get a copy of the study in advance of the introductory session, and it will be helpful if you do the homework for Lesson One ahead of time. This will make it easier for you to be able to explain the layout of the homework. It will also give you a contagious enthusiasm for what your group will be studying in the coming week. You will want to have enough books on hand for the number of people you expect so that they can get started right away with the study. You may be able to make arrangements with your church or local Christian Bookstore to bring copies on consignment. We would encourage you not to buy books for your members. Years of small group experience have taught that people take a study far more seriously when they make an investment in it.

Time—The type of group you are leading will determine the time format for your study. If you are doing this study for a Sunday school class or church study course, the time constraints may already be prescribed for you. In any case, ideally you will want to allow forty-five minutes to an hour for discussion.

WHAT TO EXPECT

When you embark on the journey of leading a small group Bible study, you are stepping into the stream of the work of God. You are joining in the process of helping others move toward spiritual maturity. As a small group leader, you are positioned to be a real catalyst in the lives of your group members, helping them to grow in their relationships with God. But you must remember, first and foremost, that whenever you step up to leadership in the kingdom of God, you are stepping down to serve. Jesus made it clear that leadership in the kingdom is not like leadership in the world. In Matthew 20:25, Jesus said, *"You know that the rulers of the Gentiles lord it over them, and their great men exercise authority over them."* That is the world's way to lead. But in Matthew 20:26–27, He continues, *"It is not so among you, but whoever wishes to become great among you shall be your servant, and whoever wishes to be first among you shall be your slave."* Your job as a small group leader is not to teach the group everything you have learned, but rather, to help them learn for themselves and from each other. It is a servant's role.

If you truly are to minister to the members of your group, you must start with understanding where they are, and join that with a vision of where you want to take them. In this introductory session, your group members will be experiencing several different emotions. They will be wondering, "Who is in my group?" and deciding "Do I like my group?" They will have a sense of excitement and anticipation, but also a sense of awkwardness as they try to find their place in this group. You will want to make sure that from the very beginning your group is founded with a sense of caring and acceptance. This is crucial if your group members are to open up and share what they are learning.

During the Session

⏳ **OPENING: 5–10 MINUTES**
GETTING TO KNOW ONE ANOTHER

Opening Prayer—Remember that if it took the inspiration of God for people to write Scripture, it will also take His illumination for us to understand it. Have one of your group members open your time together in prayer.

Introductions—Take time to allow the group members to introduce themselves. Along with having the group members share their names, one way to add some interest is to have them add some descriptive information such as where they live or work. Just for fun, you could have them name their favorite breakfast cereal, most (or least) favorite vegetable, favorite cartoon character, their favorite city or country other than their own, etc.

Icebreaker—Take five or ten minutes to get the people comfortable in talking with each other. Since in many cases your small group will just now be getting to know one another, it will be helpful if you take some time to break the ice with some fun, nonthreatening discussion. Below you will find a list of ideas for good icebreaker questions to get people talking.

_____ What is the biggest risk you have ever taken?

_____ If money were no object, where would you most like to take a vacation and why?

_____ What is your favorite way to waste time?

_____ If you weren't in the career you now have, what would have been your second choice for a career?

_____ If you could have lived in any other time, in what era or century would you have chosen to live (besides the expected spiritual answer of the time of Jesus)?

_____ If you became blind right now, what would you miss seeing the most?

_____ Who is the most famous person you've known or met?

_____ What do you miss most about being a kid?

_____ What teacher had the biggest impact on you in school (good or bad)?

_____ Of the things money can buy, what would you most like to have?

_____ What is your biggest fear?

_____ If you could give one miracle to someone else, what would it be (and to whom)?

_____ Tell about your first job.

_____ Who is the best or worst boss you ever had?

_____ Who was your hero growing up and why?

⏳ **DEFINING THE GROUP: 5–10 MINUTES**
SETTING SOME GROUND RULES

There are several ways you can lay the tracks on which your group can run. One is simply to hand out a list of suggested commitments the members should make to the group. Another would be to hand out 3x5 cards and have the members themselves write down two or three commitments they would like to see everyone live out. You could then compile these into the five top ones to share at the following meeting. A third option is to list three (or more) commitments you are making to the group and then ask that they make three commitments back to you in return.

Here are some ideas for the types of ground rules that make for a good small group:

Leader:

_____ To always arrive prepared

_____ To keep the group on track so you make the most of the group's time

_____ To not dominate the discussion by simply teaching the lesson

_____ To pray for the group members

_____ To not belittle or embarrass anyone's answers

_____ To bring each session to closure and end on time

Member:

_____ To do my homework

_____ To arrive on time

_____ To participate in the discussion

_____ To not cut others off as they share

_____ To respect the different views of other members

_____ To not dominate the discussion

It is possible that your group may not need to formalize a group covenant, but you should not be afraid to expect a commitment from your group members. They will all benefit from defining the group up front.

⧗ INTRODUCTION TO THE STUDY: 15–20 MINUTES

As you introduce the study to the group members, your goal is to begin to create a sense of excitement about the Bible characters and applications that will be discussed. The most important question for you to answer in this session is "Why should I study _____?" You need to be prepared to guide them to finding that answer. Take time to give a brief overview of each lesson.

⧗ CLOSING: 5–10 MINUTES

❑ Give homework for next week. In addition to simply reminding the group members to do their homework, if time allows, you might give them 5–10 minutes to get started on their homework for the first lesson.

❑ Key components for closing out your time are **a)** to review anything of which you feel they should be reminded, and **b)** to close in prayer. If time allows, you may want to encourage several to pray.

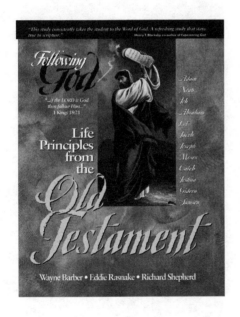

LIFE PRINCIPLES

FROM THE

OLD TESTAMENT

Table of Contents

Adam 21

Noah 24

Job 27

Abraham 30

Lot 33

Jacob 36

Joseph 39

Moses 42

Caleb 45

Joshua 48

Gideon 51

Samson 54

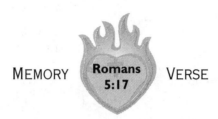

MEMORY **Romans 5:17** VERSE

"For if by the transgression of the one, death reigned through the one, much more those who receive the abundance of grace and of the gift of righteousness will reign in life through the One, Jesus Christ."

BEFORE THE SESSION

❑ One of the most important parts of leading your group is the time you spend in prayer for your group. Ask the Lord to give each member clear insight into the Scriptures. Never underestimate the importance of prayer for yourself and for the members of your group.

❑ **Suggestions for Additional Study.** Part of this study is on the "Last Adam," Jesus Christ. To better see the Person of Christ you may want to look at the lessons that refer to Christ in other Following God studies: **"The True King in Israel: Following the King of Kings"** (Lesson 12) in *Following God: Life Principles from the Kings of the Old Testament,* **"Christ the Prophet: Worshiping in Spirit and Truth"** (Lesson 12) in *Following God: Life Principles from the Prophets of the Old Testament,* **"The Bride of Christ: Walking in the Beauty of Holiness"** (Lesson 12) in *Following God: Life Principles from the Women of the Bible,* and **"The Son of Man: Following His Father"** (Lesson 12) in *Following God: Life Principles from the New Testament Men of Faith.*

❑ Spread your study time over the week instead of trying to cram everything into one afternoon or night. Perhaps you could use this as your daily quiet time.

❑ Always look for those personal applications, some of which the Lord may have you share with the group. The more impact the Word makes in your heart, the more enthusiasm you will communicate to others.

❑ Remember to mark those ideas and questions you want to discuss or ask as you go through the study. Add to those some of the questions listed below. Remember that your job is to help guide the discussion—not to teach the lesson.

WHAT TO EXPECT

Beginning at the beginning is a good way to start to study what the Scriptures say about Adam, and the "Second Adam" will surely open up many doors of insight for you and your group. This lesson looks at God's design. It also looks at how Jesus Christ fulfills that design. In this lesson there may be many questions about Adam and Creation that you may not be able to answer or to answer as fully as you would like. As you begin this study, remember that you do not need to be "the answer man" or "the answer woman" for all the things that come up. Rejoice in the new insights, and challenge the group to a deeper study of the unknowns. As you walk through the lesson, seek to keep the main focus the main focus. Emphasize what you clearly know and understand.

Then you can move on to the things that are not as clear as the Lord gives you time and insight.

> ## THE MAIN POINT
> Though Adam sinned, God did not abandon His plans for mankind. He sent His Son, Jesus Christ to fulfill those plans.

DURING THE SESSION

 OPENING: 5–10 MINUTES

Opening Prayer—Have one of the group members begin the time with prayer.

Opening Illustration—We all remember houses where we have lived or often visited—our house as a little child, a best friend's home, a grandparent's home, or our first home after we married. Scripture shows us that God is interested in houses. God Himself is Architect and Builder of the entire universe. He has a desire and design in mind for everything He does. God began showing us His design in creation, especially in the creation of Adam and the home He provided for Adam. As a result of Adam and Eve's sin, Adam was forced to abandon the home that was created for him, but God's design, plans, and desires for man were never abandoned. He is still building you and me and the members of your group.

As we think of how the concept of God as an architect and builder applies to us, we must remember that for any builder to be successful—to produce a building that looks exactly like what was originally intended in the blueprints—he must work from the architect's design. So it is with us. For us to be what God wants, we must work from His original design. You will see that truth in this study of Adam. You can also be confident that *"He who began a good work in you will perfect it until the Day of Christ"* (Philippians 1:6). In your study of Adam, may each one in your group be challenged and encouraged in how God works to build up each of us. Tell them that they can be confident in the fact that God is not finished with any of them yet!

 DISCUSSION: 30–40 MINUTES

Select one or two specific questions to get the group started. This lesson on Adam focuses on God's design for man and for His creation and how God's design is fulfilled in Jesus Christ as the **"Second Adam."** As you and your group see Christ as the One who wants to fulfill God the Father's design in and through you, you will be encouraged in your daily walk with the Lord.

Main Objective in Day One: In Day One, the main objective is to see the good design God has for man and for the created order. Some good discussion questions from Day One include these:

_____ What do you think life was like in the Garden of Eden?

_____ What would life be like if you and all those around you reflected the image of God and sought to lead by serving?

_____ How would you apply the three-fold idea of growing, guarding, and choosing to do good in the place God puts us (see p. 5 in workbook) to where you live and work?

Main Objective in Day Two: In Day Two, the main objective is to see the results of sin upon mankind and upon God's design. Some possible discussion questions for Day Two might be . . .

_____ What are some of the "cover-ups" we use and "blame games" we play today?

_____ In Day Two, we looked at some of the results of Adam and Eve's sin that would manifest themselves in the days to come. Corruption and violence marked Noah's day (Genesis 6:11). How is our day the same?

_____ Often, we have no problem recognizing the corruption of mankind as a whole, but how often do we see corruption in ourselves?

Main Objective in Day Three: Day Three focuses on God's solution to man's condition. The Lord Jesus is "the Last Adam" who fulfills the Father's plan. Some good discussion questions from Day Three might be . . .

_____ What are some ways Jesus showed Himself to be a servant?

_____ Are we really enemies of God? Talk about the deceitfulness, hurt and ugliness of sin.

_____ What is the Good News? What does it mean to you?

Main Objective in Day Four: Day Four looks at what it means to walk in oneness with God. Some good discussion questions from Day Four might be . . .

_____ What is your favorite picture in Scripture of your relationship with God? Why? (See the list at the beginning of Day Four.)

_____ What one or two things stand out in your mind that should characterize a person who walks in oneness with God?

_____ From the list on Romans 8, what is most meaningful or helpful to you and your walk?

Day Five—Key Points in Application: The most important application point seen in **Adam** is the absolute essential need for you to know Jesus Christ as your personal Savior and Lord, your **"Last Adam."** Some good discussion questions to help direct your group's focus on the applications from Day Five might be . . .

_____ What has it meant **to you** to receive Jesus Christ as your Lord and Savior, as the "Last Adam" in your life?

_____ Is there a new insight you have seen that will help you live out the truth of your relationship with God more consistently?

_____ Is there a new insight that can help you share with someone else what it means to come to Jesus and know Him personally as Lord and Savior?

⌛ CLOSING: 5–10 MINUTES

❑ **Summarize**—Restate the key points the group shared. Review the Main Point statement at the beginning of the Leader's Guide notes for this lesson. You may also want to re-read the objectives for each day's discussion. These objectives are also found in every leader's guide lesson.

❑ **Focus**—Using the memory verse (Romans 5:17), direct the group's focus to what it means to be **in Christ** and to walk in oneness with Him.

❑ **Ask** the group members to convey their thoughts concerning the key applications from Day Five.

❑ **Preview**—We have finished the first of 12 lessons in _Following God: Life Principles from the Old_

Testament. We have begun the journey and have eleven more stops. Take a few moments to preview next week's lesson on **"Noah: Following God in Reverence and Obedience."** Encourage your group members to do their homework.

❑ **Pray**—Close your time in prayer thanking the Lord for the journey you have begun.

🔧 TOOLS FOR GOOD DISCUSSION

Some who are reading this have led small-group Bible studies many times. Here is an important word of warning: experience alone does not make you a more effective discussion leader. In fact, experience can make you **less effective**. You see, the more experience you have, the more comfortable you will be at the task. Unfortunately, for some that means becoming increasingly comfortable in doing a bad job. Taking satisfaction with mediocrity translates into taking the task less seriously. It is easy to wrongly assert that just because one is experienced, he or she can successfully "shoot from the hip," so to speak. If you really want your members to get the most out of this study, you need to be dissatisfied with simply doing an adequate job and make it your aim to do an excellent job. A key to excellence is to regularly evaluate yourself to see that you are still doing all that you want to be doing. We have prepared a list of over thirty evaluation questions for you to review from time to time. The list of questions can be found on page 11 in this Leader's Guide. The examination questions will help to jog your memory and, hopefully, will become an effective aid in improving the quality of your group discussion. Review the evaluation questions list, and jot down below two or three action points for you to begin implementing next week.

ACTION POINTS:

1. _____

_____

2. _____

_____

3. _____

_____

MEMORY **Hebrews 11:7** VERSE

"By faith Noah, being warned by God about things not yet seen, in reverence prepared an ark for the salvation of his household, by which he condemned the world, and became an heir of the righteousness which is according to faith."

BEFORE THE SESSION

- ❑ Remember that your goal is not to teach the lesson, but to facilitate discussion.

- ❑ Additional study: You will benefit from reading the New Testament commentary on Noah's life found in Hebrews 11:7; 1 Peter 3:20, and 2 Peter 2:5. Some group members may find their appetites whetted by the scientific ramifications of Noah's flood. Perhaps the book that best examines the flood from a scientific point of view is the classic work *The Genesis Flood* by John C. Whitcomb and Henry Morris. There are many other resources available along these lines at your local Christian bookstore.

- ❑ Make sure your own heart is right with God. Be willing to be transparent with the group about your own life experiences and mistakes. This will make it easier for them to open up.

- ❑ Don't be afraid of chasing tangents for a while if they capture the interest of the group as a whole, but don't sacrifice the rest of the group to belabor the questions of one member. Trust God to lead you.

- ❑ You may want to keep a highlight pen handy as you study to mark key statements that stand out to you.

WHAT TO EXPECT

The danger of dealing with a character as familiar as Noah is that although most everyone will have some knowledge of certain events in his life, few will have seriously studied him. It is likely that many in your group have not studied Noah since childhood. Noah is a powerful model of obedience. God entrusted a great task to this man of faith, and Noah responded in obedience—even in the face of ridicule and opposition. We will find in this week's lesson that his life is rich in practical principles instructing us in what it means to follow God. We will also see that his is a very human example, stained by mistakes and failure. You will find that many in your group will be able to relate better to Noah after seeing his humanness. Often we place the saints of old on a pedestal too high to be relevant to most of us. Yet Noah, like all the characters of Scripture, was a person just like us. God will prompt many in your group to follow Noah's example through obedience to some calling that God is giving them. It may be faithfulness to follow God in their parenting or business. It may be a calling to ministry. Whatever God is saying, realize that He may want to use you and this study to help that particular person solidify his or her choice to obey God.

DURING THE SESSION

 OPENING: 5–10 MINUTES

Opening Prayer—Psalm 119:18 says, *"Open my eyes, that I may behold wonderful things from Thy law."* Ask the Lord to open the eyes of each one as you open the Word together as a group. Have one of the group members begin the time with prayer.

Opening Illustration—Saul was the first king in Israel, but he was rejected by the Lord and ultimately replaced by David. The proverbial "straw that broke the camel's back," leading to Saul being rejected, was his partial but self-serving obedience when God called him to utterly destroy the wicked Amalekites. These were the ones who had attacked Israel from the rear in the wilderness, killing the elderly and the children. Instead of obeying God fully and destroying everything, Saul kept back the spoils of the battle. Through the prophet Samuel, God sent a clear message: *"Has the Lord as much delight in burnt offerings and sacrifices as in obeying the voice of the Lord? Behold, to obey is better than sacrifice, and to heed than the fat of rams"* (1 Samuel 15:22). In Noah, we see that our reverence for God is revealed, not by our sacrifice, but by our obedience.

DISCUSSION: 30–40 MINUTES

Once your group gets talking, you will find that all you need to do is keep the group directed and flowing with a question or two or a pointed observation. You are the gatekeeper of discussion. Don't be afraid to ask someone to elaborate further or to ask a quiet member of the group what they think of someone else's comments. Time will not allow you to discuss every single question in the lesson one at a time. Instead, make it your goal to cover the main ideas of each day and help the group to share what they learned personally. You don't have to use all the discussion questions. They are there for your choosing. Use your own judgment as to which questions might work best for your group.

Main Objective in Day One: In Day One, the central objective is to paint a portrait of what the days of Noah were like, contrasting Noah's righteousness with the prevailing unrighteousness that surrounded him. Check the questions that are useful to your discussion on Day One.

_____ What stood out to you from the reasons Scripture gives for God judging the ancient world? How does that relate to today?

_____ What do you think it means that Noah was *"blameless in his time"*?

_____ How do Christians today stand out in our culture as we are obedient to God?

_____ Talk about the many temptations you encounter to "blend in" with the world.

Main Objective in Day Two: In Day Two, we learn an important principle about God's dealings with mankind: He doesn't always deliver His chosen ones **from** trouble. Sometimes He delivers them by taking them safely **through** the trouble. Check the discussion questions from Day Two that you will use.

_____ What stands out to you about the ark?

_____ What kind of pressures do you think Noah faced from his peers as he tried to obey God?

_____ Has God ever given you what seemed like an impossible task? What was your response?

_____ What does the idea of God delivering **through** trouble instead of **from** trouble say to you?

_____ Why do you think the Lord allows us to go through hard experiences?

Main Objective in Day Three: When Noah came to the other side of his trial, a new world awaited him. Day Three focuses on what had changed in Noah's world. Select one or two Day Three discussion questions from the list below.

_____ How do you think Noah felt toward God when he came off the ark?

_____ What jumps out at you about this new world to which Noah came?

_____ What is significant about the covenant that God made with Noah?

_____ What conclusions can we draw from Noah's experience about the results of our obedience?

Main Objective in Day Four: Although Noah was godly and used by the Lord, he was not perfect. Day Four shows us where Noah stumbled and gives us the opportunity to learn from his mistakes. Check the questions from Day Four that you will use in your group discussion.

_____ Why do you think the Bible records this failure of Noah's?

_____ Have you ever experienced a fall after a spiritual high point?

_____ What speaks to you most from Noah's failure?

_____ Did anything else stand out to you from Day Four?

Day Five—Key Points in Application: The most important application point from Noah's life is that our reverence for God is reflected in obedience to His directives in our lives. This obedience is not simply our trying hard to be good, but rather, our total surrender to God. He will always enable us to do whatever He asks of us if we are surrendered to Him. Here are a couple of discussion question possibilities:

_____ Where in life do you find your greatest struggles with obedience?

_____ Did God show you anything you need to do differently through this lesson?

⌛ CLOSING: 5–10 MINUTES

❑ **Summarize**—Restate the key points that were highlighted in the class.

❑ **Remind** the group that the victorious Christian life is not attained when we try hard to be like Jesus, but only when we surrender our lives to God and let Him work through us.

❑ **Preview**—Take time to preview next week's lesson on **"Job: Trusting God's Sovereignty."** Tell your group members to complete their homework.

❑ **Pray**—Close in prayer.

TOOLS FOR GOOD DISCUSSION

Bill Donahue, in his book, _Leading Life-Changing Small Groups_ (Grand Rapids: Zondervan Publishing House, 1996), lists four facilitator actions that will produce dynamic discussion. These four actions are easy to remember because they are linked through the acrostic method to the word, **ACTS.** You will profit from taking time to review this information in the "Helpful Hints" section of **How to Lead a Small Group Bible Study,** which is on page 5 of this Leader's Guide book.

3

MEMORY **Job 42:2** VERSE

"I know that Thou canst do all things, and that no purpose of Thine can be thwarted."

BEFORE THE SESSION

☐ Pray each day for the members of your group—that they spend time in the Word, grasp the message God wants to bring to their lives, and that they surrender to what God is saying.

☐ Do your homework—don't procrastinate!

☐ An important historical note is that many scholars believe that the book of Job was the first book of the Bible ever to be written.

☐ Mark those ideas and questions you want to discuss as you go through the study. Those, along with the questions listed below, can personalize the discussion to fit your group. Think of the needs of your group, and be looking for applicable questions and discussion starters.

☐ Remain ever teachable. Look first for what God is saying to you.

☐ Be prepared to be transparent and open about what God is teaching you.

WHAT TO EXPECT

For everyone in your group the issue of God's sovereignty over the difficulties in our lives will strike a chord. Sooner or later, everyone goes through hard times. The all-important question that surfaces in the midst of our trials is "Does God's power reach into the difficulties of my life? Is He aware? Does He care? Can He do anything about it?" You will find that this week's lesson, perhaps more than any of the others, will bring the personal struggles of your group members out into the open. When this happens, be prepared to point them to God and the truths of His word that this lesson puts forward.

> ### THE MAIN POINT
> We should always trust God's sovereignty over any adversity He allows or any blessing He chooses to take away.

DURING THE SESSION

⧗ **OPENING: 5–10 MINUTES**

Opening Prayer—Remember the Lord is the Teacher and wants us to depend on Him as we open the Scriptures.

Opening Illustration—Joseph was the favorite of Jacob's twelve sons. This was evident to all in the "coat of many colors" that Jacob gave to Joseph. Because of the jealousy this coat brought to the surface, Joseph's brothers sold him into slavery. From there it went from bad to worse. While faithfully serving as a slave, he was falsely accused by his master's wife of rape and was thrown into prison. Yet the outcome of this seemingly tragic tale was far from negative. With the 20/20 vision of hindsight, we can see that each of these difficulties was part of God's plan to place Joseph where He eventually wanted him. It was from that Egyptian prison that Joseph was promoted to Prime Minister over all of Egypt. Without his brothers' cruelty or his master's injustice, he never would have made it to the palace. We can see this truth because we know the ending of the story, but Joseph didn't have that advantage. He had to trust God's sovereignty and purposes over the adversities in his life. That he did trust God's sovereignty is evident in the statement he makes to his brothers in Genesis 50:20, *". . . you meant evil against me, but God meant it for good in order to bring about this present result. . . ."*

⏳ DISCUSSION: 30–40 MINUTES

Steer the group along the main highway of God's sovereignty. You may have a pointed observation that will help sharpen the focus of the group. Encourage some to elaborate further on a key point, or ask a quiet member of the group what he or she thinks of another member's comments. Watch the time, knowing that you can't cover every single question in the lesson. Seek to cover the main ideas of each day, and help the group to personally share what they have learned.

Main Objective in Day One: The main objective of Day One is to observe that although Satan brought all manner of adversities Job's way, God was the initiator of Job's troubles, and set the boundaries for how far Satan could go in implementing them. Some possible conversation starter questions for the discussion pertaining to Day One might be . . .

_____ Are there any trials in your life right now that you need to "accept" from God, or in which you need to "bless" God?

_____ Which do you think is harder to accept—when God takes away blessings, or when He gives adversities?

_____ What stands out to you from Satan's attacks on Job?

_____ Why do you think God allowed Job to be tested like He did?

Main Objective in Day Two: Here we learn a little of the mistakes we can make in relating to the adversities that God allows in the lives of others. We must trust God's sovereignty there as well. Check the discussion questions for Day Two that you will use.

_____ How do you think the attacks from his wife and friends added to Job's trial?

_____ Why do you think they all assumed Job had done something to deserve the trial?

_____ What are some ways we prejudge others in the midst of their trials?

_____ Have you ever said the wrong thing while trying to comfort someone because you thought you knew what God's reasons were for allowing the hard times to come?

Main Objective in Day Three: Day Three introduces us to the danger of self-justification. Even if the trial is a result of no wrong on our part, we can be wrong in how we respond to it. Select a discussion question or two from the Day Three list below.

_____ What are some ways Job was demanding an explanation from God?

_____ Psalm 119:68 states, *"Thou art good and doest good."* Have you ever been tempted to doubt God's goodness in the midst of a trial?

_____ What does 1 Corinthians 10:13 say to you in light of what we are studying?

_____ Have you ever grown impatient with any trials God has allowed to continue in your life? If so, why?

Main Objective in Day Four: The main idea for your group to seize from Day Four is that trials don't last forever, and beyond those trials lies a new view of God and of life. Place a checkmark or a "ranking number" next to the questions below that you feel are appropriate for your discussion on Day Four.

_____ What stands out to you from the lessons Job learned from his trials?

_____ What was wrong with the counsel of Job's friends? Can you relate with that?

_____ What stood out to you in the outcome of Job's trials?

_____ What are some lessons you have learned from any trials God has sent your way?

_____ Has this lesson raised any questions for you?

Day Five—Key Points in Application: The most important application point to be obtained from the Day Five reading is the truth that following God does not automatically result in a life without difficulties. Along with that thought, we can trust God to always have a distinct purpose in our difficulties. In addition to any other discussion questions that you may have in mind, the following questions might be useful:

_____ What trials are going on in your life right now?

_____ What relevance do you see from the verses on God's purpose for trials in our lives (p. 43 in workbook)?

_____ What does this lesson change most in your thinking about God?

⏳ CLOSING: 5–10 MINUTES

❑ **Summarize**—Restate the key points the group shared. Review the objectives for each of the days found in these leader notes.

❑ **Ask** your group to convey their thoughts on the key applications from Day Five.

❑ **Preview**—Take a few moments to preview next week's lesson on **"Abraham: Following God at Any Cost."** Encourage them to be sure to do their homework and to space it out over the week.

❑ **Pray**—Close in prayer.

🔨 TOOLS FOR GOOD DISCUSSION

One of the people who shows up in every group is a person we call **"Talkative Timothy."** Talkative Timothy tends to talk too much and dominates the discussion time by giving less opportunity for others to share. What do you do with a group member who talks too much? In the "Helpful Hints" section of **How to Lead a Small Group Bible Study** (p. 5), you'll find some practical ideas on managing the "Talkative Timothy's" in your group.

4

Abraham

MEMORY **Hebrews 11:9-10** VERSES

"By faith he lived as an alien in the land of promise, as in a foreign land, dwelling in tents with Isaac and Jacob, fellow heirs of the same promise, for he was looking for the city which has foundations, whose architect and builder is God."

Before the Session

❑ Be sure to do your own study far enough in advance so as not to be rushed. You want to allow God time to speak to you personally.

❑ Don't feel that you have to use all of the discussion questions listed below. You may have come up with others on your own, or you may find that time will not allow you to use them all. These questions are to serve you, not for you to serve.

❑ You are the gatekeeper of the discussion. Do not be afraid to "reel the group back in" if they get too far away from the lesson.

❑ Remember to keep a highlight pen ready as you study to mark any points you want to be sure to discuss.

What to Expect

The story of Abraham is so well-known that we run the risk of allowing familiarity to breed contempt. Yet, as you can see, there are some very practical lessons to be learned from his life—the main one being that it is not enough to **know** God's will, we must seek to **do** God's will, God's way. In Abraham's two sons,

we see two approaches to the Christian life. In Ishmael, we see Abraham striving to help God, but in Isaac, we see Abraham's spirit of total surrender to the will of God. The idea of total surrender to God is one of the most important lessons your group can ever learn. God's plan doesn't need our help. Our striving only produces "Ishmael's"—not "Isaac's." Expect people in your group to have their own "Ishmael" stories. These personal experiences will be invaluable in driving the principles home from this week's study.

> ### THE MAIN POINT
> Our relationship with God is more important than trying to help God enact His plan.

During the Session

⌛ **OPENING: 5–10 MINUTES**

Opening Prayer—Remember that if it took the inspiration of God for people to write Scripture, it will also take His illumination for us to understand it. Have one of the more serious minded members of your group open your time together in prayer.

Opening Illustration—When Jesus was betrayed and arrested in the garden of Gethsemane, the apostle

Peter tried to come to His defense. As the mob of soldiers approached, one of the disciples asked, *"Shall we strike with the sword?"* but before Jesus could answer, Peter jumped up and cut off the ear of the High Priest's slave. His motive was good—he wanted to help the Lord. But Peter didn't fully understand what God was doing, and he couldn't grasp that the Cross could be part of God's plan. Unless we follow God fully, even when we are trying to do right, we may end up doing wrong. Peter's striving, instead of rescuing Jesus, merely created a mess that the Lord had to clean up. Jesus healed the slave's wound and then allowed Himself to be arrested. In the process, He reminded Peter that at any time He could appeal to His Father and have *". . . more than twelve legions of angels"* at His disposal. God does not need our help to accomplish His plans. Abraham had to learn this lesson with Ishmael.

⌛ DISCUSSION: 30–40 MINUTES

Once your group gets talking, you will find that all you need to do is keep the group directed and the discussion flowing by asking a question or two or by mentioning a pointed observation. Don't be afraid to ask someone to elaborate further ("Explain what you mean, Barbara.") or to ask a quiet member of the group what they think of someone else's comments ("What do you think, Dave?"). Time will not allow you to discuss every single question in the lesson, one at a time. Instead, make it your goal to cover the main ideas of each day and help the group to share what they learned personally. You don't have to use all the discussion questions listed below. They are there for your choosing.

Main Objective in Day One: In Day One, the main objective is to reveal how it was God who initiated calling Abraham out of Ur. Emphasis is placed on Abraham's response of faith that allowed him to become part of God's plan. Place a checkmark or ranking number in the blank next to the questions you want to use in your discussion time.

_____ What did it cost Abraham to follow God's direction?

_____ Why do you think God's plan for Abraham was revealed a little at a time?

_____ What does Abraham being reckoned righteous by his faith say about your walk with God?

_____ Do you believe God has a specific purpose for you and for every Christian?

Main Objective in Day Two: In Day Two, we learn the key principle that it is possible to know what God's will is, and yet not pursue His will in His way. You want to make sure that your group can differentiate from merely knowing God's will and actually doing God's will. Check the discussion questions from Day Two that you will use.

_____ Why do you think Abraham listened to the worldly plan his wife brought to him?

_____ What was the result of Sarah's plan?

_____ Do you ever struggle with worrying about how God will fulfill His purpose in you?

_____ What do you struggle with more, getting ahead of God or lagging behind Him?

_____ Do you agree with the statement, "Whenever we try to help God out, we do more damage than good"?

Main Objective in Day Three: Day Three introduces us to the results of Abraham's waiting on God. What an encouragement it is that Abraham's mistake did not prevent Isaac from coming! What a beautiful picture of grace! In addition to any discussion starter questions that you may have in mind, you may want to use one or more of the questions listed below.

_____ What stands out to you from God's renewing of the vision in Genesis 17?

_____ Why do you think Abraham laughed? What about Sarah?

_____ Abraham laughed at first, but how did he ultimately respond to God's communication?

_____ What changed in Abraham's response to Sarah's suggestion here compared to Genesis 16? How does that apply to us?

Main Objective in Day Four: In Day Four, we see Abraham's ongoing surrender to God. Even though he had the son God had promised, he was willing to surrender Isaac in order to obey God. Below, check any questions that might enhance your discussion time for Day Four.

_____ What do you think went through Abraham's mind when he heard God's instructions?

_____ What do you think he believed God was going to do?

_____ What was Isaac's role in all of this?

_____ What stands out to you most from this incident?

_____ Did you have any unanswered questions from this week's lesson?

Day Five—Key Points in Application: The most important application point from the life of Abraham is that following God is a life of ongoing surrender. Check the discussion questions from Day Five that you will use.

_____ Can you think of an example in your life of something that wasn't God's doing but yours?

_____ Can you think of any issues or events in life that you have surrendered to the Lord?

_____ Are there any "Ishmael's" or "Isaac's" in your present circumstances?

_____ What applications did you see this week?

⧖ CLOSING: 5–10 MINUTES

❑ **Summarize**—Restate the key points that were highlighted in the class.

❑ **Remind** your group that the Christian life is not best exemplified in our trying hard to be like Jesus, but by our total surrender to God.

❑ **Ask** the group what they thought were the key applications from Day Five.

❑ **Preview**—Take a few moments to preview next week's lesson on **"Lot: Choosing Not to Follow."** Encourage them to be sure to do their homework.

❑ **Pray**—Close in prayer.

🔧 TOOLS FOR GOOD DISCUSSION

As mentioned earlier, there are certain people who show up in every discussion group. Last week we looked at "Talkative Timothy." Another person who is likely to show up is **"Silent Sally."** She does not readily speak up. Sometimes, her silence is because she doesn't yet feel comfortable enough with the group to share her thoughts. Other times, it is simply because she fears being rejected. Often, her silence is because she is too polite to interrupt and thus is headed off at the pass each time she wants to speak by more aggressive (and less sensitive) members of the group. In the "Helpful Hints" section of **How to Lead a Small Group Bible Study** (p. 6), you'll find some practical ideas on managing the "Silent Sally's" in your group.

5

MEMORY **Hebrews 10:38** VERSE

"But My righteous one shall live by faith; and if he shrinks back, My soul has no pleasure in Him."

BEFORE THE SESSION

❑ Resist the temptation to do all your homework in one sitting or to put it off until the last minute. You will not be as prepared if you study this way.

❑ Make sure to mark down any discussion questions that come to mind as you study.

❑ You will want to review your notes on Abraham as you look at Lot. If you want to do further study, you may want to see what you can learn about Lot from a Bible dictionary.

❑ Remember your need to trust God with your study. The Holy Spirit is always the best teacher, so stay sensitive to Him!

WHAT TO EXPECT

In this lesson, expect that all your group members need to better understand that even a child of God can wander away. Lot will be a different study since he is primarily a negative example of following God. You will need to help your group see the value in studying a negative example, as it serves as a warning to us. It offers us the opportunity to learn from Lot's mistakes instead of having to make them ourselves. It is important, however, to bring out the many evidences of God's grace in this story as well. Some in your group may have had "Lot-sized" failures of their own. They will take special comfort from seeing God's forgiveness and the gracious way He deals with Lot.

THE MAIN POINT

A man is not so much a product of his environment as he is of his own choices. In Lot we see opportunities wasted because of foolish and selfish choices.

DURING THE SESSION

⌛ **OPENING: 5–10 MINUTES**

Opening Prayer—Remember to have one of your group members open your time together in prayer.

Opening Illustration—Have you ever kicked yourself for not buying stock in Wal-Mart years ago? Think of where you would be now if you had invested in Microsoft when it first became a publicly traded company. What if you came up with the idea of "Beanie Babies"? With the 20/20 vision of hindsight, each of us can look back over our lives and think of missed economic opportunities. But what about the missed spiritual opportunities? In heaven, where gold is used for paving the streets, Microsoft stock won't matter much. However, spiritual growth holds promise not only for this life, but also for the life to come. Few in the Bible could review their missed opportunities with more regret than Lot could.

⌛ DISCUSSION: 30–40 MINUTES

Remember that your job is not to teach this lesson, but only to facilitate discussion. Do your best to guide the group to the right answers, but don't be guilty of making a point someone else in the group could just as easily make.

Main Objective in Day One: In Day One, the main objective is to see the many tremendous opportunities placed before Lot. Yet, as we will see, Lot squandered those opportunities. Check any discussion question for Day One that you might consider using in your group session.

_____ What stands out to you about the early opportunities given to Lot?

_____ What kind of influence do you think Abraham had on his life?

_____ What "Abraham's" has God placed in your life through whom you could be growing in Christ?

_____ What gets in the way of us benefiting from the "Abraham's" that God places in our lives?

_____ Were there any other questions raised by your study in Day One?

Main Objective in Day Two: In Day Two, we identify the problems that led to Abraham and Lot parting company. We see that selfish interests rather than the will of God governed Lot's choices. Below are some suggestions for your Day Two discussion starters

_____ What do you see as the root of the conflict between Lot and Abraham?

_____ What does Abraham's proposed solution say about his character and trust in God?

_____ What does Lot's choice say about the difference between appearance and reality?

_____ Are there any things in your life or in others you know that have been put in a position of priority over a relationship with God?

Main Objective in Day Three: Day Three introduces us to the consequences that begin to accrue from Lot's choices. Upon closer examination, we see that Sodom is more of a trap than a treasure. Check any discussion questions from Day Three that you might consider using in your group session.

_____ Describe the land of Sodom.

_____ What does Lot's experience say about the dangers of not seeking God's will in our decisions?

_____ Why do you think Abraham responded as he did instead of saying, "I told you so"?

_____ Have you ever experienced God's grace when you deserved the full consequences of your choices? How?

Main Objective in Day Four: In Day Four, we see another example of God's grace in action as He rescues Lot from Sodom before judgment comes. Check any questions below that might prove to be beneficial to your discussion time.

_____ Abraham asked God to spare Sodom of judgment if ten righteous persons could be found. What does Abraham's request tell you about the wickedness of Sodom?

_____ Why do you think Lot is willing to expose his daughters to danger?

_____ What does God's rescue of Lot say about grace?

_____ What do you see in Lot's choice of residence after he left Sodom?

_____ What do the actions of Lot's daughters suggest about the consequences of wrong choices?

Day Five—Key Points in Application: The important thing to see out of Day Five is God's harshness toward sin along with His compassion toward His people. Check the discussion questions from Day Five that you will use.

_____ What do you think of God's view of sin?

_____ Would anyone like to comment on God's compassion and mercy as evidenced in the story of Lot?

_____ What applications do you see from Lot about our choices in life?

_____ Is there any other aspect that strongly speaks to you from this lesson on Lot?

 CLOSING: 5–10 MINUTES

❑ **Summarize**—Restate the key points.

❑ **Remind** those in your group that the victorious Christian life is not attained when we try hard to be like Jesus, but when we totaly surrender to God and allow Him to work through us.

❑ **Ask** your group to convey what they thought were the key applications from Day Five.

❑ **Preview**—Take a few minutes to preview next week's lesson on **"Jacob: Following God in Life's Journeys."** Encourage group members to be sure to complete their homework.

❑ **Pray**—Close in prayer.

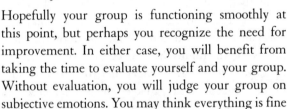

TOOLS FOR GOOD DISCUSSION

Hopefully your group is functioning smoothly at this point, but perhaps you recognize the need for improvement. In either case, you will benefit from taking the time to evaluate yourself and your group. Without evaluation, you will judge your group on subjective emotions. You may think everything is fine and miss some opportunities to improve your effectiveness. You may be discouraged by problems you are confronting when you ought to be encouraged that you are doing the right things and making progress. A healthy Bible-study group is not one without problems but is one that recognizes its problems and deals with them the right way. At this point in the course, as you and your group are nearly halfway completed with the study of the early Old Testament personalities, it is important to examine yourself and see if there are any mid-course corrections that you feel are necessary to implement. Review the evaluation questions list found on page 11 of this Leader's Guide, and jot down two or three action points for you to begin implementing next week. Perhaps you have made some steady improvements since the first time you answered the evaluation questions at the beginning of the course. If so, your improvements should challenge you to be an even better group leader for the final seven lessons in the study.

ACTION POINTS:

1. _____

_____

2. _____

_____

3. _____

_____

Jacob

MEMORY **Genesis 48:15–16** VERSES

"...The God who has been my Shepherd all my life to this day, the angel who has redeemed me from all evil, bless the lads; and may my name live on in them, and the names of my fathers Abraham and Isaac; and may they grow into a multitude in the midst of the earth."

BEFORE THE SESSION

☐ Remember the Boy Scout motto: **"Be Prepared"**? The main reason a Bible study flounders is because the leader comes in unprepared and tries to "shoot from the hip."

☐ Don't forget to pray for the members of your group and for your time studying together. You don't want to be satisfied with what **you** can do—you want to see God do what only **He** can do!

☐ Make sure to mark down any discussion questions that come to mind as you study.

☐ **Suggestions for Additional Study:** To see Jacob from the view of his son, Joseph, you may want to look ahead to the lesson on **"Joseph: Following God When the Pressure's On"** (Lesson 7).

WHAT TO EXPECT

Watching the nation of Israel come into being was certainly a wonderful privilege. Jacob's sons became the Twelve Tribes of Israel. Knowing and understanding their beginnings through Jacob will help you see the ways of the Lord in history as well as in the heart of Jacob. The Lord always works through a process to bring about the fulness of His will. That is

certainly true in the life and journeys of Jacob. There is much to see and learn in this lesson, and you probably can't cover it all in one hour. Focus on the main points and the things that proved especially meaningful to your group. Remember that you are the leader of the discussion, so try to keep the group focused on the main points in Jacob's life. The **five turning points** given in the chart at the beginning of the lesson in the workbook should be a help to you in that. Help the group see the personal applications to their lives, and rejoice in the insights the Lord has shown them during the week and for the insights brought out in the group time.

> ### THE MAIN POINT
> Trusting God and His faithfulness as He guides us through life's journey is always at the heart of following God.

DURING THE SESSION

⌛ **OPENING: 5–10 MINUTES**

Opening Prayer—As you begin your group session, have one of the group members open the time with prayer.

Opening Illustration—The noted hymn writer, Fanny Crosby, once found herself in need of five dollars, a good sum in the 1870's. She had nowhere to turn and took the need to the Lord in prayer. Soon after, there came a knock at the door. A stranger stood there with a gift in the exact amount she needed. Fanny Crosby marveled at the way the Lord had led her in praying and how He led the man to give the exact amount. Immediately, she wrote the hymn "All the Way My Savior Leads Me." Written around 1875, it was the expression of gratitude for the way the Lord had led and provided. Read the words to this hymn, and note the similarities of this song to the life of Jacob:

All the way my Savior leads me. What have I to ask beside?
Can I doubt His tender mercy, Who thru life has been my Guide?
Heav'nly peace, divinest comfort, Here by faith in Him to dwell!
For I know, whate'er befalls me, Jesus doeth all things well;
For I know whate'er befalls me Jesus doeth all things well.

Jacob certainly saw the Lord lead him in some amazing ways throughout his life. May the members of your group be encouraged as you look at the journeys of Jacob.

⧖ DISCUSSION: 30–40 MINUTES

Remember to pace your discussion so that you will be able to bring closure to the lesson at the designated time. You are the one who must balance lively discussion with timely redirection to ensure that you don't end up finishing only part of the lesson.

Main Objective in Day One: Day One is an introduction to Jacob—his parents, his birth, his brother, and the early years leading to the **first turning point** in his life. We begin to see how the Lord led him in his life journey. Some good discussion questions from Day One include these. . . .

_____ What struck you as the most significant difference between Jacob and Esau?

_____ Rebekah had a plan for Jacob. Why did she do this? Do you think it was necessary?

_____ How is God's character and ways revealed in the story of Jacob's meeting with God at Bethel?

_____ Explain the relevance of the dream that God gave to Jacob.

Main Objective in Day Two: In Day Two, the main objective is to see how the Lord works in and through the turning points of Jacob's life and our lives as well. Some discussion questions for Day Two might be . . .

_____ What did God use to get Jacob's attention about returning to Canaan? What does He sometimes use to get our attention?

_____ In your observation of Jacob praying in Haran, how could his prayer be applied to your own prayer life?

_____ Discuss the significance of Jacob's wrestling with the Angel of the Lord.

_____ What applications do you see in your life? How have you wrestled over God's will in a matter or over something He wanted you to lay down?

Main Objective in Day Three: In Day Three, we see the **fourth turning point** arising out of the pressure of the Shechemites over the actions of Jacob's children. At that point, God gave Jacob clear revelation about what he needed to do. Some possible discussion questions for Day Three might be . . .

_____ What was God's solution to the menace of the Canaanites in Shechem?

_____ What was God's focus—was it just relocation or was it also heart location? What applications do you see?

_____ God was not finished with Jacob or his sons. How do you see the faithfulness of God in the incidents of Day Three?

_____ Jacob set up a pillar—a reminder. What are some reminders—some spiritual markers— we can set up in our walk?

Main Objective in Day Four: Day Four looks at the **final turning point** in Jacob's life and how God worked to bring him to Egypt. Some good discussion questions from Day Four might be . . .

_____ Circumstances can be confusing, as when Jacob thought all things were against him. What applications do you see in these incidents?

_____ What do you see regarding the faithfulness of God in these incidents and circumstances?

_____ What do you learn from God's use of surprising turns of events in Jacob's life?

_____ From looking at Jacob, what confidence do you now have concerning how God will guide you in the turns of life?

Day Five—Key Points in Application: The most important application point seen in the study of Jacob is the faithfulness of God at every turn. Here are some pertinent questions that can be used to direct your group's attention to the main focus of Day Five.

_____ How have you seen the faithfulness of God in your life journey?

_____ As of right now, what is the most significant "spiritual milestone" in your journey with the Lord?

_____ How has Jacob encouraged you to *"run with endurance the race"* that is set before you (as the author of Hebrews [12:1] puts it)?

_____ How does Jacob give you hope for the future and for future "turns" in the road of life? What insight have you gained that can help someone else in their journey?

⏳ CLOSING: 5–10 MINUTES

❏ **Summarize**—Restate the key points the group shared. Review the main objectives for each of the days.

❏ **Remind**—Using the memory verses (Genesis 48:15–16), remind the group of how God faithfully guided Jacob (as well as Abraham and Isaac) on his life journeys, and how He will do the same for each of His children.

❏ **Ask** the group members to reveal their thoughts about the key applications from Day Five.

❏ **Preview**—Your group is now halfway-finished in your study of *Following God: Learning Life Principles from the Old Testament*. Take a few moments to preview next week's lesson on **"Joseph: Following God When the Pressure's On,"** and encourage your group members to do their homework.

❏ **Close** your time in prayer.

TOOLS FOR GOOD DISCUSSION

As discussed earlier, there are certain people who show up in every discussion group that you will ever lead. We have already looked at "Talkative Timothy" and "Silent Sally." This week, let's talk about another person who also tends to show up. Let's call this person **"Tangent Tom."** He is the kind of guy who loves to talk even when he has nothing to say. Tangent Tom loves to "chase rabbits" regardless of where they go. When he gets the floor, you never know where the discussion will lead. You need to understand that not all tangents are bad. Sometimes, much can be gained from discussion "a little off the beaten path." But these diversions must be balanced against the purpose of the group. In the "Helpful Hints" section of **How to Lead a Small Group** (p. 6), you will find some practical ideas on managing the "Tangent Tom's" that are in your group. You will also get some helpful information on evaluating tangents as they arise.

7

MEMORY VERSES

"And the patriarchs became jealous of Joseph and sold him into Egypt. And yet God was with him . . . and granted him favor and wisdom in the sight of Pharaoh, king of Egypt; and he made him governor over Egypt and all his household."

BEFORE THE SESSION

❑ It might be a good idea for you to try to get your homework done early in the week. This will allow time for you to reflect on what you have learned. Don't succumb to the temptation to procrastinate.

❑ Make sure you keep a highlight pen handy to highlight any things you want to be sure to discuss or any questions with which you think your group may have trouble. Mark down any good discussion questions that come to mind as you study.

❑ For further study on Joseph, look at Psalms 105:16–24 and Acts 7:9–15.

❑ Don't think of your ministry to the members of your group as something that only takes place during your group time. Pray for each group member by name during the week that they would receive spiritual enrichment from doing their daily homework. Encourage your group members as you have opportunity.

WHAT TO EXPECT

Genesis 30—50 presents the lives of Jacob and his family. Most of those chapters mention something about Joseph, and from chapter 37 on, the focus, for the most part, is on God's workings in and through the life of Joseph. Much of what we see in the life of Joseph is the reality of pressures. Someone has pointed out that it seems we are often just coming out of a storm, in the middle of a storm, or going into a storm. That was certainly true for Joseph from ages seventeen to thirty. We all face pressures. Your group should readily identify with the pressures Joseph faced. For some, this lesson will be preparation for coming pressures, and for others, this lesson will bring encouraging enlightenment on how God works in and through the pressures of daily life. Whatever the case, this is a good lesson to focus everyone's attention on the Lord who does "mean it for good" whatever the situation we are facing. We are not **victims**, but **victors** in Christ, and Joseph shows us that in many ways. May the members of your group see the Lord and their lives in the light of the victory Jesus has won and in the light of the plans He is carrying out even today.

> ### THE MAIN POINT
> Though we face all kinds of pressures with all kinds of intensity, we can still follow God.

DURING THE SESSION

⧗ OPENING: 5–10 MINUTES

Opening Prayer—It would be a good idea to have a different group member each week open your time together in prayer.

Opening Illustration—While in Bedford prison, John Bunyan wrote *The Pilgrim's Progress*, considered by many to be the greatest work in English literature apart from the Scriptures. In his "Apology" introducing the work he states, "Dark clouds bring waters, when the bright bring none. Yea, dark or bright, if they their silver drops cause to descend; the earth, by yielding crops, gives praise to both. . . ." Joseph faced some dark clouds, but they certainly brought the waters of God's blessing on him and his family as well as on the people of God for all time. Some in your group may be facing the dark clouds of "pressures" like Joseph faced. May your discussion of his life be refreshing to each heart like a spring rain.

⧗ DISCUSSION: 30–40 MINUTES

A key objective in how you manage your discussion time is to keep the big picture in view. Your job is not like a schoolteacher's job, grading papers and tests and the like, but more like a tutor's job, making sure they understand the subject. Keep the main point of the lesson in view, and make sure they take that main point home with them.

Main Objective in Day One: Day One is a look at the growing-up years of Joseph—his birth and his childhood through age seventeen, when he was sold into slavery. Some good discussion questions from Day One might be . . .

_____ What kinds of pressures (if any) do you think Joseph faced in the first seven years of his life?

_____ What lessons might the teenager Joseph have learned from all that went on in Shechem (Genesis 34—35)?

_____ In all that transpired going **to** and **at** Bethel, what could Joseph have learned about the Lord and His relationship to Jacob?

_____ At Bethel, what could Joseph have learned about the Lord's relationship to himself and his brothers and sister?

Main Objective in Day Two: In Day Two, the main objective is to see how the Lord works in the midst of pressures to fulfill His will. Some discussion questions for Day Two might be . . .

_____ In about a year's time, Joseph faced the birth of a new brother, the death of his mother (Rachel), and the treachery of his brothers in selling him to the Ishmaelite traders. What insights about pressure do you see so far in the life story of Joseph?

_____ How did Joseph's seeking the presence of the LORD affect him in Egypt?

_____ Name one thing you have learned from this lesson about how to face pressure.

_____ The Lord gave Joseph uncanny wisdom before Pharaoh (Acts 7:10). What does this tell you about what the Lord wants to do in your pressure points?

Main Objective in Day Three: Day Three reveals the way pressures were used not only in Joseph's life, but also in the lives of Jacob and his sons. Select one or two of the questions listed below for your discussion time.

_____ What does Joseph's testimony through the naming of his sons reveal about how he saw his troubles at that time?

_____ What comments do you have regarding how God orchestrates circumstances to accomplish His will?

_____ As Joseph worked through all that God had done over the twenty-two years since being sold into slavery, what benefits could Joseph have gained by being in Potiphar's house and in jail? How could these "rough spots" have helped him rule?

_____ How has God used some "rough spots" in your road of life to bring you to the your present place?

Main Objective in Day Four: Day Four looks at the purposes of pressure for Joseph and his family—physically, materially, and spiritually. Some good discussion questions for Day Four might include:

_____ What do you see about the care of the Lord in Joseph's life?

_____ What do you see about the care of the Lord for Jacob and his family?

_____ What is the main purpose in the pressures Joseph faced?

_____ What is God saying to you about His care for you and the pressures you are facing?

Day Five—Key Points in Application: The most important application point seen in the study of Joseph is the centrality of knowing and trusting God in whatever we go through. Place a checkmark in the blank next to the questions you feel have the best chances of enhancing your discussion time.

_____ From looking at Joseph's life, what do you know about God?

_____ How does knowing God help **you** face the pressures of life?

_____ What could you tell someone facing difficult or pressure-filled days about trusting and following God?

_____ What has the lesson on Joseph personally said to you?

⧖ CLOSING: 5–10 MINUTES

❑ **Summarize**—Restate the key points that the group shared. Review the main objectives for each of the days.

❑ **Remind**—Using the memory verses (Acts 7:9–10), remind the group of how the Lord was present with Joseph, how He rescued him from the pressures, and how He gave Joseph the grace

and wisdom to face Pharaoh, the upcoming famine, and his brothers. The Lord will give us grace and wisdom for each trial we face.

❑ **Ask** the group members to share their thoughts about the key applications from Day Five.

❑ **Preview**—Take a few moments to preview next week's lesson on **"Moses: Practicing the Presence of God"** and encourage your group members to do their homework.

❑ **Pray**—Close your time in prayer.

 **TOOLS FOR GOOD DISCUSSION**

One of the issues you will eventually have to combat in any group Bible study is the enemy of **boredom.** This nemesis raises its ugly head from time to time, but it shouldn't. It is wrong to bore people with the Word of God! Often boredom results when leaders allow their processes to become too predictable. As small group leaders, we tend to do the same thing in the same way every single time. Yet God the Creator, who spoke everything into existence is infinitely creative! Think about it. He is the one who not only created animals in different shapes and sizes, but different colors as well. When He created food, He didn't make it all taste or feel the same. This God of creativity lives in us. We can trust Him to give us creative ideas that will keep our group times from becoming tired and mundane. In the "Helpful Hints" section of **How to Lead a Small Group** (pp. 8–9), you'll find some practical ideas on adding spice and creativity to your study time.

8

Moses

MEMORY **Hebrews 11:27** VERSE

"By faith he [Moses] left Egypt, not fearing the wrath of the king; for he endured, as seeing Him who is unseen."

BEFORE THE SESSION

❑ Your own preparation is key not only to your effectiveness in leading the group time, but also in your confidence in leading. It is hard to be confident if you know you are unprepared. These discussion questions and leader's notes are meant to be a helpful addition to your own study, but should never become a substitute.

❑ For further study, look at Hebrews 11:23–29 and several references to Moses in the New Testament, such as the Transfiguration of Jesus, where Moses and Elijah were present (Matthew 17:1–8; Luke 9:28–36; Mark 9:2–8) or Jesus' references to Moses in the Gospels. Also see Psalm 106, which speaks of Moses or Psalm 90, which was written by Moses. You can find valuable information in articles on the life of Moses or on the Exodus and wilderness journeys in a good Bible dictionary. You may also want to look at the life of Moses' sister Miriam in **"Miriam: Trusting God with Your Position in Life"** (Lesson 3) in *Following God: Life Principles from the Women of the Bible.*

❑ As you do your homework, study with a view to your own relationship with God. Resist the temptation to bypass this self-evaluation on your way to preparing to lead the group.

Nothing will minister to your group more than the testimony of your own walk with God.

❑ Don't think of your ministry to the members of your group as something that only takes place during your group time. Pray for your group members by name during the week, and, as you pray, ask God to enlighten them as they do their homework. Encourage your group as you have opportunity.

WHAT TO EXPECT

Much is made of Moses in the Scriptures as well as in books on the Bible, Judaism, Christianity, the nation of Israel, and world history. He was certainly a choice servant of the Lord, and God used him in a mighty way to guide His people out of Egypt. There is much to learn from his life.

In this lesson, we will be able to touch only on a few aspects of his life, specifically, how Moses practiced the presence of God. Some in your group will know many more details than we are able to cover on this man to whom the Scripture gives so much attention. However, for some, Moses may be a new name in their list of Bible characters. Either way, it is important to keep the focus on the main ideas presented here alongside the insights you and your group members have gleaned as you have studied the Scriptures. Keeping your eyes on the main ideas will help guide the discussion and clarify some of the unanswered questions that your group members may have found in their study time this past week. Expect some questions as well as some new insights concerning this often familiar character, Moses.

> ## THE MAIN POINT
> We must understand that our faithful God is present with us wherever we go, whatever we face.

During the Session

 ## OPENING: 5–10 MINUTES

Opening Prayer—A good prayer with which to open your time is the prayer of David in Psalms 119:18, *"Open my eyes, that I may behold wonderful things from Thy law."* Remember that if it took the inspiration of God for men to write Scripture, it will take His illumination for us to understand it.

Opening Illustration—When we think of "practicing the presence of God," perhaps the clearest pictures are found in one of the most favored psalms, Psalm 23. In verses 1–2 we are reminded, *"The LORD is my shepherd. . . . He leads me beside still waters. . . ."* Notice how personal His presence is—**"my** *shepherd . . . leads* **me."** It is in the present tense—He is **now** my shepherd. He is now leading me. He is now with me. Like David, who penned those words, Moses knew that truth. He even experienced it as a shepherd in the wilderness of Midian before his experiences in Egypt or on the journeys to the Promised Land. Each of us can know the reality of His presence as well. His promises are for all His children.

DISCUSSION: 30–40 MINUTES

Remember to pace your discussion so that you don't run out of time to get to the application questions in Day Five. This time for application is perhaps the most important part of your Bible study. It will be helpful if you are familiar enough with the lesson to be able to prioritize the days for which you want to place more emphasis, so that you are prepared to

reflect this added emphasis in the time you devote to that particular day's reading.

Main Objective in Day One: In Day One, we read of the call of Moses and the promise of God to be with him as the "I AM"—ever present, ever caring for His people. Some good discussion questions from Day One might be . . .

_____ What evidence of the presence of God is there in the first years of Moses' life?

_____ What evidence is there of the presence of God in the lives of the Israelites in Egypt?

_____ God is the "I AM"—the "I will be Who I have been." What does that phrase mean to you?

_____ How does the faithfulness of God toward Moses and the Israelites apply to your life right now?

Main Objective in Day Two: In Day Two, the main objective is the difference the promise of the presence of God makes in Moses' life and by application, in our lives. Review the list of questions below, and choose the ones that best fit your group discussion.

_____ What are some of the excuses we invent when we debate God's will or God's clear Word in any matter?

_____ How has God shown Himself faithful to you or to someone you know who has been dealing with some issue concerning God's will?

_____ Can you recall a time when you experienced the presence of God as He gave you His boldness to say what needed to be said?

_____ Are there some things (or one thing) the Lord has asked you (or is asking you) to "throw down" so that you can more fully do His will?

Main Objective in Day Three: Day Three looks at how important the presence of God was to Moses personally as well as in the journey through the wilderness. Below, check any questions that you like for group discussion.

_____ What does it mean to you that God Himself wants to be present in our lives?

_____ What have you learned from Moses personally about walking in the presence of the Lord?

_____ How do we act and live when we are not practicing the presence of God?

_____ What are some substitutes (some "golden calves") we run to instead of the Lord and His Word?

Main Objective in Day Four: In Day Four, we see Moses and the Israelites at Kadesh-Barnea and the lessons they learned about how important the presence of God was for the people of God. Good discussion questions from Day Four include . . .

_____ How do "giants" and "high walls" get in the way of our walk with God?

_____ How do you run to the presence of God when things seem overwhelming?

_____ Have you ever followed a "formula" for obedience or "steps 1, 2, 3" instead of following God? What happened?

_____ What can help you practice the Lord's presence more consistently?

Day Five—Key Points in Application: The most important application point that can be acquired in the study of Moses is that we learn to practice the presence of the Lord on a moment-by-moment basis. Check the discussion questions for Day Five that you will use.

_____ What is the main hindrance to practicing the presence of God in your life right now?

_____ How have you seen His presence in your life more realistically this past week?

_____ How does the phrase, "I WILL BE WHO I HAVE BEEN" help you as you think about some of the things you are facing in your life?

_____ What is the greatest joy for you concerning the presence of God?

⌛ CLOSING: 5–10 MINUTES

❑ **Summarize**—Restate the key points. You may want to reread **The Main Point** statement at the beginning of these leader's notes on Moses.

❑ **Focus**—Using the memory verse (Hebrews 11:27), direct the group to the focus of Moses— *"Him who is unseen."* He practiced the presence of the Lord, and we can too.

❑ **Preview**—Take time to preview next week's lesson on **"Caleb: Following God Fully."** Encourage your group to do their homework.

❑ **Pray**—Close in prayer.

TOOLS FOR GOOD DISCUSSION

From time to time, each of us can say stupid things. Some of us, however, are better at it than others. The apostle Peter certainly had his share of embarrassing moments. One minute, he was on the pinnacle of success, saying, *"Thou art the Christ, the Son of the Living God"* (Matthew 16:16), and the next minute, he was putting his foot in his mouth, trying to talk Jesus out of going to the cross. Proverbs 10:19 states, *"When there are many words, transgression is unavoidable. . . ."* What do you do when someone in the group says something that is obviously wrong? First of all, remember that how you deal with a situation like this not only affects the present, but also the future. In the "Helpful Hints" section of **How to Lead a Small Group** (p. 9), you'll find some practical ideas on managing the obviously wrong comments that show up in your group.

MEMORY  VERSE

"And without faith it is impossible to please Him, for he who comes to God must believe that He is, and that He is a rewarder of those who seek Him."

BEFORE THE SESSION

❑ Pray each day for the members of your group—that they spend time in the Word, grasp the message God wants to bring to their lives, and that they surrender to what God is saying.

❑ Be sure you have searched the Scriptures carefully for each day's lesson.

❑ Walk through the discussion questions below, looking at your lesson and selecting which questions you will use.

❑ **Suggestions for Additional Study**—To better understand Caleb you will also want to refer to the companion lessons, last week's lesson on **Moses** and next week's lesson on **Joshua**.

❑ Remain ever teachable. Look first for what God is saying to you. This will help you in understanding and relating to some of the struggles that your group members may be facing in the "low places" they are going through.

WHAT TO EXPECT

This lesson may reveal some real struggles that one or a few of the members of your group are facing. Do not feel like you have to be "the answer man" or

"the answer woman." Sometimes the most faith-filled response to a question is "I don't know," followed by "but we know we can trust God, for He is faithful and trustworthy." Some members in your group will have tremendous testimonies of trusting God and seeing Him work. Like Caleb, there are some who will trust God for their own "hill country." In Caleb we also have a wonderful example of someone whose many years didn't dim his pursuit of God. We find that although he was nearly eighty years old, he didn't look for an easy task, but trusted God for one of the more difficult conquests. Caleb followed God fully all of his life. There was no coasting in his Christian life. His example should be a challenge to your entire group.

> ### THE MAIN POINT
> Faith is being willing to simply take God at His word that what He says is true, and that what He says He will do, He will do!

DURING THE SESSION

⏳ **OPENING: 5–10 MINUTES**

Opening Prayer—Remember to ask the Lord for **His** wisdom. He promised to guide us into the truth.

Opening Illustration—"Remember the Alamo" was a phrase used to cheer soldiers on in Texas' war for independence from Mexico. But why do we remember the Alamo? It was not a victory in the usual sense. All of the soldiers were eventually conquered including such notables as Sam Houston, Jim Bowie, and Davy Crockett. The fort was lost to the army of Santa Anna. Why was that battle such an inspiration to Texas? Because of the valor the men exhibited there. Though overwhelmingly outnumbered and faced with impossible odds, they refused to surrender. They fought to the very end for what they believed. Their unwillingness to quit inspired countless soldiers after them to persevere until, eventually, Texas was triumphant. The church needs an army of soldiers who are unwilling to quit no matter what they have to face. Caleb was such a man. In Deuteronomy 1:36 we are told that *"he has followed the Lord fully."*

⏳ DISCUSSION: 30–40 MINUTES

Select one or two specific questions to get the group started. Keep the group directed along the main highway of Caleb. By this point in the course (Week Nine), you know both the talkative ones and the quiet ones. Continue to encourage each member in the importance of his or her input. Some of the greatest applications ever to be learned from this study course may come from someone who has said very little up to this point.

Main Objective in Day One: In Day One, the main objective is to see Caleb's role in the first venture into Canaan and his faithful response even when every one else doubted. Check which discussion questions from Day One that you will use.

_____ Describe your thoughts about Caleb as he is introduced.

_____ What do you think was going through the minds of Israel's leaders as they prepared to enter Canaan?

_____ Why do you think Caleb's report was different than the rest of the group?

_____ Are there any other aspects of Day One that you feel are worth discussing?

Main Objective in Day Two: Here we learn the difference perspective makes. We see that **focusing on God** fortifies faith, while **focusing on our circumstances** erodes faith. Check the questions from the Day Two list below that you will use in your discussion time.

_____ What role do you think the lack of faith on the part of the majority of the leaders played in the fears of the people?

_____ Can you relate with **focusing on your circumstances** instead of **focusing on God?**

_____ What is significant about Caleb and Joshua's response to the unbelief of the people?

_____ Why do you think Caleb and Joshua had to suffer the consequences of the people's unbelief?

_____ Are there times in your life when you have suffered the consequences of someone else's unbelief or wrong choice?

Main Objective in Day Three: Day Three introduces us to Caleb and the people after the forty years of wandering in the wilderness. Below, check any discussion questions for the Day Three reading that are useful to your group discussion.

_____ What stood out to you from looking at God's judgments through the plagues?

_____ What do we learn about God from His dealings with Israel in the wilderness?

_____ How do you think Joshua and Caleb felt about going into the Promised Land without Moses?

_____ At what age do you think Caleb had his most significant ministry?

_____ What does that say to you?

Main Objective in Day Four: Here we see the conquest of Canaan and how God fulfilled His promises to Caleb and to Israel. In addition to any questions or observations that you or your group have in mind, the following questions may be essential to your discussion time:

_____ Why did Caleb want the hill country?

_____ Why was he the right person to take on the giants of Hebron?

_____ Why do you think God wanted Israel to fight for the promised land?

_____ What do you think Caleb and the people learned through the process?

_____ Did this lesson raise any questions for you, or leave any questions unanswered?

Day Five—Key Points in Application: The most important application point we can learn from this lesson on Caleb is that we are to trust God by taking Him at His word. Check the discussion questions from Day Five that you will use.

_____ Why do you think Caleb made the hard choices he did?

_____ What are some choices we face today where faith and obedience are more difficult than taking the easy way out?

_____ What applications stand out to you most personally from this lesson?

⌛ CLOSING: 5–10 MINUTES

❑ **Summarize**—Restate the key points the group shared. Review the objectives for each of the days found in the leader's notes for **Caleb**.

❑ **Focus**—Using the memory verse (Hebrews 11:6), refocus the group on what faith is—to believe that God is, and that He rewards those who seek Him.

❑ **Ask** them to convey their thoughts about the key applications from Day Five.

❑ **Encourage**—We have finished nine lessons. This is no time to slack off. Encourage your group to keep up the pace. We have three more lessons full of life-changing truths. Take a few moments to preview next week's lesson on **"Joshua: The Necessity of Humility."** Encourage your group members to do their homework in proper fashion by spacing it out over the week.

❑ **Close** in prayer.

 ## TOOLS FOR GOOD DISCUSSION

The Scriptures are full of examples of people who struggled with the problem of pride. Unfortunately, pride isn't a problem reserved for the history books. It shows up just as often today as it did in the days the Scriptures were written. In your group discussions, you may see traces of pride manifested in a "know-it-all" group member. **"Know-It-All Ned"** may have shown up in your group by this point. He may be an intellectual giant, or he may be a legend only in his own mind. He can be very prideful and argumentative. If you want some helpful hints on how to deal with "Know-It-All Ned," look in the "Helpful Hints" section of **How to Lead a Small Group Bible Study** (p. 7).

10

MEMORY **Joshua 1:9** VERSE

*"Have I not commanded you? Be strong and courageous!
Do not tremble or be dismayed, for the LORD your God
is with you wherever you go."*

BEFORE THE SESSION

❑ Never underestimate the importance of prayer for yourself and for the members of your group. Ask the Lord to give them understanding in their time in the Word and bring them to a new level of knowing Him.

❑ Spread your study time over the week.

❑ Remember to mark those ideas and questions you want to discuss or ask as you go through the study.

❑ To grasp the big picture, you may want to familiarize yourself with the chart, "A Look at Joshua's Life," found at the end of this lesson.

❑ **Suggestions for Additional Study**—To better understand the life of Joshua and all he experienced in the wilderness and in conquering the Promised Land, you may want to read some of the articles in a good Bible dictionary on the Exodus, the wilderness, Canaan, Joshua, and the conquests of Joshua. You may also want to review the last two lessons on **Moses** and **Caleb**.

❑ Be sensitive to the needs of your group. Be prepared to stop to pray for a member who may be facing a difficult struggle or challenge.

WHAT TO EXPECT

Many have heard about Joshua and the Battle of Jericho, while others know about the Book of Joshua in the Old Testament. However, many do not know the entire story that Scripture shows us about his life (from age 50 to age 110). The many ways God used Joshua as Moses' servant and the many other battles he fought in Canaan have much to teach us all.

In this lesson we will focus on how Joshua first followed Moses as a humble servant and learned much about following God. Then we will look at how he continued following God with that same heart of a humble servant. As you guide the discussion, seek to keep the focus on the character of Joshua, particularly the qualities of humility, teachability, and availability to the Lord. May Joshua be an encouragement to you and to each one in your group.

THE MAIN POINT

If we are not teachable, we cannot truly learn. If we are not obedient to what we hear, we will not experience all that God wants for us.

DURING THE SESSION

 OPENING: 5–10 MINUTES

Opening Prayer—Have one of the group members open the time with prayer.

Opening Illustration—What does humility look like? Sometimes we fail to recognize humility when we see it and so we fail to understand what it really is. Think of the time Jesus went to the home of Mary and Martha in Bethany (Luke 10:38–42). In that incident, at first glance, some would say Martha was acting with humility as a humble servant—preparing a meal for everyone. We must hear what Jesus says about the situation to see it as it really is. Martha was certainly busy with the meal preparations, while Mary chose to sit at Jesus' feet and listen to His Word. When Martha suggested that Mary should come help her, Jesus stated simply, *"Martha, Martha, you are worried and bothered about so many things; but only a few things are necessary, really only one, for Mary has chosen the good part, which shall not be taken away from her"* (10:41–42). Here was a picture of humility, because humility is always teachable. In Mary, we see just such a heart. Martha, on the other hand was busy and promoting her own agenda. In humility, Mary chose to sit and listen to Jesus. What she learned would be with her forever—an eternal investment.

There are times when the busy preparations can wait. Something eternal is at hand. A humble heart will submit to the Lord's ways at that point. That was true of Mary of Bethany, and it was true of Joshua. We will see that in many ways as we walk through this week's lesson.

 DISCUSSION: 30–40 MINUTES

Select one or two specific questions to get the group started in discussion. This lesson on Joshua covers most of the life of Joshua and has many application points. Pay attention to the process through which God took Joshua. Remember to look at the heart of Joshua—humble, teachable, and available to the Lord—and how important that heart attitude is in following God. Continue to encourage each member in the importance of his or her insights and input.

Main Objective in Day One: Day One looks at the early years of Joshua under the leadership of Moses and how he remained ever teachable, staying mold-

able before the Lord. Some good discussion questions for Day One might be . . .

_____ What has Joshua shown you about the importance of depending on the Lord in the battles of life?

_____ What are some ways we can learn from one another like Joshua did from Moses? How can we spend beneficial time together?

_____ How can we set apart the time and the place we need to spend quality and quantity time with the Lord?

_____ Joshua and Caleb believed the Lord would give them victory in Canaan. How does time with the Lord and time in His Word affect our trust-level?

Main Objective in Day Two: In Day Two, the main objective is to see the importance of being available to the Lord. Some good discussion questions for Day Two might be . . .

_____ What does it mean to be "available"?

_____ How is a personal relationship with the Lord important in serving the Lord?

_____ How important is it to have a servant's heart if you are going to lead others?

_____ In contrast, what would it be like to have a leader who is not available to the Lord, not teachable, and not servant-hearted?

Main Objective in Day Three: In Day Three, the main objective is to see the faithfulness of God and the faithful response of Joshua in leading the people of God. Possible discussion questions for Day Three include . . .

_____ How important is it to know God's Word in accomplishing the will of God in our lives?

_____ What are some essentials in being prepared for a task in which the Lord may want to use you?

_____ How can we begin to see sin as God sees sin? What difference will it make in our lives?

_____ What can be the results of surrender and obedience to the Lord where we live?

Main Objective in Day Four: Day Four looks at the importance of faithfulness to God in what He has given us to do. Check any questions below that might serve as good discussion starters in your group time.

_____ The Lord led Joshua in a pattern—first of all in worship, then in His Word, and then in the work he was to do. What is significant about that order? What applications do you see?

_____ What do you learn from the events at Jericho and Ai about dealing with temptation and sin?

_____ Joshua continually brought the people back to God's Word. What does that say to us today about leadership and followship?

_____ Fill in the blank with the one thing that is needed in your life now: "As for me, I will

_____

_____

Day Five—Key Points in Application: The most important application point seen in the study of **Joshua** is the necessity of humility—a humility that remains teachable and available to the Lord. Some questions to help your group focus on the applications from Day Five are . . .

_____ How can we walk in humility on the job today? At home? At church? At school?

_____ Since we never know the ultimate impact of our choices, how important could our influence be in the lives of those around us day after day?

_____ What has this lesson on Joshua said to you personally?

⌛ CLOSING: 5–10 MINUTES

❑ **Summarize**—restate the key points the group shared. You may want to repeat the statement at the beginning of the leader notes, called **"The Main Point."** Also, ask them to express their thoughts on the key applications from Day Five

❑ **Focus**—Using the memory verse (Joshua 1:9), focus the group's attention to Joshua's relationship with God. As Joshua humbly followed the Lord, he would experience the Lord's presence wherever he went and the Lord's power to fulfill His will. The same is true for each of your group members.

❑ **Remind** your group that the same Lord who commanded and empowered Joshua is their **power source** for today. As each one humbles himself before the Lord, he or she can experience the Lord walking **with them,** working **in them,** and then working **through them** as He did with Joshua.

❑ **Preview**—Take a few moments to preview next week's lesson on **"Gideon: Little Is Much When God Is in It."** Encourage your group to complete their homework.

❑ **Pray**—Close in prayer.

 **TOOLS FOR GOOD DISCUSSION**

So, group leaders, how have the first nine weeks of this study been for you? Have you dealt with anyone in your group called **"Agenda Alice"**? She is the type that is focused on a Christian "hot-button" issue instead of the Bible study. If not managed properly, she (or he) will either sidetrack the group from its main study objective, or create a hostile environment in the group if she fails to bring people to her way of thinking. For help with "Agenda Alice," see the "Helpful Hints" section of **How to Lead a Small Group Bible Study** (pp. 7–8).

11

MEMORY **2 Corinthians 12:9** VERSE

"...'My grace is sufficient for you, for power is perfected in weakness.' Most gladly, therefore, I will rather boast about my weaknesses, that the power of Christ may dwell in me."

BEFORE THE SESSION

❑ Pray for your group as they walk through this week's lesson.

❑ Spread your study time over the week. Think of the lesson as a large meal. You need time to chew each truth and digest it fully.

❑ Remember to mark those ideas and questions you want to discuss or ask as you go.

❑ **Suggestions for Additional Study**—To better understand the condition of Israel at this time, you may want to look at the period of the Judges in a Bible dictionary.

WHAT TO EXPECT

Most everyone in your group has probably heard of Gideon before. Yet they will be unfamiliar with many of the details in his life other than his seeking God's will through the means of the "fleece." Recognize that many in your group will be encouraged and challenged by Gideon's smallness. They will perhaps be able to identify better with him than with most of the characters we have studied. Remind those in your group that Gideon is an "example" to us (1 Corinthians 10:11). Be patient. Study diligently in your preparation time. You may want to consult a

Bible dictionary about some of these things. As you walk through the lesson seek to keep the main point the main point. Emphasize what you clearly know and understand. Then you can move on to the things that are not as clear as the Lord gives you time and insight.

> ### THE MAIN POINT
> When God does His work through the small, all the glory goes to Him—where it belongs.

DURING THE SESSION

⧗ **OPENING: 5–10 MINUTES**

Opening Prayer—Have one of the group members open the time with prayer.

Opening Illustration: It's the Little Things That Count—Often we are tempted to think that only the big things in life, or the big events, or the "big name" people are of any real importance. But a small rudder turns the greatest of ships, and the tongue, though it is one of the smallest members of our bodies, is often the most powerful. How many times we have found that it is not a whole book or a whole chapter of the Bible that impacts—but a small verse or part of a verse or phrase empowered by the Spirit of God that pierces us in soul and spirit. The study of Gideon has this potential. Throughout his story we see that God wanted to work through the small instead of the large, to guard man from pride and from taking credit for what God had done.

⌛ DISCUSSION: 30–40 MINUTES

Once your group gets talking you will find that all you need to do is keep the group directed and flowing with a question or two or a pointed observation. Don't be afraid to ask someone to elaborate further or to ask a quiet member of the group what he or she thinks of someone else's comments. Time will not allow you to discuss every single question in the lesson one at a time. Instead, make it your goal to cover the main ideas of each day, and help the group members to personally share what they learned. You don't have to use all the discussion questions. They are there for your choosing, so use your own judgment as to which ones are best suited for your group.

Main Objective in Day One: The reading for Day One is designed to help you to gain a feel for the days in which Gideon lived, and to see that it is God who sought Gideon out. Gideon didn't come to God and ask for an assignment. Decide which discussion questions from Day One you will use.

_____ What stands out to you about the "sin cycle" of the book of Judges?

_____ What does God "giving Israel into the hands of Midian" say to you? Have you ever experienced anything like that?

_____ Why do you think the Lord picked someone like Gideon through which to work?

_____ What else stood out to you from Day One?

Main Objective in Day Two: In Day Two, we see that God doesn't start Gideon out with the biggest task. He gives him a smaller task both so Gideon can show himself faithful and so God can build his faith. Choose which discussion questions from Day Two that you will use.

_____ Why do you think God wanted to deal with Israel before he dealt with Midian?

_____ What do you learn about Gideon from how he tackled the problem of the altar of Baal?

_____ What stands out to you from the way Gideon's father defends him?

_____ Can you think of any situations in your own walk with God where He gave you an opportunity to show yourself faithful? Did you pass the test?

Main Objective in Day Three: Day Three focuses on Gideon's humanness and how God tolerates that. You want to be sure your group members see this. Place a checkmark next to the questions that are most suitable to your group, or rank the questions in order of your preference.

_____ What do you think about "the Spirit of the Lord" coming upon Gideon and the others mentioned in the book of Judges?

_____ What is different for us today? How do we let the Spirit "put us on like a garment"?

_____ Can you relate to Gideon's struggling with taking God at His word?

_____ How does the "fleece" method of seeking God's will relate to us today?

_____ What aspect from Day Three has the most significance to you?

Main Objective in Day Four: Day Four looks at how the Lord dealt with Gideon to show him the difference between what man does for God and what God does through man. Check the discussion questions from Day Four that you will use.

_____ Why did God not want to deliver Israel through the large army that Gideon originally gathered?

_____ What can we learn from God reassuring Gideon's weak faith?

_____ Can you think of a time in your life when God had you in a position where the only way to have victory was if He did something miraculous?

_____ Why do you think the Lord sent the men into battle with pots and torches instead of swords?

_____ Did this week's lesson raise any questions for you that weren't answered?

Day Five—Key Points in Application: The most important application point seen in the ministry of

Gideon was his "smallness." He was the youngest child, from the least family, in the smallest "half-tribe" of Israel. Yet he saw God do great things through him. The same can be true of us. Select a discussion question or two from the list below.

_____ Can you think of a time when you've felt inadequate for a task set before you?

_____ How has this lesson changed how you look at your inadequacies and "smallness"?

_____ Is there any weakness in your life upon which you need to boast?

_____ How are you going to apply this lesson personally?

⌛ CLOSING: 5–10 MINUTES

❑ **Summarize**—Restate the key points.

❑ **Ask** the group to reveal their thoughts on the key applications from Day Five.

❑ **Preview** next week's lesson on **"Samson: The Downward Spiral of Sin."** Encourage your group to do their homework.

❑ **Pray**—Close in prayer.

TOOLS FOR GOOD DISCUSSION

Well, it is evaluation time again! You may be saying to yourself, "Why bother evaluating at the end? If I did a bad job, it is too late to do anything about it now!" Well, it may be too late to change how you did on this course, but it is never too late to learn from this course what will help you on the next. Howard Hendricks, that peerless communicator from Dallas Theological Seminary, puts it this way: "The good teacher's greatest threat is satisfaction—the failure to keep asking, 'How can I improve?' The greatest threat to your ministry is **your ministry.**" Any self-examination should be an accounting of your own strengths and weaknesses. As you consider your strengths and weaknesses, take some time to read through the evaluation questions list found in the **How to Lead a Small Group Bible Study** section on pages 11–12 of this leader's guide. Make it your aim to continue growing as a discussion leader. Jot down below two or three action points for you to implement in future classes.

ACTION POINTS:

1. _____

_____

2. _____

_____

3. _____

_____

12

MEMORY **Genesis 4:7** VERSE

"... if you do not do well, sin is crouching at the door; and its desire is for you, but you must master it."

BEFORE THE SESSION

❑ Never underestimate the place of prayer for yourself and for the members of your group. Pray for each of them by name.

❑ Spread your study time over the week.

❑ Remember to mark those ideas and questions you want to discuss or ask as you go through the study. Add to those some of the questions listed below.

❑ Be sensitive to the working of the Spirit in your group meeting, ever watching for ways to help one another truly follow God.

WHAT TO EXPECT

Samson is a powerful example that being used by God does not make one immune to temptation or sin. His life stands as a warning to us all to watch our weaknesses lest they sideline us in the service of the Lord. Be prepared for the fact that although everyone in your group sins (including the leader), they may not be comfortable in discussing that. This is where you must lead by example. Your willingness to be open and honest in sharing stories of your own struggles will go a long way toward making it easier for others to open up. Hopefully, you have built an environment of trust in your group over these weeks of the study. Rejoice in the new insights, and challenge the group to delve into a deeper study of the unknowns. As you walk through the lesson, seek to keep the main point the main point. Emphasize what we clearly know and understand. Then you can move on to the things that are not as clear as the Lord gives you time and insight.

> ### THE MAIN POINT
> The downward spiral of sin will take you further, keep you longer, and cost you more than you can ever imagine.

DURING THE SESSION

⏳ **OPENING: 5–10 MINUTES**

Opening Prayer—Psalm 119:18 says, *"Open my eyes, that I may behold wonderful things from Thy law."* Ask the Lord to open your eyes as you meet together. Have one of the group members open the time with prayer.

Opening Illustration—King David was a man after God's own heart. He led the people well and still ministers today through his writings. But he also committed great sin. One particular year in the spring, at a time when kings usually went abroad to do battle, David decided to take a sabbatical from the weary struggles of war. During this time, he stayed up late and slept late, while others fought his battles for him. He awoke one evening and went out on his roof where he spied a beautiful neighbor taking a bath. He probably thought, "it won't hurt anything if I just look." But he didn't just look. He invited her over and ended up having sexual relations with her. Soon, he heard her utter those frightening words, "I'm pregnant." What could he do? He invited her husband home from the war in the hopes that he would sleep with his wife and no one would ever know that the child was not his. But that didn't work. This problem kept getting more complicated. He had to get this woman's husband out of the way. So David orchestrated his betrayal and death. He had hidden his actions from everyone but God. He thought for a time that he had gotten away with it, but that wasn't the case. In the end, his sin was revealed, and the child conceived in that sin was dead. Sin will take you further than you thought you'd stray, keep you longer than you thought you'd stay, and cost you more than you thought you'd pay. David could have learned that lesson from Samson instead of having to learn it the hard way. So can we.

⌛ DISCUSSION: 30–40 MINUTES

Remember that your job is not to teach the lesson, but to guide discussion. It is a servant's job. If you do most of the talking you are talking too much. You want to keep the discussion flowing with timely questions, and you will need to work to stay on track with the lesson. You will need to monitor the time to make sure that you can bring the discussion to closure. But don't say something someone else in the group could have said. You can share your own insights of course, but don't dominate the sharing. Let the group learn from each other.

Main Objective in Day One: Your main objective for Day One is that you and your group members begin to see Samson's weakness and his failure to manage that. Make sure your group sees that sin is always a choice. Check any discussion questions from Day One that you will use.

_____ What stands out to you from God's choosing of Samson?

_____ What do you see in Samson's weakness? How did his parents deal with that weakness? Why do you think they didn't deal with it more?

_____ Why do you think Samson did not make progress in dealing with his weaknesses? What consequences did he later endure as a result of his actions in those early years?

_____ Have you seen a "Samson" in your experience, or have you been a "Samson"?

Main Objective in Day Two: In Day Two, we see the reality that when sin gets us in its clutches, it keeps us longer than we intend. Check the questions from Day Two that you will use in your discussion.

_____ Why do you think Samson was attracted to a girl like Delilah?

_____ What do you suppose Samson was thinking when Delilah began her attempt to trick him?

_____ Why do you think he stayed in the relationship after Delilah had proved that she couldn't be trusted?

_____ Why do you think Samson foolishly revealed the true secret of his strength?

_____ What could he have done to avoid staying so long?

Main Objective in Day Three: In Day Three, the main objective is to see that although the bill may come later, sin always costs, and usually more than we thought it would. In addition to any questions or observations that you and your group may have, the following discussion starter questions may be helpful:

_____ Were there any questions that this lesson raised for you? What stands out to you about the things Samson's sin cost him?

_____ Why do you think he wasn't aware that the Lord had departed from him? Have you ever experienced that?

_____ Why do you think there are personal consequences when we sin?

_____ What would you say to someone faced with the same kinds of choices that Samson faced?

Main Objective in Day Four: Day Four looks at the message of hope that even when we sin, God's grace and mercy is able to rescue us from the mess in which our sin has snared us. Some good discussion questions from Day Four include. . . .

_____ What kind of treatment did Samson deserve from God?

_____ Why do you think God gives us grace and mercy instead of just giving us what we deserve?

_____ What was significant about the fact that Samson "called to the Lord"?

_____ What role does repentance play in our experiencing mercy instead of the consequences of our sin?

_____ Has God ever allowed you to lose something in order to realize your need for Him?

Day Five—Key Points in Application: The most important application point in Samson is that although there are consequences to sin, repentance allows us to draw on His mercy. Review the possible discussions question listed below, and choose one or two for use in your group session.

_____ Can you think of an example in your life where a "small" sin took you further than you intended? . . . kept you longer? . . . cost you more?

_____ In what ways have you experienced God's mercy when you should have encountered worse consequences?

_____ Have you ever been caught in the "downward spiral of sin" like the diagram illustrates? (This diagram is on p. 186 in the workbook.)

_____ Do you know how to break free from that spiral now?

 CLOSING: 5–10 MINUTES

❑ **Summarize**—Restate the key points the group shared.

❑ **Ask** your group members to share their thoughts about the key applications from Day Five.

❑ **Pray**—Close your time in prayer, thanking the Lord for the journey He has led you on over the past 12 weeks.

 TOOLS FOR GOOD DISCUSSION

Congratulations! You have successfully navigated the waters of small group discussion. You have finished all 12 lessons in *Following God: Life Principles from the Old Testament*, but there is so much more to learn, so many more paths to take on our journey with the Lord, so much more to discover about what it means to follow Him. Now what? It may not be wise for you and your group to stop with this study. In the front portion of this leader's guide (in the "Helpful Hints" section of **How to Lead a Small Group Bible Study,** pp. 9–10), there is information on how you can transition to another study and share those insights with your group. Encourage your group to continue in some sort of consistent Bible study. Time in the Word is much like time at the dinner table. If we are to stay healthy, we will never get far from physical food, and if we are to stay nourished on "sound" or "healthy" doctrine, then we must stay close to the Lord's "dinner table" found in His Word. Job said it well, *"I have not departed from the command of His lips; I have treasured the words of His mouth more than my necessary food"* (Job 23:12).

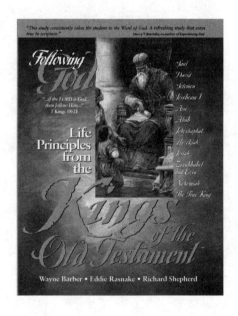

LIFE PRINCIPLES

FROM THE KINGS OF THE

OLD TESTAMENT

Table of Contents

Saul 61

David 64

Solomon 67

Jeroboam I 70

Asa 73

Ahab 76

Jehoshaphat 79

Hezekiah 82

Josiah 85

Zerubbabel and Ezra 88

Nehemiah 91

The True King 94

MEMORY **I Samuel 15:22–23** VERSES

"And Samuel said, 'Has the Lord as much delight in burnt offerings and sacrifices as in obeying the voice of the Lord? Behold to obey is better than sacrifice, and to heed than the fat of rams."

Before the Session

❑ Be sure to familiarize yourself with the timeline chart showing where Saul stands in the history of Israel.

❑ Spread out your homework instead of trying to cram everything into one afternoon or night. Perhaps use this as your daily quiet time.

❑ Always look for those personal applications, some of which the Lord may have you share with the group. The more impact the Word makes in your heart, the more enthusiasm you will communicate.

❑ Be transparent before the Lord and before your group. We are all learners—that is the meaning of the word "disciple."

❑ A good Bible dictionary article on "Saul" will give you more background information. Tools like these can often help you see the historical or cultural setting in which the man or woman lived.

❑ **Additional Study**—For a good companion to this study you can look at **"Samuel: Hearing God—Following His Word"** in *Following God: Life Principles from the Prophets of the Old Testament.*

As you study, write down any good discussion questions as they come to mind.

What to Expect

Many in your group may have experienced new insights or rich applications from their study this week. Some will understand for the first time the danger of remorse without repentance. Expect the Lord to do a fresh work in you as well as in the members of your group. He waits to show Himself strong toward *"those whose heart is fully His."* (See 1 Chronicles 16:9a.) Some may have questions about the study or even about the validity of some portions of the Word of God. You can help them see this as God's Word written in love. They can discover that this Book is eternal wisdom and is ever able to teach, reprove, correct, and train in righteousness (2 Timothy 3:16–17).

THE MAIN POINT

It is not our sin alone that brings consequences from God, but, more importantly, how we deal with our sin when He confronts us with it.

During the Session

 OPENING: 5–10 MINUTES

Opening Prayer—You or one of your group members should open in prayer. Remember that if it took the inspiration of God for people to write Scripture, it will also take His illumination for us to understand it.

Opening Illustration—In the early 1970's, our nation was rocked by the "Watergate" scandal, which eventually led to the resignation of President Richard Nixon and seriously eroded our country's confidence in its elected leaders. High-ranking officials in the Nixon administration had masterminded a break-in at the Democratic Headquarters (located in the Watergate Hotel) in hopes of gaining a political advantage. When all was said and done, several of President Nixon's closest advisors were convicted and served time in prison for "Watergate" related crimes. One of those aides to the President was John Dean. At his sentencing hearing, the judge asked Dean if he regretted his role in the "Watergate" scandal, to which he replied, "Yes." The judge then reportedly asked Dean, "Why do you regret it?" Dean's answer was very telling. He said, "Because of all that my family has had to go through." He didn't speak to the wrongness of his actions, but to the pain of their consequences. You see, he wasn't repentant about what he had done. He was merely remorseful about what getting caught had done to him. In the same way, Saul was remorseful over the consequences of his sins, but exhibited no true heart of repentance. No wonder God rejected him as king—he didn't have a heart after God's heart.

DISCUSSION: 30–40 MINUTES

Main Objective in Day One: The main objective for Day One is to see the context of Israel's request for a king and why Saul fit what they were looking for. Below, check which discussion questions you will use for Day One.

_____ Why did Israel want a king?

_____ What are some ways we struggle today with letting the world (instead of God) shape what we want?

_____ What else stood out to you from Day One?

_____ What evidences of judgment did you see in your reading of Day One? What evidences of grace did you see?

Main Objective in Day Two: In Day Two, we look closely at what kind of man Saul was relating to his character. Check which discussion questions you will use for Day Two.

_____ What worldly features did Saul have that made him seem like leader material?

_____ What flaws do you see?

_____ What does Saul's unwillingness to wait on the prophet say about his character?

_____ What applications does this offer to today's leaders?

Main Objective in Day Three: Day Three continues our look into Saul's actions as king, and what they reveal about him as a leader. Examine the suggested discussion starter questions below, and pick one or two questions for your Day Three discussion on Saul.

_____ What consequences did Saul's leadership bring to the people?

_____ What priority did seeking God hold for him?

_____ What do you learn from Jonathan's mistake?

_____ Can you see similarities between Saul and any modern leaders?

Main Objective in Day Four: Day Four focuses on the event that led to Saul being rejected as king. It stands as a fitting contrast to the king who would follow him—David. In addition to any discussion questions that may have come to your mind in your studies of Saul, the following suggested questions may prove beneficial to your group session:

_____ How did Saul do at obeying God in 1 Samuel 15?

_____ Why do you think Saul receives no credit for his partial obedience?

_____ What evidences do you see in this story of a lack of true repentance?

_____ What did Saul think would satisfy God?

Day Five—Key Points in Application: The most important application point from our study of Saul is seeing that remorse is not the same thing as repentance. Check which discussion questions you will use for Day Five.

_____ What made Saul such a poor king?

_____ What negative lessons do you learn from how Saul dealt with his sin?

_____ Have you ever experienced God giving you what you wanted so that you could see that what He wants is better?

_____ What other personal applications do you see from this lesson?

⧖ CLOSING: 5–10 MINUTES

❑ **Summarize**—Restate the key points highlighted in the class.

❑ **Preview**—Take just a few moments to preview next week's lesson on **"David: A Heart to Follow God."**

❑ **Encourage** the group to be sure to do their homework.

❑ **Pray**—Close in prayer.

 TOOLS FOR GOOD DISCUSSION

Some who are reading this have led small group Bible studies many times. Here is an important word of warning: experience alone does not make you a more effective discussion leader. In fact, experience can make you **less effective**. You see, the more expe-

rience you have, the more comfortable you will be at the task. Unfortunately, for some that means becoming increasingly comfortable in doing a bad job. Taking satisfaction with mediocrity translates into taking the task less seriously. It is easy to wrongly assert that just because one is experienced, he or she can successfully "shoot from the hip," so to speak. If you really want your members to get the most out of this study, you need to be dissatisfied with simply doing an adequate job and make it your aim to do an excellent job. A key to excellence is to regularly evaluate yourself to see that you are still doing all that you want to be doing. We have prepared a list of over thirty evaluation questions for you to review from time to time. This list of questions can be found on page 11 in this Leader's Guide. The examination questions will help to jog your memory and, hopefully, will become an effective aid in improving the quality of your group discussion. Review the evaluation questions list, and jot down below two or three action points for you to begin implementing next week.

ACTION POINTS:

1. _____

_____

2. _____

_____

3. _____

_____

David

MEMORY VERSE

Acts 13:22

"And after He had removed him, He raised up David to be their king, concerning whom He also testified and said, 'I HAVE FOUND DAVID the son of Jesse, A MAN AFTER MY HEART, who will do all My will.'"

BEFORE THE SESSION

❑ Remember that your goal is not to teach the lesson, but to facilitate discussion.

❑ For additional study, you will benefit from reading the Old Testament narrative on David's life found in 2 Samuel.

❑ Make sure your own heart is right with God. Be willing to be transparent with the group about your own life experiences and mistakes. This will make it easier for them to open up.

❑ Don't be afraid of chasing tangents for a while if the diversions capture the interest of the group as a whole, but don't sacrifice the rest of the group to belabor the questions of one member. Trust God to lead you.

❑ You may want to keep a highlight pen handy as you study to mark key statements that stood out to you.

WHAT TO EXPECT

The danger of dealing with such a familiar character as David is that although most everyone will have some knowledge of certain events in his life, few will have seriously studied him. Many, if not most, will never have studied David against the backdrop of his predecessor, Saul. Looking at David's kingship will give your group greater understanding into the man and his writings. We will find in this week's lesson that his life is rich in practical principles, instructing us in what it means to follow God. We will also see that his is a very human example, stained by mistakes and failure. You will find that many in your group will be able to relate better to David after studying his humanness. Often we place the saints of old on a pedestal too high to be relevant to most of us. Yet David, like all the characters of Scripture, was a person just like us.

> ### THE MAIN POINT
> Having a heart after God's own heart does not imply living a life without sin, but rather, having a willingness to deal with sin in God's way when it does show up.

DURING THE SESSION

 OPENING: 5–10 MINUTES

Opening Prayer—Ask someone in your group to open the session in prayer.

Opening Illustration—A worldly kind of person came to the preacher, defending her practice of attending worldly entertainment. She said, "But, pastor, I can take Jesus Christ with me wherever I go." The pastor after a few moments of thought quietly replied, "Indeed, is that so? I didn't know that was the order of the Bible. Is it for you to lead Jesus to where you want to go, or for Him to lead you where He wants you to be?" In David and Saul, we see just such a contrast: one who would take the Lord with him, and the other who would follow where the Lord would lead.

⌛ DISCUSSION: 30–40 MINUTES

Once your group gets talking, you will find that all you need to do is keep the group directed and flowing with a question or two or a pointed observation. You are the gatekeeper of discussion. Don't be afraid to ask someone to elaborate further or to ask a quiet member of the group what they think of someone else's comments. Time will not allow you to discuss every single question in the lesson one at a time. Instead, make it your goal to cover the main ideas of each day, and help the group to personally share what they learned. You don't have to use all the discussion questions. They are there for your discretion.

Main Objective in Day One: In Day One, the central objective of the study is to paint a portrait of the early years of David and what those early years reveal of his heart. Below, check any discussion questions that you might consider using in your group session.

_____ Describe your thoughts on the incident of David and Goliath.

_____ What is the most recent situation God has used in your life to teach you to trust and rely on Him?

_____ What do you think God was saying to the unbelievers through the David and Goliath incident?

_____ What evidences did you see in David of a heart after God's heart?

Main Objective in Day Two: In Day Two, we see the important principle illustrated of doing God's will God's way in David's life and ascension to the throne. Check any discussion questions you will use.

_____ Why do you think David was unwilling to take matters into his own hands and put Saul out of the way?

_____ What do you see of David's heart in how he responds to Saul's death?

_____ When you are faced with someone who is working against you, and perhaps God as well, how do you usually respond?

_____ How do you think Jesus' instruction in Luke about responding to our enemies should be lived out today?

_____ Are there any other areas of Day Two that you would like to discuss?

Main Objective in Day Three: Day Three gives us the stained, very human, portrait of David's sins. His heart is revealed not in perfection, but in his willingness to deal with his sin God's way. Look over the discussion-starter questions below to see if any are applicable to your group.

_____ Concerning the incident with the Ark of the Covenant, how does having a heart after God's heart affect the way we handle mistakes?

_____ What do you gather from David's response to the death of his child with Bathsheba?

_____ Did you think of a time when God, in His grace, took sin in your life and worked it to His purpose and your good?

_____ What did you learn from David's mistake with the census?

_____ Did today's lesson raise any questions for you?

Main Objective in Day Four: Day Four shows us the process of David dealing with his sins, and sets this up as a model for us. Review the discussion question list below, and choose any that you feel are good questions for your session.

_____ Why do you think the Bible records the failures of David?

_____ What do you see as the biggest differences between how Saul dealt with his sin and how David dealt with his?

_____ Did anything in particular stand out to you from Psalm 51? What about Micah 6:6–8?

_____ Do you have any questions about how to deal with sin?

Day Five—Key Points in Application: The most important application point from David's life is that having a heart after God's own heart does not mean that we will never sin, but that when we do, we deal with it and turn back to God. Some good application questions for Day Five include . . .

_____ What does it mean to you to have a heart after God's heart?

_____ Have you ever seen in your own life or someone around you the heaviness of unconfessed sin weighing on the heart?

_____ Have you seen the release of confession?

⌛ CLOSING: 5–10 MINUTES

❑ **Summarize**—Review the main objectives for each day.

❑ **Remind** those in your group that living a victorious Christian life is not attained when we try hard to be like Jesus, but only when we surrender our lives to God and let Him work through us.

❑ **Preview**—Take a few moments to preview next week's lesson on **"Solomon: Guarding your Heart."** Encourage your group members to complete their homework.

❑ **Pray**—Close in prayer.

TOOLS FOR GOOD DISCUSSION

Bill Donahue, in his book, *Leading Life-Changing Small Groups* (Grand Rapids: Zondervan Publishing House, 1996), lists four facilitator actions that will produce dynamic discussion. These four actions are easy to remember because they are linked through the acrostic method to the word, **ACTS.** You will profit from taking time to review this information in the "Helpful Hints" section of **How to Lead a Small Group Bible Study,** which is on page 5 of this Leader's Guide book.

3

Solomon

MEMORY **Proverbs 4:23** VERSE

*"Watch over your heart with all diligence,
for from it flow the springs of life."*

BEFORE THE SESSION

❑ Pray each day for the members of your group. Pray that they spend time in the Word, grasp the message God wants to bring to their lives, and that they surrender to what God is saying.

❑ Thoroughly prepare for your group session—don't procrastinate!

❑ Remember that Solomon is the son of David (last week's lesson) and that much of what he did and said was learned from David.

❑ As you go through the study, jot down any ideas or questions you want to discuss. Those, along with the suggested questions listed throughout this Leader's Guide, can personalize the discussion to fit your group. Think of the needs of your group, and look for applicable questions and discussion starters.

❑ To better understand the times of Solomon, you may want to look at articles on "Solomon," "The Temple," or "Israel" in a Bible dictionary.

❑ Remain ever teachable. Look first for what God is saying to you.

❑ Be prepared to be transparent and open about what God is teaching you. Nothing is quite as contagious as the joy at discovering new treasures in the Word.

WHAT TO EXPECT

Most in your group know something about Solomon. They have heard of his riches or the book of Proverbs, or Ecclesiastes, or even the Song of Solomon. However, many are not cognizant of the defeat Solomon suffered as a result of his refusal to listen to his own counsel. Solomon did not always guard his heart and, eventually, was caught in the snare of idolatry. For many in your group the danger of idolatry is something reserved for some tribe on an island in the middle of the Pacific, not for modern society. The reality concerning the snare of idolatry (or of anything that distracts and divides our hearts) will be one of the key truths taught in this study of Solomon. Allow this study to give you and your group a guided tour down the "halls of wisdom." Take this opportunity to sharpen your group's awareness of the idols of today. Help them see the subtlety of idolatry. Hearing what Solomon said and seeing what he did can help lead the members of your group onto more solid ground for a Christian walk that comes from "guarded" hearts.

> **THE MAIN POINT**
> A person with a guarded heart is able to rejoice in the ways of God because he is walking in those same ways.

DURING THE SESSION

 OPENING: 5–10 MINUTES

Opening Prayer—Remember the Lord is the Teacher and wants us to depend on Him as we open the Scriptures. Ask Him to teach you as you meet together.

Opening Illustration—One of the evident truths in any age is that men will only guard what is valuable. There are few guards posted at a city landfill. There are many guards and security measures at banks, jewelry stores, and top secret military installations. Why? Because of the value there. That says something about God's view of the heart. He knows that the heart is of great value to Him and to the one who possesses it. The Hebrew word for "guard" or "keep" (*natsar*) in Proverbs 4:23 carries the idea of "continual watching" and sometimes refers to a "watchman" on security duty. "Watching" includes two things—**1)** you keep anything bad from coming in, and **2)** you keep anything good from being stolen. So it is with our hearts. As you walk through this lesson on Solomon, look at him and the Word of God through the eyes of a "watchman," who must guard the "city" of your heart. What do you want to keep out of your heart, and what do you want to secure, making sure no one steals it out of your heart? Seek to answer those questions as you guide your group through this lesson.

 DISCUSSION: 30–40 MINUTES

Keep the group directed along the main highway of Solomon. You may have a pointed observation that helps sharpen the focus of the group. Encourage some to elaborate further on a key point or ask a quiet member of the group what they think of someone's comments. Watch the time, knowing you can't cover every single question in the lesson. Seek to cover the main ideas of each day and help the group to personally share what they have learned.

Main Objective in Day One: In Day One, the main objective is for you and your study group to see the importance of obedience in following the Word of God. Obedience is the key to a well-guarded heart. Check which discussion questions you will use from Day One.

_____ How tempting is it today to try to gain personal power, position (business, political, or even religious), or financial power? In what ways do we try to gain these?

_____ How does the Word of God help guard us against the abuse of personal power and position?

_____ David sought to teach his son, Solomon. How can others help us in guarding our hearts?

_____ What difference does it make whether we simply hear wise words or obey wise words?

Main Objective in Day Two: Day Two focuses on a hearing heart, a heart hungry to learn and eager to obey. The following questions may serve as excellent discussion starters for your group session:

_____ How important is wisdom for a leader, whether that leader is a king, governor, mayor, parent, older sibling, employer, or even a small group Bible-study leader?

_____ How does wisdom compare with all the other things many leaders think they must have to lead?

_____ What does it mean to follow God in leading others? Why is that important?

_____ What value can you place on knowing and experiencing the presence and the guiding hand of God in your life, in your family, in your work or school?

Main Objective in Day Three: Day Three introduces us to the dangers, first, of an unguarded heart and then, of a divided heart. Check which discussion questions you will use from Day Three.

_____ How valuable are the warnings of a loving Father? What do you know about those warnings?

_____ What is the danger we face when everything is running smoothly and we have abundance?

_____ What things can crowd out the voice of the Lord and His Word? What can make our hearing dull?

_____ What does the discipline of the Lord tell you about His love and care for you? (You may want to refer to Hebrews 12:5–13.)

Main Objective in Day Four: In Day Four, we look back over the wisdom Solomon gained over the years. The wisdom God gave him can guide us if we will listen! Check which discussion questions you will use from Day Four.

_____ What is the difference between being rich in "riches" and being rich in "life"?

_____ What is the significance of remembering our Creator? What would He be able to tell us about how to live life?

_____ How can you gain wisdom for every circumstance of life? What does "diligence" have to do with wisdom?

_____ What has God been teaching you about guarding your relationships or about guarding your time?

Day Five—Key Points in Application: The most important application point is in applying the wisdom and truths that we know. Otherwise, we become arrogant in our knowledge and led astray by our self-directing pride. Below, select a question or two for your Day Five discussion.

_____ What can help us walk in humility before the Lord and His Word?

_____ What are some potential idols in our lives today? (They can be subtle.) How do we recognize them?

_____ Is the Lord dealing with you about any aspect of this lesson?

❑ **Summarize**—Restate the key points the group shared. Review the objectives for each of the days found in these leader notes.

❑ **Remind**—Using the memory verse (Proverbs 4:23), remind the group of the importance of each one guarding his or her heart. Idols and other deceptions are still around today. We must stay on guard.

❑ **Ask** them to share their thoughts about the key applications from Day Five.

❑ **Preview**—Take a few moments to preview next week's lesson on **"Jeroboam I: The Ruin of Following the Devices of One's Own Heart."** Encourage your group to do their homework and to space it out over the week.

❑ **Pray**—Close in prayer.

TOOLS FOR GOOD DISCUSSION

One of the people who show up in every group is a person we call **"Talkative Timothy."** Talkative Timothy tends to talk too much and dominates the discussion time by giving less opportunity for others to share. What do you do with a group member who talks too much? In the "Helpful Hints" section of **How to Lead a Small Group Bible Study** (p. 5), you'll find some practical ideas on managing the "Talkative Timothy's" in your group.

Jeroboam I

MEMORY **Luke 9:23–25** VERSES

"If anyone wishes to come after Me, let him deny himself, and take up his cross daily, and follow Me. For whoever wishes to save his life shall lose it, . . . For what is a man profited if he gains the whole world and loses or forfeits himself?"

BEFORE THE SESSION

☐ Be sure to do your own study far enough in advance so as not to be rushed. You want to allow God time to speak to you personally.

☐ Familiarize yourself with the chart, "The Life of Jeroboam I and His Impact on Israel," at the end of this lesson.

☐ Don't feel that you have to use all of the discussion questions listed below. You may have come up with others on your own, or you may find that time will not allow you to use them all. These questions are to serve you, not for you to serve.

☐ You are the gatekeeper of the discussion. Do not be afraid to "reel the group back in" if they get too far away from the subject of the lesson.

☐ Remember to keep a highlight pen ready as you study to mark any points you want to be sure to discuss.

☐ Pray each day for the members of your group—that they spend time in the Word, grasp the message God wants to bring to their lives, and that they surrender to what God is saying.

WHAT TO EXPECT

Jeroboam I is not one of the better-known kings of Ancient Israel, but his life needs to be studied and understood. Many times we learn the attitudes to have and the choices to make by looking at someone who has chosen foolishly. As you study the life of Jeroboam, look for his foolish choices. You should also look for ways the Lord sought to mercifully bring Jeroboam back to following Him. Look for the consequences that developed when Jeroboam stubbornly and arrogantly refused to obey God. There are many lessons to be learned from such a study.

> ### THE MAIN POINT
> People who are wrapped up in themselves are destined for defeat and loss unless they repent.

DURING THE SESSION

⌛ **OPENING: 5–10 MINUTES**

Opening Prayer—Remember that if it took the inspiration of God for people to write Scripture, it will also take His illumination for us to understand it. Have one of the members of your group open your time together in prayer.

70 FOLLOWING GOD LEADER'S GUIDE

Opening Illustration—We are always in danger of following the devices of our own hearts instead of the desires of God. When we do not follow Him, we will move **backward** and **downward** in our walk. Second Timothy 3:13–14 says, *"But evil men and impostors will grow worse and worse, deceiving and being deceived. But you must continue in the things which you have learned and been assured of, knowing from whom you have learned them. . . ."* The Puritan author, Thomas Watson, commenting on those verses, wrote:

> Such as do not grow in grace, decay in grace. . . . There is not standing in religion, either we go forward or backward. If faith does not grow, unbelief will; if heavenly-mindedness does not grow, covetousness will. A man who does not increase his stock, diminishes it: so if you do not improve your stock of grace, your stock will decay. . . . The more we grow in grace, the more we shall flourish in glory. Though every vessel of glory shall be full, yet some vessels hold more than others. He whose pound gained ten, was made ruler over ten cities (Luke 19:17). Such as do not grow much, though they lose not their glory, they lessen it. If any shall follow the Lamb in whiter and larger robes of glory than others, they shall be such as have shone most in grace here. Lament the want of growth. Religion in many is grown into a form and profession only: this is to grow in leaves, not in fruit. Many Christians are like a body in an atrophy, which does not thrive. They are not nourished by the sermons they hear. . . . It is to be suspected where there is no growth, there wants a vital principle. Some instead of growing better, grow worse; they grow more earthly, more profane (2 Timothy 3:13). . . . Many grow hell-ward—they grow past shame (Zephaniah 3:5). [Thomas Watson, *A Body of Divinity*: p. 276]

Those dangers of spiritual decline were real in Jeroboam's day, and they are just as undeniable today. As your group walks through the life of Jeroboam I, be watching for those common dangers of the devices of one's own heart.

⧗ DISCUSSION: 30–40 MINUTES

Once your group gets talking you will find that all you need to do is keep the group directed and flowing with a question or two or a pointed observation. You are the gatekeeper of discussion. Don't be afraid to ask someone to elaborate further ("Explain what you mean, Barbara.") or to ask a quiet member

of the group what they think of someone else's comments ("What do you think, Dave?"). Time will not allow you to discuss every single question in the lesson one at a time. Instead, make it your goal to cover the main ideas of each day and help the group to share what they learned personally. You don't have to use all the discussion questions above. They are there for your choosing and discretion.

Main Objective in Day One: Day One focuses on the opportunity Jeroboam had to follow God and to be greatly honored by Him. But Jeroboam squandered his opportunity. Below, check which discussion questions you will use from Day One.

_____ How should we treat the opportunities the Lord gives us?

_____ What does it mean to wait on God? How can we trust in His timing?

_____ What must we do with our desires? How can we discern between godly desires and selfish desires?

_____ There are always those who are ready to "help" you, even if it is against what God wants. How would you caution someone about the "help" they are receiving?

Main Objective in Day Two: Day Two studies the foolish choices of Jeroboam (and of Rehoboam) and the destructive path upon which he began to walk. Check which discussion questions you will use from Day Two.

_____ What does it matter whether we seek and follow godly counsel or wicked counsel?

_____ How do you see someone getting his own way as part of God's judgment on that way?

_____ Why do people so easily follow lies, half-truths, and the things that corrupt?

_____ What does Jeroboam's influence on Israel (Northern Kingdom) say to you about **your influence** at home, at school, at work, on the playing field, or at church?

Main Objective in Day Three: In Day Three, we see God's warning to Jeroboam. The Lord is patient, but He is also serious when He gives a warning. It is an opportunity to repent and follow God. In addition to any discussion-starter questions that you may have in mind, the following questions may also prove useful to your group time.

_____ Why do you think the Lord wanted Israel to come to a **specific place** to worship instead of just letting them choose any place they wanted?

_____ God sent a man of God from Judah with His message. What does that say to you about the Lord?

_____ How important is prompt, exact obedience?

_____ To what depths of degradation can selfishness take someone? What do you see in Jeroboam?

Main Objective in Day Four: In Day Four, the judgment of God is clearly revealed after repeated attempts to bring Jeroboam back to the truth. Below, place a checkmark next to the questions that you feel are worthy of mention in your session. Or you may want to place ranking numbers next to each question to note your order of preference.

_____ What does God's judgment on Jeroboam tell you about God?

_____ Jeroboam's son, Abijah, had a heart for God. What does this tell you about the work of God even in the midst of corrupt family leadership?

_____ Why do you think Jeroboam continually refused to repent?

_____ How can we walk with God in mercy instead of judgment?

Day Five—Key Points in Application: The most important application point your group can glean from the lesson on Jeroboam I is the importance of listening to the warnings that God sends our way and paying attention to the correcting ways of God in our lives. Examine the question list below, and decide if there are any that fit your group discussion for the Day Five application time.

_____ When God speaks or gives a command, He gives the grace and strength to fulfill what He wants done. What has the lesson on the life of Jeroboam said to you? What applications have you seen?

_____ What kind of leader would you like to be?

_____ How can we help one another pay heed to the warnings that God sends our way?

_____ God speaks our language. Name some incidents in Scripture where God warned others. What are some ways He warns us today?

⌛ CLOSING: 5–10 MINUTES

❑ **Summarize**—Restate the key points that were highlighted in the class. You may want to briefly review the objectives for each of the days found at the beginning of these leader notes.

❑ **Focus**—Using this lesson's memory verses (Luke 9:23–25), focus on the heart that Jesus wants us to have—a heart of daily surrendering our wills and our lives to Him. He does not want us to lose out on His best for us. He wants us to know His will and experience His Life working in us and through us.

❑ **Ask** the members of your group to reveal their thoughts about the key applications from Day Five.

❑ **Preview**—Take a few moments to preview next week's lesson on **"Asa: The Lord Is with You When You Are with Him."**

❑ **Pray**—Close in prayer.

TOOLS FOR GOOD DISCUSSION

As mentioned earlier, there are certain people who show up in every discussion group. Last week we looked at "Talkative Timothy." Another person who is likely to show up is **"Silent Sally."** She does not readily speak up. Sometimes, her silence is because she doesn't yet feel comfortable enough with the group to share her thoughts. Other times, it is simply because she fears being rejected. Often, her silence is because she is too polite to interrupt and thus is headed off at the pass each time she wants to speak by more aggressive (and less sensitive) members of the group. In the "Helpful Hints" section of **How to Lead a Small Group Bible Study** (p. 6), you'll find some practical ideas on managing the "Silent Sally's" in your group.

MEMORY  VERSE

"For the eyes of the Lord move to and fro throughout the earth that He may strongly support those whose heart is completely His."

BEFORE THE SESSION

❑ Resist the temptation to do all your homework in one sitting or to put it off until the last minute. You will not be as prepared if you study this way.

❑ Make sure to mark down any discussion questions that come to mind as you study. Don't feel that you have to use all of the suggested discussion questions included in this leader's guide. Feel free to pick and choose based on your group and the time frame with which you are working.

❑ If you want to do further study, you may want to see what you learn of Asa from a Bible dictionary.

❑ Remember your need to trust God with your study. The Holy Spirit is always the best teacher, so stay sensitive to Him!

WHAT TO EXPECT

In this lesson, expect that all your group members will need a better understanding of the key principle of keeping their hearts completely His. Anticipate that only a few of your group members will have ever heard of Asa, let alone studied him. For most, this will be uncharted territory, and they will be experiencing the excitement of new discovery in the Word of God. Some will be surprised to discover how practical and application-filled this lesson will be. Make every effort to steer the study away from being just a history lesson by reminding your group members to look to their own lives and circumstances for how these principles can apply to them.

> ### THE MAIN POINT
> God is with us when we are with Him. If our hearts are completely His, we will enjoy His strong support.

DURING THE SESSION

⏳ **OPENING: 5–10 MINUTES**

Opening Prayer—Remember to have one of your group members open your time together in prayer.

Opening Illustration—It is related that once when Queen Victoria was in the Highlands of Scotland, she stopped at the cottage of a poor woman. The Queen sat for a few minutes in this woman's old armchair. When the party was leaving, someone told the old woman who her visitor was. She was awed by the thought of the honor that had been hers, and she carried the old chair into the spare room, saying, "No one shall ever sit in that chair again, because my queen sat in it." How much more sacredly should we preserve our hearts for our Lord—the greatest Guest! How is it, just now, in your heart? Is there any need for Christ to come with His whip of cords to drive out the traders, the sellers of cattle and doves, and the moneychangers? Asa began well and for most of his life, his heart belonged completely to the Lord, but his downfall came when he allowed other things into that place reserved for the Lord.

⌛ DISCUSSION: 30–40 MINUTES

Remember that your job is not to teach this lesson, but to facilitate discussion. Do your best to guide the group to the right answers, but don't be guilty of making a point someone else in the group could just as easily make.

Main Objective in Day One: The main point here is to gain a feel for the days in which Asa grew up and to set his early godliness against the dark backdrop of his family situation. Choose a discussion question or two from the list below.

_____ What are your thoughts on Rehoboam and Abijah?

_____ Why do you think the Queen mother, Maacah, was tolerated? How hard do you think it was for Asa to come to the decision of banishing her from her position?

_____ What else stood out to you from the first ten years of Asa's reign?

_____ What does Asa say to you about today's popular belief that we are products of our environment?

Main Objective in Day Two: In Day Two, we see how Asa handled his first real test as a military leader. We see his heart for God reflected in how he responded to this test. Below, check any discussion questions you might use from Day Two.

_____ Describe the battle with the Ethiopians and how Asa responded to their threat.

_____ Why do you think the Lord allowed this army to come against Judah?

_____ How did Asa view himself and his army?

_____ What parallels do you see to our lives in this battle and its outcome?

Main Objective in Day Three: Day Three introduces us to the years immediately following Asa's victory and the impact they had on his following God. It is encouraging to see that he did not let up in his pursuit of God. Review the questions below, and see if any are suitable to your group discussion on Day Three.

_____ What stands out to you about the message God sent to Asa?

_____ How did Asa respond to the prophetic message?

_____ Has God shown you any idols in your own life that need to be torn down?

_____ What principles for today do you see in the people defecting from Israel to Judah?

_____ Did anything else grab your attention in your studies in Day Three?

Main Objective in Day Four: In Day Four, we see the other side of the coin in Asa's life. We have seen him enjoy God's strong support as his heart is completely surrendered. Now we see what happens when his heart wanders. Check which discussion questions you will use from Day Four.

_____ How does the strife with Baasha compare with the threat of the Ethiopians in the early years of Asa's reign?

_____ Why do you think Asa chose to place his trust in Ben-hadad instead of with God?

_____ What do you think would have happened if Asa had repented at the rebuke of Hanani?

_____ How do you tend to respond when God confronts you with your sin?

_____ What were the consequences of Asa's failure to repent?

Day Five—Key Points in Application: The important thing to see out of Day Five is God's desire for our hearts to be completely His. It is in surrender that we enjoy His strong support. Decide on some discussion-starter topics for the application section of Day Five. The following questions are suggested questions that you may want to use for your discussion:

_____ Has God placed you in any difficult situations right now?

_____ What are some other places we turn to instead of trusting God?

_____ What would you tell someone who was struggling with trusting God in an area?

_____ Were there any areas in particular where this lesson touched your heart?

⌛ CLOSING: 5–10 MINUTES

❑ **Summarize**—Go over the key points of your study of Asa.

❑ **Remind** those in your group that living a victorious Christian life is not attained when we try hard to be like Jesus, but only when we surrender our lives to God and let Him work through us.

❑ **Ask** them what they thought were the key applications from day five

❑ **Preview**—Take a few moments to preview next week's lesson on **"Ahab: The Sins of Serving Self."** Encourage them to do their homework.

❑ **Pray**—Close in prayer.

TOOLS FOR GOOD DISCUSSION

Hopefully your group is functioning smoothly at this point, but perhaps you recognize the need for improvement. In either case, you will benefit from taking the time to evaluate yourself and your group. Without evaluation, you will judge your group on subjective emotions. You may think everything is fine and miss some opportunities to improve your effectiveness. You may be discouraged by problems you are confronting when you ought to be encouraged that you are doing the right things and making progress. A healthy Bible-study group is not one without problems, but is one that recognizes its problems and deals with them the right way. At this point in the course, as you and your group are nearly halfway-completed with the study of the Old Testament kings, it is important to examine yourself and see if there are any mid-course corrections that you feel are necessary to implement. Review the evaluation questions list found on page 11 of this Leader's Guide, and jot down two or three action points for you to begin implementing next week. Perhaps you have made steady improvements since the first time you answered the evaluation questions at the beginning of the course. If so, your improvements should challenge you to be an even better group leader for the final seven lessons in the study.

ACTION POINTS:

1. _____

   _____

2. _____

   _____

3. _____

   _____

Ahab

MEMORY **Philippians 2:3** VERSE

"Do nothing from selfishness or empty conceit, but with humility of mind let each of you regard one another as more important than himself."

BEFORE THE SESSION

❑ Remember the Boy Scout motto: **BE PRE-PARED!** The main reason a Bible study flounders is because the leader comes in unprepared and tries to "shoot from the hip."

❑ Make sure to jot down any discussion questions that come to mind as you study.

❑ If you want to do further study, you may benefit from doing the lesson on Elijah from *Following God: Life Principles from the Prophets.* He was the prophet who ministered to Israel during the reign of Ahab.

❑ Don't forget to pray for the members of your group and for your time studying together. You don't want to be satisfied with what you can do—you want to see God do what only He can do!

WHAT TO EXPECT

In studying this lesson, you should realize that all of us, sooner or later, will fall prey to selfishness. It is at the very core of what sin is—enthronement of self and dethronement of God. While most of us will never relate to the level of Ahab's wickedness, we all fall victim to the sin of selfishness, and there will be much we can learn of what not to do from Ahab's

negative example. Realize that there may be some sin brought to the surface that God wants to deal with so that He can make each member more useable to Him in His work. Be sensitive to any discussion questions that may surface in this lesson, and guard your group from applying it only to others rather than to themselves.

> ### THE MAIN POINT
> There are tragic consequences of following self. Yet even with wicked Ahab, we see the accessibility of grace to all who will repent.

DURING THE SESSION

 OPENING: 5–10 MINUTES

Opening Prayer—Remember to have one of your group members open your time together in prayer.

Opening Illustration—Centuries ago, Nicolaus Copernicus studied the sky and declared, "If man is to know the truth, he must change his thinking! Despite what we have said for years, our earth is not the center of the cosmos—but just one celestial body among many. The sun does not move around us; we move around the sun."

That was a radical adjustment—a revolution in thought. Years later, Jean Piaget studied children and declared, "Each child must experience his or her own 'Copernican revolution.' They must learn that they are not the center of their world." This is a private, radical adjustment for everyone to make. "After all," each infant thinks, "My wants have always been met. Let life continue that way! Walls should move out of the way before I run into them. The floor should become soft just as I fall. Everyone should give me their toys if I want them. The rules of games should change so I can always win. And big things like cars should never drive where I might want to run or play." Sooner or later, life does not cooperate, and the child is shocked. Like many adults today, King Ahab was one who never learned the childhood lesson that he was not the center of the universe.

⏳ DISCUSSION: 30–40 MINUTES

Remember to pace your discussion so that you will be able to bring closure to the lesson at the designated time. You are the one who must balance lively discussion with timely redirection to ensure that you don't end up finishing only part of the lesson.

Main Objective in Day One: In Day One, the main objective is to see how selfishness stained Ahab's spiritual life. Check which discussion questions you will use from Day One.

_____ Which do you think is more accurate—did Jezebel pull Ahab down, or was it his low state that led him to marry Jezebel?

_____ How do you see selfishness reflected in the things Ahab was unwilling to confront?

_____ Describe Ahab's encounter with Elijah on Mount Carmel?

Main Objective in Day Two: In Day Two, we learn some of the specific ways that selfishness manifested itself in Ahab's battles. Choose a discussion question or two from the Day Two list below.

_____ What lessons can we learn from King Ahab's encounter with Ben-hadad?

_____ What do you see in Ahab's lack of gratitude for God's deliverance?

_____ Why do you think God continually delivered Ahab?

_____ Does it remind you at all of King Saul?

_____ What does Ahab's failure to destroy Ben-hadad say to you about selfish leadership?

Main Objective in Day Three: Day Three introduces us to what Ahab's possessions have to say about his heart. Decide on some discussion-starter questions for your session on Ahab. Below are some possible discussion questions for you to consider.

_____ What stands out to you in the contrast between Ahab's view of his possessions and that of King David's?

_____ What do we see of Ahab in Jezebel's obtaining the vineyard he desired?

_____ When Elijah confronts Ahab's sin, he is called an "enemy." Can you think of any examples where someone speaking truth is made out to be the bad guy?

_____ Why do you think God was so responsive to Ahab's repentance?

Main Objective in Day Four: In Day Four, we see the reality that selfishness often stains our ability to hear truth. People dominated by self are always in danger of surrounding themselves with counselors who will tell them what they want to hear. Check which discussion questions you will use from Day Four.

_____ What ways have we seen God pointing Ahab toward truth? What do you think about that?

_____ Why was Ahab so willing to take Jezebel's counsel?

_____ What do you see as the message of Ahab's life and death?

Day Five—Key Points in Application: The most important application point out of Day Five is that all of us must guard against the stains of selfishness. Below, check any discussion questions that are best suited to your group for application.

_____ Which of the three temptations do you struggle with the most?

_____ What are some ways selfishness stains the different areas of life?

_____ Do you ever struggle with only taking counsel from people who will tell you what you want to hear?

_____ Do you understand each of the steps to getting right with God (confession, repentance, restitution, surrender, growth)?

⏳ CLOSING: 5–10 MINUTES

❑ **Summarize**—Highlight the key points of the lesson on Ahab. Review "The Main Point" statement and the memory verse for this lesson.

❑ **Remind** those in your group that living a victorious Christian life is not attained when we try hard to be like Jesus, but only when we surrender our lives to God and let Him work through us.

❑ **Preview**—Take time to preview next week's lesson on **"Jehoshaphat: Unequally Yoked."** Discuss the importance of the assigned homework.

❑ **Ask** your group to discuss the key applications from Day Five.

❑ **Pray**—Close in prayer.

TOOLS FOR GOOD DISCUSSION

As discussed earlier, there are certain people who show up in every discussion group that you will ever lead. We have already looked at "Talkative Timothy" and "Silent Sally." This week, let's talk about another person who also tends to show up. Let's call this person **"Tangent Tom."** He is the kind of guy who loves to talk even when he has nothing to say. Tangent Tom loves to "chase rabbits" regardless of where they go. When he gets the floor, you never know where the discussion will lead. You need to understand that not all tangents are bad. Sometimes, much can be gained from discussion "a little off the beaten path." But these diversions must be balanced against the purpose of the group. In the "Helpful Hints" section of **How to Lead a Small Group** (p. 6), you will find some practical ideas on managing the "Tangent Tom's" in your group. You will also get some helpful information on evaluating tangents as they arise.

Jehoshaphat

MEMORY **2 Corinthians 6:14a** VERSE

"Do not be bound together with unbelievers; for what partner-ship have righteousness and lawlessness, or what fellowship has light with darkness?"

BEFORE THE SESSION

❏ Try to get your lesson plans and homework done early this week. This gives time for you to reflect on what you have learned and process it mentally. Don't succumb to the temptation to procrastinate.

❏ Make sure you keep a highlight pen handy to highlight any things you intend to discuss, including any questions that you think your group may have trouble comprehending. Jot down any good discussion questions that come to your mind as you study.

❏ Don't think of your ministry to the members of your group as something that only takes place during your group time. Pray for your group members by name during the week that they would receive spiritual enrichment from doing their daily homework. Encourage them as you have opportunity.

WHAT TO EXPECT

In this lesson we are afforded a very practical Old Testament example of the New Testament admonition to not be unequally yoked with unbelievers. Although there are many commendable things to see in Jehoshaphat's life, he stands as a warning to us of how being bound with unbelievers can negate the effect of our testimony and our impact in the world in which we live. Expect that everyone in your group will have areas of life to which these principles will apply. Be prepared to share your own struggles as well as you guide them toward personal evaluation of their lives and personal application to the different areas their lives touch.

> ### THE MAIN POINT
> A good and godly life can be robbed of its full impact if it is allowed to be unequally yoked with unbelievers.

DURING THE SESSION

⏳ **OPENING: 5–10 MINUTES**

Opening Prayer—It would be a good idea to have a different group member each week open your time together in prayer.

Opening Illustration—Olivia ("Livey") Langdon was married to the American author and beloved humorist, Samuel Langhorne Clemens, better known by his pseudonym—Mark Twain. Although "Livey" at one time held strongly to her faith in God that was rooted in her solid Christian family upbringing, she knew that Mark was not a believer—but married him anyway. Early in their marriage he allowed praying at mealtimes, but he never once made a commitment to Christ. Later on in their marriage he began attacking her belief in the Bible. Bit by bit, Twain's lack of faith chipped away at Livey's trust in God. It eroded her faith so badly that at one point, when the couple faced the pressing sorrow of the death of their daughter, Twain said to Livey, "Why don't you fall back upon your personal faith?" to which Livey replied, "Mark, I can't, for I haven't any." She learned the hard way the painful consequences of being unequally yoked with unbelievers. We see that same painful principle played out this week in the life of Jehoshaphat.

⏳ DISCUSSION: 30–40 MINUTES

A key objective in how you manage your discussion time is to keep the big picture in view. Your job is not like a schoolteacher's job, grading papers and tests and the like, but more like a tutor's job, making sure your group understands the subject. Keep the main point of the lesson in view, and make sure they take that main point home with them.

Main Objective in Day One: In Day One, the main objective is to look at Jehoshaphat's heart for God and the righteous choices he made during his reign as king of Judah. Start thinking now about what discussion starters you will use in your session devoted to Jehoshaphat. Review the question list below. Perhaps there is a question or two below that might be essential to your group time.

_____ What impact do you think Jehoshaphat's father, Asa, had on the kind of man he was?

_____ What stands out to you from Jehoshaphat's relationship with God?

_____ How do you think Jehoshaphat's reforms affected the nation of Judah?

_____ What do you think it would be like to have a leader like that today?

_____ What else stood out to you from Day One?

Main Objective in Day Two: In Day Two, we look at one of the greatest challenges to arise during the reign of Jehoshaphat—the invasion by Moab and Ammon. This is perhaps the single most familiar event from his life and reign. Check which discussion questions you will use from Day Two.

_____ Can you imagine what it would have been like to live in Judah when this challenge arose? What do you think was the response of the average citizen?

_____ What stands out to you from Jehoshaphat's response to the crisis?

_____ How did you respond the last time that you faced a crisis?

_____ What stood out to you from the prayer of Jehoshaphat?

_____ Do you see any principles from God's deliverance here that apply to us today?

Main Objective in Day Three: Day Three introduces us to the details of Jehoshaphat's ill-fated alliances with wicked King Ahab of Israel and some of their consequences. Take a look at the discussion question list below to see if any are applicable to your group session.

_____ What do you think motivated Jehoshaphat in allying himself to Ahab by marriage?

_____ What thoughts came to mind as you looked at the way Jehoshaphat was drawn into a military alliance with Ahab?

_____ Why do you think Jehoshaphat ignored the counsel of Micaiah?

_____ What aspects of this battle (if any) particularly intrigued you?

_____ Were there any questions raised by your study in Day Three?

Main Objective in Day Four: Day Four examines the final example of Jehoshaphat's weakness for ungodly alliances—the economic alliance with Ahab's son, Ahaziah. We also investigate some of the far-reaching consequences of this fleshly tendency. Choose some discussion starters for your group session.

_____ What do you think motivated the economic alliance Jehoshaphat forged with Ahaziah?

_____ Why do you think it turned out the way it did?

_____ How do you see Jehoshaphat's foolish choices affecting his children?

____ What were the long-term consequences of Jehoshaphat's choices?

Day Five—Key Points in Application: The most important application point out of Day Five is to recognize the dangers of allowing ourselves to be unequally yoked with unbelievers. Make sure your members understand that they cannot walk with the world and remain untarnished by it. Below, check any discussion questions that you might consider using for your application time.

____ What are the areas where you are tempted to compromise with unholy alliances?

____ What motivations make such alliances attractive?

____ Can you think of any examples in your own life where unity was wrongly sought at the expense of truth?

____ What is the biggest application point you observed this week?

⧖ CLOSING: 5–10 MINUTES

❑ **Summarize**—You may want to read "The Main Point" statement at the beginning of the leader's notes on Jehoshaphat.

❑ **Preview**—If time allows, preview next week's lesson on **"Hezekiah: Following God in the Crises of Life."** Encourage your group to complete their homework.

❑ **Pray**—Close in prayer.

  ## TOOLS FOR GOOD DISCUSSION

One of the issues you will eventually have to combat in any group Bible study is the enemy of **boredom.** This enemy raises its ugly head from time to time, but it shouldn't. It is wrong to bore people with the Word of God! Often boredom results when leaders allow their processes to become too predictable. As small group leaders, we tend to do the same thing in the same way every single time. Yet God the Creator, who spoke everything into existence is infinitely creative! Think about it. He is the one who not only created animals in different shapes and sizes, but different colors as well. When He created food, He didn't make it all taste or feel the same. This God of creativity lives in us. We can trust Him to give us creative ideas that will keep our group times from becoming tired and mundane. In the "Helpful Hints" section of **How to Lead a Small Group** (pp. 8–9), you'll find some practical ideas on adding spice and creativity to your study time.

Hezekiah

MEMORY **2 Chronicles 31:20–21** VERSES

"And thus Hezekiah did throughout all Judah; and he did what was good, right and true before the Lord his God. And every work which he began in the service of the house of God in law and in commandment, seeking his God, he did with all his heart and prospered."

BEFORE THE SESSION

❑ Your own preparation is key not only to your effectiveness in leading the group session, but also in your **confidence** in leading. It is hard to be confident if you know you are unprepared. These discussion questions and leader's notes are meant to be a helpful addition to your own study, but should never become a substitute.

❑ As you do your homework, study with a view to your own relationship with God. Resist the temptation to bypass this self-evaluation on your way to preparing to lead the group. Nothing will minister to your group more than the testimony of your own walk with God.

❑ If you want to do further study, you may benefit from studying the lesson on **Isaiah** from *Following God: Life Principles from the Prophets of the Old Testament.*

❑ Don't think of your ministry to the members of your group as something that only takes place during your group time. Pray for your group members by name during the week that they would receive spiritual enrichment from doing their daily homework. Encourage them as you have opportunity.

WHAT TO EXPECT

Every life is punctuated with some measure of crisis. It is not the whole of our lives, yet sometimes these times of distress and the choices made in them go a long way toward shaping the flow of our lives. In Hezekiah, we have a healthy reminder of both the positive and negative impact our response to the crises of our lives can have. Be prepared for the possibility that someone in your group may be in a crisis situation that they feel is hopeless, perhaps with an unbelieving spouse or a prodigal child. While these truths from Hezekiah should be a great comfort, they may also bring to the surface some hidden pain. Don't be afraid of some honest emotion spilling out into the group time.

THE MAIN POINT
The most important thing to see about times of crisis is that it is not the crisis that shapes us as much as it is our response to the crisis.

DURING THE SESSION

⌛ **OPENING: 5–10 MINUTES**

Opening Prayer—A good prayer with which to

open your time with is the prayer of David in Psalm 119:18, *"Open my eyes, that I may behold Wonderful things from Thy law."* Remember, if it took the illumination of God for men to write Scripture, it will take the same for us to understand it.

Opening Illustration—The Duke of Luxemburg, on his death-bed, declared, "That I would then much rather have had it to reflect upon, that I had administered a cup of cold water to a worthy poor creature in distress, than that I had won so many battles as I had triumphed in." All the sentiments of worldly grandeur vanish at that unavoidable moment which decides the eternal state of men. At the end of our lives, what we are is a result of the defining choices we have made over the course of the circumstances of our lives. We can clearly see this reality in the study of Hezekiah.

⌛ DISCUSSION: 30–40 MINUTES

Remember to pace your discussion so that you don't run out of time to get to the application questions in Day Five. This time for application is perhaps the most important part of your Bible study. It will be helpful if you are familiar enough with the lesson to be able to prioritize the days for which you want to place more emphasis, so that you are prepared to reflect this added emphasis in the time you devote to that particular day's reading.

Main Objective in Day One: In Day One, the main objective is to understand that every choice we make in life is a crisis of sorts. In the right choices Hezekiah made, we see an example we can follow. Choose a discussion question or two from the Day One list below.

____ What stands out to you about Hezekiah's father?

____ What was the connection between the sordid state of affairs in the temple worship and the difficulties that the nation of Judah experienced?

____ Why do you think the temple and the priesthood was the first place Hezekiah started his reforms?

____ What stood out to you from the reinstatement of the Passover?

____ Are there any other thoughts from Day One that you would like to discuss?

Main Objective in Day Two: We learn in Day Two some of the specifics of how Hezekiah responded when he was faced with the crisis of invasion by Sennacherib of Assyria. Check which discussion questions you will use from Day Two.

____ What do you see reflected in Hezekiah's response to Sennacherib's invasion?

____ How did Hezekiah help to keep the focus of God's people on the Lord instead of the invaders?

____ How did Hezekiah keep his own focus on the Lord?

Main Objective in Day Three: Day Three introduces us to the crisis of sickness that came to Hezekiah and how he responded. In addition to any discussion questions you may have in mind for your group session, the following questions may also be useful:

____ Why do you think God allows sickness to come to His people?

____ What is significant about Hezekiah's response?

____ How did God confirm Hezekiah's healing?

____ What do you think this good news did for Hezekiah's faith?

____ Were there any other questions raised by your study in Day Three?

Main Objective in Day Four: In Day Four, our study of Hezekiah takes us to the reality that the hardest crisis to navigate may not be adversity, but prosperity. Place a checkmark next to the discussion question you would like to use for your group session. Or you may want to place a ranking number in each blank to note your order of preference.

____ What was Hezekiah's response to his healing?

____ Have you ever witnessed God do something great for someone only to have that person act ungratefully?

____ Why do you think Hezekiah showed off the temple treasures?

____ What are some ways our present life on earth tests our faith in God?

Day Five—Key Points in Application: The most important application point from Day Five is that we must trust God with the trials in our lives, for it is in the trials that He tests our trust. Make sure your members understand this correlation between trials and trust. Check which discussion questions you will use from Day Five.

_____ What usually occurs when you encounter a crisis?

_____ What do you sense the Lord is saying to you from the example of Hezekiah?

_____ Is there any request you have withheld from the Lord because you didn't think He would be interested in it?

_____ What other applications did you see from this week?

⌛ CLOSING: 5–10 MINUTES

❑ **Summarize**—Restate the key points. You may want to reread "The Main Point" statement for Hezekiah.

❑ **Preview**—If time allows, preview next week's lesson on **"Josiah: The Impact of Following the Word of God."**

❑ **Ask** them to discuss the key applications from Day Five.

❑ **Pray**—Close in prayer.

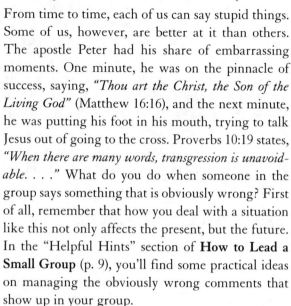 ## TOOLS FOR GOOD DISCUSSION

From time to time, each of us can say stupid things. Some of us, however, are better at it than others. The apostle Peter had his share of embarrassing moments. One minute, he was on the pinnacle of success, saying, *"Thou art the Christ, the Son of the Living God"* (Matthew 16:16), and the next minute, he was putting his foot in his mouth, trying to talk Jesus out of going to the cross. Proverbs 10:19 states, *"When there are many words, transgression is unavoidable. . . ."* What do you do when someone in the group says something that is obviously wrong? First of all, remember that how you deal with a situation like this not only affects the present, but the future. In the "Helpful Hints" section of **How to Lead a Small Group** (p. 9), you'll find some practical ideas on managing the obviously wrong comments that show up in your group.

9

MEMORY **Proverbs 27:17** VERSE

"Iron sharpens iron, so one man sharpens another."

BEFORE THE SESSION

❏ Pray each day for the members of your group—that they spend time in the Word, grasp the message God wants to bring to their lives, and that they surrender to what God is saying.

❏ Be sure you have searched the Scriptures carefully for each day's lesson.

❏ Familiarize yourself with the chart, "The Life of Josiah, King of Judah" (pp. 163–64) in the workbook.

❏ While preparing for this lesson, read through the discussion questions on the following pages, and select which questions you will use.

❏ To better understand the condition of Judah at this time you may want to look at *Following God: Life Principles from the Prophets of the Old Testament* (Lesson 9), **"Jeremiah: Trusting in God When Life Looks Hopeless"** and Lesson 10 entitled, **"Habakkuk: Following God in the Low Places of Life."**

❏ Remain ever teachable. Look first for what God is saying to you. This will help you in relating to some of the situations your group members may be facing as they are seeking to make an impact on those around them.

WHAT TO EXPECT

Studying the life of Josiah can be one of the most encouraging adventures in all of Scripture. He was sterling in character, in purpose, and in his leadership of the people of God. This lesson can give your group members a new vision for making an impact on the lives of people at work, at school, in the church, and even in their homes. For some, Josiah will be a new (and welcome) name from the pages of Scripture. Continually look for those "velcro points" where you can attach a clear application to the challenges of today. Use this lesson as an example of what can be done when we seek the Lord and His Word. Encourage the members of your group who may come from less than ideal situations. The Lord can work in the most desperate circumstances, and, as He worked through Josiah, He can certainly work through the members of your group. Help them see this truth so that they may be all God wants them to be.

THE MAIN POINT

Following God can make an impact upon the lives of others that will last forever.

During the Session

 OPENING: 5–10 MINUTES

Opening Prayer—Remember to ask the Lord for His wisdom. He promised to guide us into the truth.

Opening Illustration—In 1858, a man named Mr. Kimball went into a shoe store in Boston and led a young man to Christ. Later as an evangelist, that young shoe clerk, D. L. Moody, had a significant impact on a pastor in England by the name of F. B. Meyer. When F. B. Meyer was preaching in America, a college student named J. Wilbur Chapman came to Christ. He became a noted evangelist. In the 1890's a young man named Billy Sunday labored with him in evangelistic work. Years later, Mr. Sunday held evangelistic meetings in Charlotte, North Carolina. That effort so impacted the town that a group of laymen planned another revival with evangelist, Mordecai Ham. One of the young men touched by God in that meeting was Billy Graham.

We can never know the power of our influence on the lives of others. Faithfulness to the Lord and to His Word will make a difference in our lives, and, because of that difference, we too will make a difference in the places the Lord puts us. We can see this faithfulness in the life of Josiah. He was influenced by godly men and women in Jerusalem who directed him to the Word of God. That made the difference in his life and ultimately made the difference in many, many lives in the land of Judah. Josiah's influence is still making a difference in lives today as we study his life and how he followed God.

 DISCUSSION: 30–40 MINUTES

Select one or two specific questions to get the group started. Keep the group directed along the main highway of Josiah. By this point in the course (Week 9), you know the talkative and the quiet. Continue to encourage each member in the importance of his or her input. Some of the greatest life lessons we ever learn may come from someone who has said very little up to this point.

Main Objective in Day One: In Day One, the main objective is to see the impact of others on the young Josiah. Review the question list below, and decide upon some discussion starters for your group session on Josiah.

_____ What do you think Josiah could learn about the ways of God from his grandfather, Manasseh?

_____ What could he learn about the ways of God from his father Amon's reign and death?

_____ How important are the friends we choose?

_____ How important is input from the Word of God in the relationships we have?

Main Objective in Day Two: Day Two focuses on the impact of seeking the Lord. Josiah is our example. Check which discussion questions you will use from Day Two.

_____ Josiah did what was right. How do we know what is right in God's sight?

_____ How do our beliefs and actions go together?

_____ Josiah began to deal with the idolatry of the land. How can we recognize idols in our lives?

_____ Why is it important to cleanse our lives (God's temple today) of anything He says is wrong?

Main Objective in Day Three: Day Three introduces us to the strong, ongoing impact of the Word of God. Some good discussion questions for Day Three include . . .

_____ Have you ever entered into prayer through reading something in the Word of God? What difference did it make?

_____ How does the Word of God help us in seeking the Lord?

_____ How do new insights in the Word of God affect relationships?

_____ How can we lead others by using the Word of God?

Main Objective in Day Four: Day Four examines how Josiah followed God **only** and the impact that made on others. Check which discussion questions you will use from Day Four.

_____ The more of the Word of God that Josiah knew, the more he saw sin (his own sin included) and idolatry. How have you experienced this in your life?

_____ What does it mean to obey God fully in any matter—not partial obedience—but full obedience to what He has shown you?

_____ As we learn more of God's Word, we often see a lot of things to deal with in our lives and in our relationships. Why is it so important to deal with these things?

_____ What has God shown you this week about seeking Him?

Day Five—Key Points in Application: The most important application point in the lesson on Josiah is found in making the Word of God the foundation of all we think, say, or do. Below, are some suggestions for discussion questions. Feel free to come up with your own questions as well.

_____ Name some of the changes the Word of God can make in a person's life.

_____ What has been the greatest benefit of the Word of God in your life?

_____ How can knowing the Word of God unify people? Why does it sometimes divide?

_____ Learning God's Word is wonderful! But what can help you and others close to you **do** (not just learn) what the Word of God says?

⧖ CLOSING: 5–10 MINUTES

❑ **Summarize**—Restate the key points the group shared. Review the objectives for each of the days found at the beginning of these leader notes.

❑ **Focus**—Using the memory verse (Proverbs 27:17), focus the group on the power of influ-

ence. Each one of them has the potential to influence another in following God.

❑ **Ask** them to express their thoughts about the key applications from Day Five.

❑ **Encourage**—We have finished nine lessons. This is no time to slack off. Encourage your group to keep up the pace. We have three more lessons full of life-changing truths. Take a few moments to preview next week's lesson on **"Zerubbabel and Ezra: Following God's Will."** Encourage your group members to do their homework in proper fashion by spacing it out over the week.

❑ **Pray**—Close in prayer.

 TOOLS FOR GOOD DISCUSSION

The Scriptures are replete with examples of people who struggled with the problem of pride. But pride isn't a problem reserved for the history books. It shows up just as often today as it did in the days the Scriptures were written. In your group discussions, you may see traces of pride manifested in a "know-it-all" group member. **"Know-It-All Ned"** may have shown up in your group by this point. He may be an intellectual giant, or he may be a legend only in his own mind. He can be very prideful and argumentative. If you want some helpful hints on how to deal with "Know-It-All Ned," look in the "Helpful Hints" section of **How to Lead a Small Group Bible Study** (p. 7).

10

Zerubbabel and Ezra

MEMORY   Romans 12:2   VERSE

"...do not be conformed to this world, but be transformed by the renewing of your mind, that you may prove what the will of God is, that which is good and acceptable and perfect."

BEFORE THE SESSION

❏ Never underestimate the importance of prayer for yourself and for the members of your group. Ask the Lord to give your group members understanding in their time in the Word and to bring them to a new level of knowing Him.

❏ Spread your study time over the week.

❏ Remember to mark those ideas and questions you want to discuss or ask as you go through the study.

❏ To grasp the big picture you may want to familiarize yourself with the chart, "A Chronology of Ezra-Nehemiah-Haggai-Zechariah-Malachi," at the end of this lesson in the workbook (pp. 185–87).

❏ To better understand the times of Zerubbabel and Ezra, you may want to read some of the articles in a good Bible dictionary on "The Book of Ezra," or on "The Babylonian Captivity (or Exile)." You may also want to look at **"Haggai: A Call to Consider Your Ways"** (Lesson 11) in *Following God: Life Principles from the Prophets of the Old Testament.*

❏ Be sensitive to the needs of your group. Be pre-pared to stop and pray for a member who may be facing a difficult struggle or challenge.

WHAT TO EXPECT

Zerubbabel will be a new name to many in your group. While Ezra may be more familiar, few know how either of these men fit into Old Testament history. Understanding the time frame of their lives will help in understanding the Scriptures that tell their stories. The chart at the end of the lesson in the workbook will help you in seeing where they fit and where other events fit around them.

In this lesson, we will focus on how Zerubbabel followed the will of God in the first return of the exiles from Babylon (around 536 BC) and in the rebuilding of the Temple in Jerusalem. Then we will look at Ezra as he faithfully followed God's will in bringing the people back to Israel in the second return of the exiles (458 BC). As you guide the discussion seek to keep the focus on the faithfulness of these men even in the face of their numerous difficulties. While Zerubbabel had to be called to begin the Temple building after several years' delay, he finished the task. Ezra faithfully taught the people to fully follow the Lord and His Word. May your group be encouraged and challenged by the example of these men.

THE MAIN POINT

Knowing and obeying God's will are the vital signs for following God.

During the Session

⏳ OPENING: 5–10 MINUTES

Opening Prayer—Have one of the group members open the time with prayer.

Opening Illustration—Do you remember playing "hide and seek" as a child? For many, finding God's will is like that game. We are sure God knows His will for us and where it is, but we sometimes think He likes to play "hide and seek" with it. Of course, that is not true, but we still sometimes have difficulty "finding" God's will. That is why we must carefully and consistently read and study and meditate on the letters God has already written to us. In His Word, we learn the "vocabulary" of the Spirit. We find how He thinks, how He acts, His ways, what is "for sure" His will and what is "for sure" not His will. As you walk through the journeys of Zerubbabel and Ezra, note how clearly God directed them by His Word and through the leaders He raised up. May your group gain insight into God's will for their lives and begin to follow Him more fully and consistently.

⏳ DISCUSSION: 30–40 MINUTES

Select one or two specific questions to get the group started in discussion. This lesson on Zerubbabel and Ezra covers 80 years of Israel's history, but the main points are not in the history. They will be found in the hearts of these two men and how they led the people of God in following God and His will. Continue to encourage each member in the importance of his or her insights and input.

Main Objective in Day One: Day One looks at the call of the people to return with Zerubbabel and rebuild the Temple. Good discussion starters for Day One include . . .

_____ What do Cyrus' actions say about the ways of God with His people?

_____ What does the evident supply of provision for the Temple say about God's will in the rebuilding of that Temple?

_____ What principles about God's will do the incidents in Ezra 1—3 reveal?

_____ What applications about following God's will do you see for your life in Day One?

Main Objective in Day Two: In Day Two, the main objective is to see the importance of the Temple and worship in the life of the people of God. Below are some suggested questions for your discussion on Day Two. Which questions will you use for your group session?

_____ It is evident that God wanted the Temple rebuilt. Why do you think this is so?

_____ What is the importance of pure worship, of worship in line with the Word of God?

_____ What is significant about the opposition Israel faced in rebuilding the Temple?

_____ What applications from Israel's experiences do you see for worship in your life?

Main Objective in Day Three: In Day Three, the main objective is to see **how** Ezra followed the will of God. What discussion questions do you plan to use for Day Three? Below are some suggestions.

_____ How important is a clear sense of purpose (like that which Ezra had)?

_____ How does knowing that God works through various leaders give you confidence in knowing and doing the will of God?

_____ How needful is humility in doing God's will?

_____ How does seeking God in prayer relate to knowing and doing God's will?

Main Objective in Day Four: Day Four looks at the importance of dealing with sin in following God and His will. Check which questions you will use for your discussion on Day Four.

_____ Ezra took care to do all things with integrity. How do integrity and worship go together?

_____ How important is it to know the Word of God in dealing with any sin?

_____ Israel was to be set apart from all of the other nations as the people of God. How are we as Christians to be set apart? What marks us as God's children?

_____ What are some kinds of "leaven" that we have to deal with as believers?

Day Five—Key Points in Application: The most important application point seen in Zerubbabel and Ezra is that seeing sin God's way **and** seeing God's will God's way are necessary if we are to walk in the will of God. Select a discussion question or two from the list below.

_____ While we should never live in the past, what can we learn from it?

_____ What is the greater struggle for you—doing something you shouldn't do or not doing something that you should do?

_____ How can you best deal with sin?

_____ How would you describe the will of God? What is essential to experience God's will to the fullest?

⏳ CLOSING: 5–10 MINUTES

❑ **Summarize**—Review the key points the group shared. You may want to review "The Main Point" statement for Zerubbabel and Ezra. Also, ask your group to express their thoughts about the key applications from Day Five

❑ **Focus**—Using the memory verses (Romans 12:1-2), focus the group on the heart of the will of God—a heart of worship. God wants a surrendered heart first, then a transformed mind that can know and experience the will of God.

❑ **Remind** your group that both Zerubbabel and Ezra knew and experienced the will of God. Each of your group members can do the same.

❑ **Preview**—Take just a few moments to preview next week's lesson on **"Nehemiah: Leading by Following God."**

❑ **Pray**—Close in prayer.

TOOLS FOR GOOD DISCUSSION

So, group leaders, how have the first nine weeks of this study been for you? Have you dealt with anyone in your group called **"Agenda Alice"**? She is the type that is focused on a Christian "hot-button" issue instead of the Bible study. If not managed properly, she (or he) will either sidetrack the group from its main study objective, or create a hostile environment in the group if she fails to bring people to her way of thinking. For help with "Agenda Alice," see the "Helpful Hints" section of **How to Lead a Small Group Bible Study** (pp. 7–8).

11

Nehemiah

MEMORY **Nehemiah 6:15–16** VERSES

"So the wall was completed on the twenty-fifth of the month Elul, in fifty-two days. And it came about when all our enemies heard of it, and all the nations surrounding us saw it, they lost their confidence; for they recognized that this work had been accomplished with the help of our God."

BEFORE THE SESSION

❑ Pray for your group as they study through this week's lesson.

❑ Spread your study time over the week. Think of the lesson as a large meal. You need time to chew each truth and digest it fully.

❑ For further study, you may want to familiarize yourself with the chart, "A Chronology of Ezra–Nehemiah–Haggai–Zechariah–Malachi" at the end of Lesson 10 on Zerubbabel and Ezra (Workbook pp. 185–87). This will help you see how all the events fit together.

❑ Remember to jot down those ideas and questions you want to discuss or ask as you go.

❑ To better understand the times of Nehemiah, you may want to look at an article on Nehemiah in a Bible dictionary.

WHAT TO EXPECT

Some will readily recognize the name of Nehemiah, the name of the man who led in rebuilding the wall around Jerusalem. The city at that time measured some 200 acres, and the wall around it was broken and in shambles. Completing the repair and construction of the wall around Jerusalem in 52 days

was no small task. Many lives are like that. The way Nehemiah followed God in rebuilding gives us a pattern for following God and seeing lives rebuilt. He also shows us how we can follow God and help others finish what God has called them to do.

Help your group see the importance of finishing what God has called them to do—even finishing this study in *Following God*. (We have one more lesson to go.) Encourage them to share insights that God has shown them.

> ### THE MAIN POINT
> We must learn to follow God if we are to lead in any fashion.

DURING THE SESSION

⌛ **OPENING: 5–10 MINUTES**

Opening Prayer—Have one of the group members open the time with prayer.

Opening Illustration—What does it mean to "follow"? When Jesus called His disciples and commanded them to "follow Me," He used a Greek word that paints a beautiful picture for us. The word *akoloutheo* comes from a root word meaning "road" and conveys the meaning to walk the same path or road. In Jesus' day, people usually walked wherever they went. The students of a Rabbi would often walk with him as he walked about or went on a journey. When Jesus urged others to follow Him, He promised that if they walked with Him they would never walk in darkness (John 8:12). He would be like a torch or lamp to light the way wherever they went, whenever they went with him. Paul told the Corinthians to *"be imitators of me just as I also am of Christ"* (1 Corinthians 11:1). In other words Paul is saying, "I am following Christ. I am walking in the same road with Him. Where He turns, I turn. When He stops, I stop. When He goes, I go. It is a walk in the light because He Himself is the light. Now, you imitate me. Follow Christ and walk in the light."

Nehemiah followed the God of Heaven **in** Babylon, **from** Babylon **to** Jerusalem, and **in** Jerusalem. As a result, he continually walked in the light and knew which path to take. When others tried to trip him up, he did not stumble, because he knew whom he was following. All those who followed Nehemiah walked in that same light and rejoiced in the successful completion of the wall that God called them to build. You and your group can follow the Lord God of Heaven, Jesus, the Light of the World, and you can lead others to do the same.

⧗ DISCUSSION: 30–40 MINUTES

Don't let the details of history hide the insights found in the life and work of Nehemiah. There are many insights concerning God's ways with Israel that also speak of His ways with us and His care of us today. Study diligently in your preparation time. You may want to consult a Bible dictionary about some of the details just to make sure they are clear in your mind. Many Old Testament facts and information can be very new simply because we have not spent as much time in the Old Testament as in the New Testament. Don't let that discourage you. Help your group see the adventure of new discoveries. Also, as you trek through the lesson, seek to keep the main point the main point. Emphasize what you clearly know and understand. Then you can move on to the things that are not as clear as the Lord gives you time and insight.

Main Objective in Day One: In Day One, the main objective is to see the crucial place of prayer in following God. In addition to any discussion questions you may have in mind, the list of questions below may also contain useful discussion-starter ideas.

____ When we hear of a need, what do we often do instead of pray? What other options do we run to instead of to God in prayer?

____ What difference does your view of God make when it comes to prayer or in trying to solve a problem?

____ Nehemiah acknowledged the sin of the people. What place should acknowledging (or confessing) have in our praying? (Confession means agreeing with God.)

____ In his prayer, Nehemiah spoke of God's Word to Moses. How important is the Word of God in our praying?

Main Objective in Day Two: In Day Two, the main objective is to see how following God does not alleviate distractions. In following Him, He shows us how to handle distractions. Check which discussion questions you will use from Day Two.

____ What kinds of distractions can oppose us or get in the way today?

____ How important is it to get God's perspective in dealing with distractions?

____ What part does planning play in what God has called us to do? How should we make our plans?

____ How do we keep God's perspective? How do we "stay at it"—How do we stay with what God has given us to do?

Main Objective in Day Three: In Day Three, our main objective is to see how a leader leads by serving others. Nehemiah's example can show us much. Below, are some suggested discussion starters for you to consider.

____ Serving does not mean being a doormat. How does Nehemiah's firmness about how God's Word addressed their problems reveal a servant's heart?

____ When we seek to serve God first, how does that affect the way we serve people?

____ How does the fear of God affect our attitude and actions toward people, especially as it relates to serving them?

____ Nehemiah stayed focused. What keeps us focused on what God has given us to do? What are some things that can help us stay focused?

Main Objective in Day Four: Day Four's main objective is for you and your group to see the central place of the Word of God in following God. Check any questions that are applicable for your Day Four discussion time.

____ How does a present-day testimony of God's work encourage you in what God has given you to do?

____ How does the Word of God reveal sin?

____ How does the Word of God give joy?

____ When we follow God and do His will and finish the task He has given us to do, what is often our response? What response pleases God?

Day Five—Key Points in Application: The most important application point in Nehemiah is found in following God in prayer and in His Word in all of life. Then, we can lead others and build them up the way God intends. Check which discussion questions you will use to help focus the applications from Day Five.

____ What has this study of Nehemiah said to you about prayer?

____ What do you plan to do differently when the next distraction or problem arises?

____ What has Nehemiah shown you about how to handle a spiritual burden?

____ What has Nehemiah shown you about your personal knowledge of God's Word?

⌛ CLOSING: 5–10 MINUTES

❏ **Summarize**—Restate the key points the group shared.

❏ **Focus**—Using the memory verses (Nehemiah 6:15–16), focus the group again on what it means to follow God in the tasks He wants done.

Remind them it must be done by His power, wisdom, and grace.

❏ **Ask** them to share their thoughts about the key applications from Day Five.

❏ **Preview**—Take time to preview next week's lesson on **"The True King in Israel: Following the King of Kings."** Encourage your members to do their homework in proper fashion by spacing it out over the week.

❏ **Pray**—Close in prayer.

TOOLS FOR GOOD DISCUSSION

Well, it is evaluation time again! You may be saying to yourself, "Why bother evaluating at the end? If I did a bad job, it is too late to do anything about it now!" Well, it may be too late to change how you did on this course, but it is never too late to learn from this course what will help you on the next. Howard Hendricks, that peerless communicator from Dallas Theological Seminary, puts it this way: "The good teacher's greatest threat is satisfaction— the failure to keep asking, 'How can I improve?' The greatest threat to your ministry is **your ministry.**" Any self-examination should be an accounting of your own strengths and weaknesses. As you consider your strengths and weaknesses, take some time to read through the evaluation questions listed in **How to Lead a Small Group Bible Study** on pages 11–12 of this leader's guide. Make it your aim to continue growing as a discussion leader. Jot down below two or three action points for you to implement in future classes.

ACTION POINTS:

1. _____

_____

2. _____

_____

3. _____

_____

12

The True King

MEMORY **Revelation 11:15b** VERSE

"The kingdom of the world has become the kingdom of our Lord, and of His Christ; and He will reign forever and ever."

Before the Session

❑ You will certainly need to pray for your group as they walk through this last lesson in the study on the Kings. Never underestimate the importance of prayer for yourself and for the members of your group. Pray for each of them by name.

❑ Spread your study time over the week.

❑ Remember to mark those ideas and questions you want to discuss or ask as you go through the study. Add to those some of the questions listed below.

❑ To better see the Person of Christ, you may want to look at the lessons that refer to Christ in other Following God studies: **"Adam: Following God's Design"** (Lesson 1) in *Following God: Life Principles from the Old Testament,* **"Christ the Prophet: Worshiping in Spirit and Truth"** (Lesson 12) in *Following God: Life Principles from the Prophets of the Old Testament,* **"The Bride of Christ: Walking in the Beauty of Holiness"** (Lesson 12) in *Following God: Life Principles from Women of the Bible,* and **"The Son of Man: Following His Father"** (Lesson 12) in *Following God: Life Principles from the New Testament Men of Faith.*

❑ Be sensitive to the working of the Spirit in your group meeting, ever watching for ways to help one another truly follow God.

What to Expect

We know that Jesus is Savior and Lord, but many times we forget about His role as the prophesied King of Israel. When Nathaniel first met Jesus, he called Him the King of Israel. At His triumphal entry, the people cried out *"Hosanna! Blessed is He who comes in the name of the Lord,* **even the King of Israel"** (John 12:13 emphasis added). His "crime" written over His cross in Hebrew, Latin, and Greek was simply "King of the Jews." He is the King of the Jews, and He is sovereign King over all.

When we come to any discussion on the True King, Jesus Christ, there will often be many interpretations expressed that are related to prophecy and the Second Coming of Christ. The purpose of this study is not to turn your group study into a prophecy forum or debate, though the subject of prophecy will enter into your discussion. The goal for this study is for you and your group to look solely at the kingship of Christ, His right to rule, and our responsibility to yield, obey, and worship Him as our King.

The Scriptures have much to say about the kingship of Jesus, the Messiah. Many in your group will receive increased understanding into the kingship of Jesus both as to the future and as to their day-to-day walk under His Lordship. Hopefully, they will see many new application points for His reign as King in their lives. Encourage them to share their insights as you guide the discussion.

> ### THE MAIN POINT
> Jesus Christ is The True King. His reign over all exists now and will last forever!

During the Session

 OPENING: 5–10 MINUTES

Opening Prayer—Psalm 119:18 says, *"Open my eyes, that I may behold wonderful things from Thy law."* Ask the Lord to open your eyes as you meet together. Have one of the group members open the time with prayer.

Opening Illustration—The story is told of Alexander the Great that a very young soldier was brought to him after a fierce battle. This soldier had acted cowardly in battle, so Alexander questioned the young man, probably no more than he would have questioned a lad. Throughout the interrogation, Alexander began to feel a measure of pity toward the soldier and asked him to reveal his name. "Alexander, sir," came the reply. The great leader stiffened and demanded, "What did you say?" "Alexander, sir." With that, Alexander the Great looked the young man in the face and commanded him, "Either change your conduct or change your name!" That incident illustrates the call placed upon each of us to serve our King in a way that reveals the honor of His Name. Jesus is the King of kings who deserves our undying devotion, our unquestioned loyalty, and our unfailing service.

 DISCUSSION: 30–40 MINUTES

Select one or two specific questions to get the group started. This lesson on The True King offers many application points in which to look at how each of us is following (or faltering in our following) our True King. He is continually guiding us in places of serv-

ice in His kingdom, and we need to encourage one another in those places of service. Remember to look for those "Velcro" points where members can see something that applies to their own lives. Encourage them to share the insights the Lord has shown them during the week.

Main Objective in Day One: In Day One, the main objective is to see the kind of king God has always wanted to reign on earth. Place a checkmark next to the suggested discussion questions that you would like to use in your group session. Or you may want to use ranking numbers and rank the questions in preferential order.

_____ What are some of the characteristics of a righteous king?

_____ What do you think it would be like to live under a king who followed God's will?

_____ Imagine living during the Old Testament times. What do the promises of a coming king (who would reign God's way) mean to you?

_____ How important is the Word of God in leading others? What difference would it make for a king?

Main Objective in Day Two: In Day Two, the main objective is to see the promise of the coming of a righteous king. Check which discussion questions you will use from Day Two.

_____ What do the promises made to Adam and Eve, to Abraham, and to David concerning the "seed to come" say about God?

_____ How do you see God's faithfulness in His actions toward the descendants of King David?

_____ When you look at the prophecies of a ruler to come and then look at the life and ministry of Jesus, what is most significant to you? Do you see any personal applications to your relationship with God?

_____ Seeing what God has already done, what confidence do you have in what God is planning to do?

Main Objective in Day Three: Day Three focuses on the war against the True King and His people. Some good discussion questions for Day Three include . . .

_____ What does pride have to do with war against The True King? Do you see any applications to your own life?

_____ In the long war against The True King, what do you see about the wisdom and ways of God?

_____ What new insights do you have about the Christmas story and the victory the Lord had even in that?

_____ Even in the face of Pilate, Jesus knew He was the King, and that His Kingdom would stand. What insights and/or personal applications do you see in the events surrounding Jesus' trials, crucifixion, and resurrection?

Main Objective in Day Four: In Day Four, the main objective is to see the promises of the coming of the King and His prophesied reign. Select a discussion question or two from the list of questions below.

_____ If you were one of the disciples, and you knew the many Old Testament prophecies and heard the many teachings of Jesus, what would you have expected after the forty days following Jesus' resurrection?

_____ What assurance do we have of the return of Jesus Christ?

_____ For you, what is the most comforting promise about the future? What is the most significant or the most important promise to you?

_____ How do the promises of His return affect the way you live today? How should they affect you?

Day Five—Key Points in Application: The most important application point seen in The True King is the danger of pride and the importance (even the adventure) of surrendering to and following Jesus as King day by day. Check which discussion questions you will use to help focus the applications from Day Five.

_____ King Nebuchadnezzar was marked by self-will, self-effort, and self-glory. How can we learn to recognize and avoid those in our walk with the Lord?

_____ What does it mean to daily surrender to the Lord? Can you give a practical example?

_____ The Word of God is the King's Word to us. How can the Word of God help us in surrendering and following King Jesus?

_____ What is the most significant insight the Lord has shown you concerning His status as King of Kings (in the present and/or in the future)?

⧖ CLOSING: 5–10 MINUTES

❑ **Summarize**—Restate the key points the group shared. Review the main objectives for each of the days found in these leader notes.

❑ **Focus**—Using the memory verse (Revelation 11:15b), direct the group's focus to the reality of the eternal reign of Jesus Christ as King of kings. Note the practical applications to everyday life that His reign as Lord has for each life now.

❑ **Ask** the group to express their thoughts about the key applications from Day Five.

❑ **Pray**—Close your time in prayer thanking the Lord for the journey He has led you on over the past 12 weeks.

⚒ TOOLS FOR GOOD DISCUSSION ⚒

Congratulations! You have successfully navigated the waters of small group discussion. You have finished all 12 lessons in *Following God: Life Principles from the Kings of the Old Testament*, but there is so much more to learn, so many more paths to take on our journey with the Lord, so much more to discover about what it means to follow Him. Now What? It may be wise for you and your group to pursue another study. In the front portion of this leader's guide (in the "Helpful Hints" section of **How to Lead a Small Group Bible Study:** pp. 9–10), there is information on how you can transition to the next study and share those insights with your group. Encourage your group to continue in some sort of consistent Bible study. Time in the Word is much like time at the dinner table. If we are to stay healthy, we will never get far from physical food, and if we are to stay nourished on "sound" or "healthy" doctrine, then we must stay close to the Lord's "dinner table" found in His Word. Job said it well, *"I have not departed from the command of His lips; I have treasured the words of His mouth more than my necessary food"* (Job 23:12).

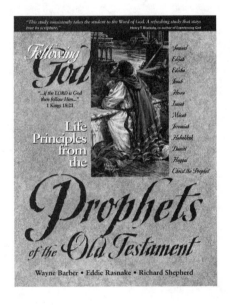

LIFE PRINCIPLES
FROM THE PROPHETS
OF THE OLD TESTAMENT

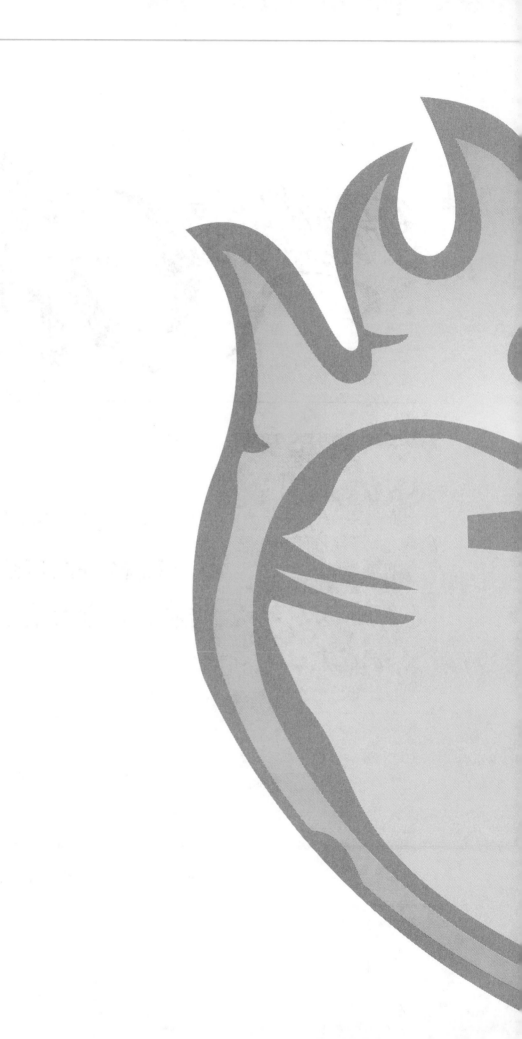

Table of Contents

Samuel 101

Elijah 104

Elisha 107

Jonah 110

Hosea 113

Isaiah 116

Micah 119

Jeremiah 122

Habbakuk 125

Daniel 128

Haggai 131

Christ the Prophet.....................134

Samuel

MEMORY **I Samuel 12:24** VERSE

"Only fear the LORD and serve Him in truth with all your heart; for consider what great things He has done for you."

BEFORE THE SESSION

❏ Be sure to familiarize yourself with the chart on the life and ministry of Samuel at the end of Lesson 1.

❏ Spread your homework out rather than trying to cram everything into one afternoon or night. Perhaps use this as your daily quiet time.

❏ Always look for some personal applications which the Lord may have you share with the group. The more impact the Word makes in your heart the more enthusiasm you will communicate.

❏ As you study, write down any good discussion questions as they come to mind.

❏ Additional Study: To grasp the times in which Samuel lived and better prepare yourself towards leading the discussion, you may want to read the book of Judges and/or Ruth. You may also want to look at some of the other **Following God** lessons centered around this period—**Gideon** and **Samson** in *Following God: Life Principles from the Old Testament*, **Ruth** and **Hannah** in *Following God: Life Principles from the Women of the Bible*, and **Saul** and **David** in *Following God: Life Principles from the Kings of the Old Testament*. The lessons in these **Following God** titles will help

you see the times and the ways of the people in Samuel's day.

❏ A good Bible dictionary article on "Samuel" will give you more background information. Dictionaries often help you see the historical setting in which the man or woman lived.

❏ Be transparent before the Lord and before your group. We are all learners—that's the meaning of the word "disciple."

WHAT TO EXPECT

Samuel was born because of the surrender of his mother, Hannah, to the Lord's will. This attitude of surrender became an indelible characteristic of Samuel's life. Samuel's attitude was not genetically inherited, but it became evident as he learned to walk with the Lord, hearing Him and obeying His Word. Samuel's life, as is the case in all our lives, was a process of growth, of knowing the Lord at deeper and deeper levels, of hearing and obeying by faith. Studying the life of Samuel can help us know the Lord at greater depths of faith when we listen to His Word. If we will listen with a teachable heart we will learn much more readily.

It is quite possible that many in your group will experience new insights or rich applications from their study this week. Some will realize how far they have strayed from the Word of God. Others will be affirmed in the steps of obedience they have taken. Expect the Lord to do a fresh work in you as well as in the members of your group. He waits to show Himself strong toward *"those whose heart is fully His"* (see 1 Chronicles 16:9a). Some may have questions about the study or even about the validity of some portions of the Word of God. You can help them see the Bible as God's Word written in love. They can discover that this Book is eternal wisdom and is ever able to teach, reprove, correct, and train in righteousness (2 Timothy 3:16–17).

> ## THE MAIN POINT
> It is necessary to pay close attention to God's Word and obey Him promptly and fully.

DURING THE SESSION

 ## OPENING: 5–10 MINUTES

Opening Prayer—You or one of your group members should open your time together in prayer.

Opening Illustration—A very dear missionary to China, Miss Bertha Smith, was part of the great Shantung Revival there in the 1930's. During her time in China, she faced the attack of the Japanese and was one of those expelled by the Communists in 1949. For years (until she died at the age of 100), she used countless opportunities to testify of the redemption found in Christ, the power of the Holy Spirit, and the sufficiency of the Word of God. Often when she gave her testimony, she would sing "How Firm a Foundation," a hymn she sang during the shelling of Yenchow by the Communists and also a hymn that she declared had seen her through three or four wars. The first verse declares:

> "How firm a foundation, ye saints of the Lord,
> Is laid for your faith in His excellent Word!
> What more can He say than to you He hath said,
> To you who for refuge to Jesus have fled?"

The members of your group can find that to be true for their lives as well. Ask God to solidify the faith of each one as you study the life of Samuel.

DISCUSSION: 30–40 MINUTES

Main Objective in Day One: The days in which Samuel was born were a time of spiritual decline when *"everyone did what was right in his own eyes"* (Judges 21:25). We want to see the heart and life of Hannah, Samuel's mother, and the life of Samuel (even as a young boy) against this backdrop. Below are some possible discussion questions for the Day One discussion. Check which questions you will use.

_____ What do you sense Samuel's home was like?

_____ How would you describe Hannah, Samuel's mother?

_____ What stands out about the spiritual atmosphere around the Tabernacle at Shiloh?

_____ How was Samuel different from Eli's sons?

Main Objective in Day Two: Just as the Word of God was the final word in Samuel's life, it is vital for us to make the Word central to all we think, say, and do. Check which discussion questions you will use for Day Two.

_____ Someone has well said, "You can choose your sin, but you cannot choose your consequences." How do you see that being worked out in the lives of Eli's sons?

_____ What does Samuel show us regarding how we are to respond to the Word of God?

_____ How would a fresh, clear understanding of the Word of God change the way things are in your home? At your job? In your community?

Main Objective in Day Three: The people of Israel had to learn that **knowing** the Word of God meant they were accountable to follow the will of the Lord as a nation and as individuals. Day Three focuses on surrender to the will of the Lord. Check which discussion questions for Day Three you might use.

_____ Israel did not have an in-depth knowledge of the Word of God. They treated the Ark of the Covenant in a somewhat superstitious way, almost like a "good-luck" charm. In what ways do we act like that in our Christian lives?

_____ Why do you think 1 Samuel 3:1 indicates that the *"word from the Lord was rare in those days"*?

_____ What are some "idols" that we must deal with? How do they distract us from hearing and seeing God and His will for our daily lives?

Main Objective in Day Four: Just as important as finding God's will is **doing** His will **in His way.** In Day Four, we see that Samuel learned this lesson when God made His choice for king of Israel. We must learn this lesson too. Some good discussion questions from Day Four might be . . .

_____ What have you learned from Samuel's life about dealing with sin (from both good or bad examples)?

_____ As Samuel grew older, he still had some things to learn about the Lord's ways. How does that relate to us?

_____ Like Samuel, we live in an era of spiritual decline. What does Samuel's life and ministry say to us today?

Day Five—Key Points in Application: The most significant application point from the life of Samuel is the importance of following the Word of the Lord with a humble, teachable heart. Choose one or two discussion questions from the list below.

_____ Samuel was **available** to the plan of God. Being available means being surrendered to do His will His way—when He says, how He says. Do you ever struggle with "I'm not available for that" attitudes? As leaders, you may want to share some struggles you have had.

_____ Samuel was also **teachable.** What do you think gets in the way of us being teachable?

_____ What are some ways you are honoring the Word of God as your source of wisdom and direction?

_____ What do you think of people who treat the Scriptures as just another book of good opinions, another option on the shelf of options?

⌛ CLOSING: 5–10 MINUTES

❑ **Summarize**—Restate the key points highlighted in the class. Take a few moments to preview next week's lesson, **"Elijah: Following God When Those Around You Do Not."**

❑ **Encourage** the group to do their homework.

❑ **Pray**—Close in prayer.

⚒ TOOLS FOR GOOD DISCUSSION ⚒

Some who are reading this have led small-group Bible studies many times. Here is an important word of warning: experience alone does not make you a more effective discussion leader. In fact, experience can make you **less effective**. You see, the more experience you have the more comfortable you will be at the task. Unfortunately, for some that means becoming increasingly comfortable in doing a bad job. Taking satisfaction with mediocrity translates into taking the task less seriously. It is easy to wrongly assert that just because one is experienced, he or she can successfully "shoot from the hip," so to speak. If you really want your members to get the most out of this study, you need to be dissatisfied with simply doing an adequate job and make it your aim to do an excellent job. A key to excellence is to regularly evaluate yourself to see that you are still doing all that you want to be doing. We have prepared a list of over thirty evaluation questions for you to review from time to time. The list of questions can be found on page 11 in this Leader's Guide. The examination questions will help to jog your memory and, hopefully, will become an effective aid in improving the quality of your group discussion. Review the evaluation questions list, and jot down below two or three action points for you to begin implementing next week.

ACTION POINTS:

1. _____

_____

2. _____

_____

3. _____

_____

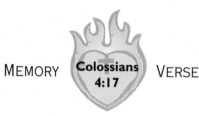

MEMORY **Colossians 4:17** VERSE

"Take heed to the ministry which you have received in the Lord, that you may fulfill it

BEFORE THE SESSION

☐ An important historical note is that Elijah ministered after the division of Israel into two kingdoms—the conservative Southern Kingdom (Judah), ruled over by the descendents of David, and the liberal Northern Kingdom (still called Israel), ruled by whoever could seize power. Elijah was a prophet to that Northern Kingdom.

☐ Remember that your goal is not to teach the lesson, but to facilitate discussion. Think of open-ended questions that will generate dialogue.

☐ For an enhanced understanding of the times in which Elijah ministered, see *Following God: Life Principles from the Kings of the Old Testament*, Lesson 6, on **"King Ahab: The Sins of Serving Self."** This wicked king reigned in Israel during the ministry of the prophet Elijah.

☐ Make sure your own heart is right with God. Be willing to be transparent with the group about your own life experiences and mistakes. This will make it easier for them to open up.

☐ Don't be afraid of chasing tangents for a while if they capture the interest of the group as a whole, but don't sacrifice the rest of the group to belabor the questions of one member. Trust God to lead you.

WHAT TO EXPECT

The danger of dealing with a character as familiar as Elijah is that, although most everyone will have some knowledge of certain events in his life, few will have seriously studied him. What they know of Elijah is woven from the snippets they have heard of him in sermons and the like. Make sure that, if nothing else, everyone goes away with some kind of grasp on the "received vs. achieved" principle. Many will find this principle to be an unfamiliar concept, but hopefully the concept will be a liberating one to them. God will be prompting many in your group to follow Elijah's example. They will need to be reminded that the keys are **a) walking** with God, and **b) waiting** on God. To experience "received" ministry and a "God-initiated" life, we have to be willing to be patient and let God have His way with us.

> ### THE MAIN POINT
> True ministry is "received, not achieved." Elijah models for us what it means to live a God-initiated life instead of a self-initiated, self-directed life.

During the Session

 OPENING: 5–10 MINUTES

Opening Prayer—Ask someone to open your time in prayer.

Opening Illustration—The great hymn, "Have Thine Own Way" was written in 1902 by Adelaide Pollard during a time she referred to as suffering "a great distress of soul." Shortly before, she had tried unsuccessfully to raise funds for a missionary trip to Africa. God met with her in a prayer meeting, and the result was these words to this powerful hymn:

"Have Thine own way, Lord! Have Thine own way!
Thou art the Potter; I am the clay.
Mould me and make me after Thy will,
While I am waiting, yielded and still."

She had learned that true ministry is **received**, not achieved.

 DISCUSSION: 30–40 MINUTES

Once your group gets talking, you will find that all you need to do is keep the group directed and flowing with a question or two or a pointed observation. You are the gatekeeper of discussion. Don't be afraid to ask someone to elaborate further or to ask a quiet member of the group what they think of someone else's comments. Time will not allow you to discuss every single question in the lesson one at a time. Instead, make it your goal to cover the main ideas of each day and help the group to share what they learned personally. You don't have to use all the discussion questions. They are there for you to pick and choose from.

Main Objective in Day One: The main objective here is to see the central role in Elijah's life of *"the Word of the Lord."* This refers not just to the Scriptures, but specifically to his hearing from God and being directed by God as he walked in fellowship with Him. While we will not experience God audibly speaking to us on a day-to-day basis, we are going to experience His leading as we walk with Him. Check which discussion questions you will use.

_____ What do you think the text means by the phrase, *"the word of the Lord"*?

_____ How was Elijah's hearing from God different than what we experience today?

_____ How was it the same?

_____ A companion idea here is that "where God guides, He provides." How do we see that in Elijah's experience?

_____ What things get in the way of us hearing from God?

Main Objective in Day Two: Here we see that the miracle on Mt. Carmel was not a matter of Elijah coming up with a good idea and asking God to bless it, but rather doing all, Elijah says, *"at thy word"* (1 Kings 18:36).

_____ From where does the idea come for Elijah's challenge?

_____ What do you think God is trying to show Israel through His dealings here at Mt. Carmel? Why?

_____ James says Elijah's prayer is an example of "effective prayer." What do you learn about prayer from his example?

_____ Does prayer have to be long to be effective?

_____ What keeps our prayers from being effective?

Main Objective in Day Three: Day Three introduces us to some of Elijah's humanness. There is always the danger of placing the people God uses on such a pedestal that we lose our ability to relate with them. Not only does Elijah show us that the Christian life is going to have its share of "highs" and "lows," but through him we also see that the highs are often followed by lows. Examine the discussion questions below, and determine which questions you might want to use in your discussion for Day Three.

_____ How is this experience of Elijah different than what we saw on Mt. Carmel?

_____ Why do you think Elijah struggled with trusting God with the threat on his life?

_____ What is the good news in how God dealt with Elijah's suicidal prayer?

_____ What conclusions can we draw from Elijah's experience concerning how we manage our own spiritual highs and lows?

Main Objective in Day Four: In Day Four we see the potential pitfall into which each of us can stumble: that is, thinking we are the only one standing for God. Like Elijah, we can convince ourselves that God needs us and wrongly assume that without us His purposes cannot be realized. Check which discussion questions you will use from Day Four.

_____ What is wrong with Elijah's perspective here?

_____ Have you ever felt that you were the only one standing for God?

_____ What does Elijah's experience say to you about loneliness?

_____ Did anything else stand out to you from Day Four?

Day Five—Key Points in Application: The most important application point from Elijah's life is that he followed God's initiation and direction most of the time. When he followed God, he was able to see God do more for him than anything he could do for God. Check which discussion questions you will use for Day Five.

_____ Can you see any examples in your own life or those around you of ministry that is **achieved** (man-initiated) instead of **received** (initiated by God)?

_____ Did God show you anything through this lesson you need to do differently?

⏳ CLOSING: 5–10 MINUTES

❑ **Summarize**—restate the key points that were highlighted in the class.

❑ **Remind** your group that the Christian life is not about trying hard to be like Jesus, but it is about totally surrendering our lives to God and letting Him work through us.

❑ **Preview**—Take a few moments to preview next week's lesson on **"Elisha: Putting Down the Idols in our Lives."** Encourage the group to be sure to do their homework.

❑ **Pray**—Close in prayer.

TOOLS FOR GOOD DISCUSSION

Bill Donahue, in his book, _Leading Life-Changing Small Groups_ (Grand Rapids: Zondervan Publishing House, 1996), lists four facilitator actions that will produce dynamic discussion. These four actions are easy to remember because they are linked through the acrostic method to the word, **ACTS.** You will profit from taking time to review this information in the "Helpful Hints" section of **How to Lead a Small Group Bible Study,** which is on page 5 of this Leader's Guide book.

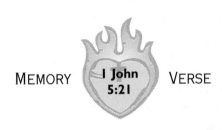

3

MEMORY **I John 5:21** VERSE

"Little children, guard yourselves from idols."

BEFORE THE SESSION

❑ Pray each day for the members of your group—that they spend time in the Word, grasp the message God wants to bring to their lives, and that they surrender to what God is saying.

❑ Do your homework—don't procrastinate!

❑ Remember, Elijah (last week's lesson) was mentor to Elisha. Keep that connection in view.

❑ Mark those ideas and questions you want to discuss as you go through the study. Those, along with the questions listed below, can personalize the discussion to fit your group. Think of the needs of your group and be looking for applicable questions and discussion starters.

❑ To better understand the times and the depths of Israel's idolatry, see *Following God: Life Principles from the Kings of the Old Testament,* Lesson 6, entitled **"Ahab: The Sins of Serving Self"** as well as Lesson 7 on **"Jehoshaphat: Unequally Yoked."**

❑ Ever remain teachable. Look first for what God is saying to you.

❑ Prepare yourself to be transparent and open about what God is teaching you. Nothing is quite as contagious as the joy of discovering new treasures in the Word.

WHAT TO EXPECT

For some in your group the dangers of idolatry are something reserved for some tribe on an island in the middle of the Pacific, not for modern society. However, we see in the life of Elisha just how close idols can be—as close as the breath we breathe. This can be an eye-opening and heart-revealing truth. Take this opportunity to sharpen your group's awareness of the idols of today, and then help them see the subtlety of idolatry. Elisha can be a true friend to help lead them out of the pit of idolatry and onto the solid ground of a surrendered walk with the true and living God.

> ### THE MAIN POINT
> We are to faithfully follow the true and living God and ever guard ourselves against idolatry in any form.

DURING THE SESSION

⧗ OPENING: 5 MINUTES

Opening Prayer—Remember that the Lord is the Teacher, and He wants us to depend on Him as we open the Scriptures.

Opening Illustration—In one of His acts of judgment on faithless Israel in the wilderness, God sent poisonous serpents among the people. In Numbers 21, we read the story of God directing Moses to make a bronze serpent and lift it on a pole. All who had been bitten by these snakes need only look at the pole and be healed. The bronze serpent pole is an Old Testament picture of Christ (John 3:14). Yet in King Hezekiah's day, we learn that it had to be destroyed. It had become an idol to the people (2 Kings 18:4). They named it *"Nehushtan"* and burned incense to it. The human heart is able to take things that should point us to God and turn them into objects of worship. Whether it is creation or our blessings or even the past working of God, there is ever the danger of placing something ahead of God in our hearts. That is the danger we see Elisha confronting.

⌛ DISCUSSION: 30–40 MINUTES

Keep the group directed along the main highway of Elisha. You may have a pointed observation that helps sharpen the focus of the group. Encourage some to elaborate further on a key point, or ask a quiet member of the group what he or she thinks of someone's comments. Watch the time, knowing that you cannot cover every single question in the lesson. Seek to cover the main ideas of each day and help the group to share what they learned personally.

Main Objective in Day One: You should desire that you and your group see the necessity of following the true God in the midst of any tests or challenges that you may face. Elisha faced certain tests concerning his willingness to follow Elijah. He learned to trust in God's ways and experienced God's power as Elijah had done. He also had to trust God that the people would listen to him as God's spokesman. Check which discussion questions you will use from Day One.

_____ What was Israel like in the days of Elijah and Elisha? What parallels do you see today?

_____ Elijah faced some struggles. How did the Lord deal with him and with his struggles? How did the Lord encourage Elijah?

_____ What do you think it meant for Elisha to leave behind his parents and the family business? Are you facing a similar challenge or call on your life?

_____ How did Elisha respond to the various tests he faced? What can we learn from Elisha's responses for the tests we face?

Main Objective in Day Two: Here we learn that the Lord is the **living** God, the true provider, who longs for His people to look to Him and to follow Him—not some **dead** idol. You want to make sure your group catches that one point. Check which discussion questions you will use for your discussion of Day Two.

_____ Why do you think many in Israel superstitiously followed Baal and Baal worship like the nations around them? How did Elisha show them the truth about the true God?

_____ What are some modern "gods/idols" today? How do we follow the "popular" gods of those around us? How can we show them the truth about the true God?

_____ Think of the many ways God used Elisha to reveal Himself as the **Living God** in today's Scriptures. Name or list those ways or write them on a marker board.

_____ How has God revealed Himself as the **Living God** today? Some in your group may want to share ways they have seen God alive in their lives and circumstances this week or in recent weeks.

Main Objective in Day Three: Day Three introduces us to the ways of God among "the nations." He is Lord of all the earth, not just Israel. Check a discussion question or two below that you find to be useful for your discussion about Day Three.

_____ How does God deal with those from other nations? What does God's dealings with Naaman tell you about the ways of God?

_____ How did Elisha deal with someone from another nation? What was his focus? In the New Testament, Peter declared *"I most certainly understand now that God is not one to show partiality"* or is *"no respecter of persons"* (Acts 10:34). Neither was Elisha partial. What does that say to you?

_____ What do you see about God's protective care for His people in the incident of the army surrounding Elisha? Ask different members of your group to give one of the purposes of the angels according to Hebrews 1:14.

_____ What is God's desire for the nations? You may want to read some additional Scriptures not found in this lesson, such as Joshua 4:19–24 (especially verse 24), 1 Kings 8:41–43, and Matthew 28:18–20.

Main Objective in Day Four: For Day Four, we want to emphasize the faithfulness of God. He is faithful to His people in every detail of their lives and is committed to seeing them walk with Him, following Him as their God. Therefore, He is committed to child-training and discipline. Check which discussion questions you will use from Day Four .

_____ What kind of discipline did God bring upon Israel through Hazael of Syria? What does this show us about God's faithfulness to His people?

_____ What role did Jehu play in God's dealings with Israel? What do you discover about the faithfulness and the ways of God in all Jehu did?

_____ What does 2 Kings 13:22–23 mean to you personally?

_____ Read Hebrews 12:1–13. How does that passage speak to you about the faithfulness of God in training and dealing with His children?

Day Five—Key Points in Application: The most important application point is found in the delight of walking with the true and living God, while always being aware of the ever-present danger of idolatry. Below, check the questions that you might consider using in your discussion.

_____ We need to be nourished on "sound" or "healthy" doctrine—the Word of God. How can you be sure to guard yourself from unhealthy teaching?

_____ Has this lesson brought to mind any worldly opinions that have gotten mixed in with what you know in Scripture? Share some of these.

_____ What about idolatry in **your** life? Remember when the apostle John was writing 1 John, he was talking to Christians (*"little children"*) who knew the Scriptures. The dangers of idolatry are always near. That's why we must "guard" ourselves. Review some of the idols we may face in today's world.

_____ What can you do to increase your intake of the Word of God and intensify your watchfulness against idolatry?

⌛ CLOSING: 5–10 MINUTES

❑ **Summarize**—Restate the key points the group shared (Review the objectives for each of the days found at the beginning of these leader notes).

❑ **Remind**—Using the memory verse (1 John 5:21), remind the group that idols are still around today. We must stay on guard.

❑ **Preview**—Take time to preview next week's lesson, **"Jonah: Following God When You Don't Want To."**

❑ **Pray**—Close in prayer.

TOOLS FOR GOOD DISCUSSION

One of the people who shows up in every group is a person we call **"Talkative Timothy."** Talkative Timothy tends to talk too much and dominates the discussion time by giving less opportunity for others to share. What do you do with a group member who talks too much? In the "Helpful Hints" section of **How to Lead a Small Group Bible Study** (p. 5), you'll find some practical ideas on managing the "Talkative Timothy's" in your group.

# Jonah

MEMORY **I Samuel 15:22** VERSE

"Has the Lord as much delight in burnt offerings and sacrifices as in obeying the voice of the Lord? Behold, to obey is better than sacrifice, and to heed than the fat of rams."

BEFORE THE SESSION

❑ Be sure to do your own study far enough in advance so as not to be rushed. You want to allow God time to speak to you personally.

❑ Don't feel that you have to use all of the discussion questions listed below. You may have come up with others on your own, or you may find that time will not allow you to use them all. These questions are to serve you, not for you to serve.

❑ You are the gatekeeper of the discussion. Do not be afraid to "reel the group back in" if they get too far away from the lesson.

❑ Remember to keep a highlight pen ready as you study to mark any points you want to be sure to discuss.

WHAT TO EXPECT

The story of Jonah is the most human portrait of any of the prophets. It accurately records his rebellion against God's plan for him and shows how God dealt with him to bring him to a place of obedience. The account of Jonah and the great fish is so familiar that we run the risk of resembling that old adage, "familiarity breeds contempt." Yet, as you can see, there are some very practical lessons to be learned

from his life—the main one being that we cannot succeed in running from God. Because God is who He is, He is able to keep turning up the heat through the circumstances of our lives, until we yield to His will and way. An important point to acknowledge, however, is that even submitting to God's will can be done with a wrong heart. To do the right actions alone is not enough. God desires that our hearts become yielded to Him, not simply that we acquiesce to His will because we have to.

THE MAIN POINT
The main point to be seen here is God's grace in the midst of Jonah's very reluctant obedience.

DURING THE SESSION

 OPENING: 5–10 MINUTES

Opening Prayer—Remember that if it took the inspiration of God for people to write Scripture, it will also take His illumination for us to understand it. Have one of the more serious minded members of your group open your time together in prayer.

Opening Illustration—A good hook for introducing this lesson might be the story of the little school boy who was made to sit in the corner during class as punishment for repeatedly standing when he should not. When the teacher came by and said, "Now, that is more like it," he replied in rebellion, "I may be sitting down on the outside, but I am standing up on the inside!" Such reluctant submission is not what the Lord desires. Yet that is what we see in Jonah.

⌛ DISCUSSION: 30–40 MINUTES

Here is a little tip to enhance the quality of your group's discussion. Don't be afraid to ask someone to elaborate further on their comments ("Explain what you mean, Barbara.") or to ask a quiet member of the group what he or she thinks of someone else's comments ("What do you think, Dave?"). Time will not allow you to discuss every single question in the lesson one at a time. Instead, make it your goal to cover the main ideas of each day, and help the group to share what they learned personally.

Main Objective in Day One: In Day One the main objective is to reveal the downward spiral Jonah experiences when he runs from God's plan and purpose. Jonah was called to a purpose that he didn't like, so instead of obeying, he rebelled and ran from God. Every Christian has done the same thing at some point, so you should have no trouble getting your group members to identify with Jonah. Check which discussion questions from Day One you will use.

_____ Have someone restate the assignment God gave to Jonah in verses 1 and 2.

_____ Can you think of a purpose God has given to you at some time that you have struggled with?

_____ How did God deal with Jonah's rebellion?

_____ What do you think was going through Jonah's mind as he was running?

Main Objective in Day Two: In Day Two we learn the key principle, "If you don't get right when God sends the storm, you will get right when troubles grow far worse!" You'll want to make sure that your group understands that God is willing and able to turn up the heat if we are unwilling to submit to Him. Check the discussion questions below that might apply to your group.

_____ What was Jonah's response to the storm God sent his way?

_____ What are some of the storms God brings into our lives to get our attention?

_____ Why do you think it took Jonah so long to surrender to the Lord's call?

_____ We see that it wasn't until Jonah prayed that God commanded the fish to vomit him onto the land. What is the message for us in that?

_____ The last statement of Day Two says, "When God brings calamity upon us for our rebellion, He will not relent until we repent." Do you agree or disagree with that statement?

Main Objective in Day Three: Day Three introduces us to the results of Jonah's repentance. The fruit his preaching at Ninevah bore is the greatest evangelistic response recorded in Scripture—greater even than Peter's preaching at Pentecost. Jonah's repentance allowed him to be a part of a mighty moving of God. Check which discussion questions from Day Three you will use.

_____ What stands out to you from Jonah's message to Ninevah?

_____ Why do you think the people of Ninevah responded as they did?

_____ How does our preaching today differ from what you see here?

_____ Verse 10 tells us that when the people repented, God relented concerning the calamity. How does that apply to us?

_____ What do you think true repentance is?

Main Objective in Day Four: In Day Four we see more of Jonah's humanness. Sadly, though he was finally obedient to God's charge, he was disappointed that God did not judge the Ninevites anyway. Below, check any discussion questions from Day Four that may be appropriate for your group.

_____ What are some reasons we don't rejoice when God shows mercy to the guilty?

_____ What prejudices do you struggle with?

_____ We see that Jonah's reluctance was rooted in the fact that he did not agree with God's plan. Are there any areas in your life where you struggle with disagreeing with God's plan?

_____ Did you have any unanswered questions from this week's lesson?

Day Five—Key Points in Application: The most important application point from the life of Jonah is that God did not allow him to succeed in running away from His will. Check which discussion questions you will use from Day Five.

_____ Can you think of a time where you ran from God's will?

_____ Hebrews 12 indicates two wrong responses to God's disciplines: **a)** to regard it lightly, and **b)** to faint when we are reproved. What would these wrong responses look like in practical terms?

_____ What are some areas where you struggle with recognizing people *"...according to the flesh"*?

⌛ CLOSING: 5–10 MINUTES

❑ **Summarize**—Restate the key points that were highlighted in the class. You may also want to briefly review the main objectives for each of the days found in these leader notes.

❑ **Remind** your group that the victorious Christian life is not attained when we try hard to be like Jesus, but when we surrender our lives to God and let Him work through us.

❑ **Ask** your group what they think the key applications from Day Five are.

❑ **Preview**—Take a few moments to preview next week's lesson on **"Hosea: Returning to the Lord."** Encourage your group to do their homework.

❑ **Pray**—Close in prayer.

 ## TOOLS FOR GOOD DISCUSSION

As mentioned earlier, there are certain people who show up in every discussion group. Last week we looked at "Talkative Timothy." Another person who is likely to show up is **"Silent Sally."** She does not readily speak up. Sometimes, her silence is because she doesn't yet feel comfortable enough with the group to share her thoughts. Other times, it is simply because she fears being rejected. Often, her silence is because she is too polite to interrupt and thus is headed off at the pass each time she wants to speak by more aggressive (and less sensitive) members of the group. In the "Helpful Hints" section of **How to Lead a Small Group Bible Study** (p. 6), you'll find some practical ideas on managing the "Silent Sally's" in your group.

5

MEMORY **2 Corinthians 11:2–3** VERSES

"I am jealous for you with a godly jealousy; for I betrothed you to one husband, that to Christ I might present you as a pure virgin. But I am afraid, lest as the serpent deceived Eve by his craftiness, your minds should be led astray from the simplicity and purity of devotion to Christ."

BEFORE THE SESSION

❑ Resist the temptation to do all your homework in one sitting or to put it off until the last minute. You will not be fully prepared if you study in this fashion.

❑ Make sure to mark down any discussion questions that come to mind as you study.

❑ If you want to do further study, look at 1 and 2 Kings and 1 and 2 Chronicles and read about the kings who ruled while Hosea ministered.

❑ Remember your need to trust God with your study. The Holy Spirit is always the best teacher, so stay sensitive to Him!

WHAT TO EXPECT

In this lesson, assume that all your group members need to better understand how to return to the Lord when they stray. They will all eventually need this for their own walk, and they will all, sooner or later, be in a position to help someone else who will need it. Don't worry so much about covering all the details of the study. Make sure that you devote adequate time to clearly explaining and answering any questions they have about returning to the Lord.

THE MAIN POINT

The main call of Hosea is to "return to the Lord," and the main point to be seen in this lesson is how we do that.

In order to understand Hosea's instruction, it is necessary to look at the day in which he lived and the sins of Israel that he confronted. His powerful showdown with the spiritual adultery of Israel was made more personal by the physical adultery of his own wife.

DURING THE SESSION

⏳ **OPENING: 5–10 MINUTES**

Opening Prayer—Remember to have one of your group members open your time together in prayer.

Opening Illustration—Winston Churchill, Prime Minister of Great Britain during World War II, not only was a great leader, but also earned a reputation as the "king of the verbal comeback." He seemed to be at his best while sparring with his main political adversary, Lady Astor. On one occasion, being quite put out with him, she uttered, "Sir Churchill, if I were your wife, I would put arsenic in your tea!" to which Churchill retorted, "Lady Astor, if I were your husband, I would drink it!" On another occasion at a party the two met in the elevator as they were leaving. Lady Astor remarked with contempt, "Sir Churchill, I perceive that you are drunk." The quick-witted Churchill returned, "Yes Lady Astor, and you are ugly," and then added, "and tomorrow I shall be sober!" No one, however, was armed with a greater comeback than the prophet Hosea. Every time someone would comment about his unfaithful, harlot wife, he could return, "And that is exactly what you are to God."

⏳ DISCUSSION: 30–40 MINUTES

By now, you should realize that your job is not to teach this lesson, but to facilitate discussion. Do your best to guide the group to the right answers, but don't be guilty of making a point **someone else** in the group could easily make.

Main Objective in Day One: In Day One, the main objective is to see how God worked His message into Hosea's life. Through his marriage to an unfaithful bride, he was able to feel the heart of God toward prodigal Israel. Check which questions you might use for your discussion on Day One.

_____ Why do you think God wanted Hosea to have a harlot for a wife?

_____ What struggles do you think Hosea had in ministry because of his wife?

_____ How is Gomer's harlotry a good parallel to Israel's wanderings from God?

_____ What do you think about Hosea's children?

_____ Were there any questions raised by your study?

Main Objective in Day Two: In Day Two, we learn some of the specifics of the sins in Israel God confronted through the prophet Hosea. Make sure that your group grasps the concept that Israel had committing "spiritual" adultery by their dalliance with other religions. Not mentioned in the workbook study, but something worth discussing, is that the words used in Hosea 2:2 are similar to those used in the Jewish formula for divorce. Check which discussion questions you will use from Day Two.

_____ What kinds of actions in Israel does God associate with "spiritual adultery"?

_____ What are some equivalents to "spiritual adultery" in our day?

_____ What correlation do you see between Israel's straying and their lack of gratitude for God's blessings?

_____ Israel's unfaithfulness to the Lord included the hypocrisy of rituals with no meaning in their hearts. What are some things that can become meaningless rituals to us today?

Main Objective in Day Three: Day Three introduces us to the heart of God through His message to "return to the Lord." It is a powerful reminder that at the heart of the Scriptures is God's willingness to accept us back when we stray. Every member of your group will be able to relate in some way with wandering from the Lord, and will benefit from Hosea's invitation. It is worth reminding the group that the word "return" appears 22 times in Hosea. Check the discussion questions for Day Three you that appeal to you.

_____ What stands out to you most about the way God draws His unfaithful spouse back in Chapter 2?

_____ What similarities do you see between Hosea and what God did with us through Christ?

_____ Hosea 2:6 indicates that God would _hedge up her way with thorns._ Have you ever experienced God doing that as you wandered?

_____ Have you ever experienced God "winning" your love back? How?

_____ Do you agree with the statement, "We don't 'find' God—He finds us"?

Main Objective in Day Four: In Day Four, we see how God woos His prodigal people back to Himself. Some key points you want your group members to catch are: **1)** confession is for our benefit, not just God's, **2)** repentance **always** accompanies true confession, and, most importantly, **3)** repentance will involve "plowing the fallow (unplowed) ground." Make sure they see that any area of our lives from which we exclude God will become hard, fallow ground. It takes a choice to allow the plow of His Word into those areas to break up the hardness. Check the questions for Day Four that you will use in your discussion on Hosea.

_____ Why do we need to confess sin if God already knows everything?

_____ Do you think it is possible to truly confess without repenting?

_____ Hosea 14:5–8 pictures the freshness of life after repentance. Have you ever experienced this repentance?

_____ How do you think "fallow" ground (hard, unplowed ground) develops in our lives?

_____ Name some examples of "fallow ground" that you have seen or experienced.

Day Five—Key Points in Application: The most important application out of Day Five is that we are all prodigals, and therefore we all need to know how to return to the Lord. Express to your group that the keys to repentance and returning to God are: **a)** remembering what it was like to walk with God, and **b)** making a choice to return. Check which discussion questions from Day Five you will use.

_____ What stands out to you about the parable of the prodigal son?

_____ What gets in our way of returning to the Lord?

_____ Have you ever tried to "return" to God, expecting God to place you on "probation"?

_____ Is there anything you still don't understand about returning to the Lord when you stray?

CLOSING: 5–10 MINUTES

❑ **Summarize**—Restate the key points.

❑ **Ask** your group what they consider to be the key applications for Day Five.

❑ **Sing**—If your meeting space allows, you may want to sing together the last verse of "Come Thou Fount of Every Blessing." Explain the relevance of this song to the Hosea study. (See p. 77 in *Following God: Life Principles from the Prophets of the Old Testament*.)

❑ **Pray**—Ask someone in your group to close your session with prayer.

TOOLS FOR GOOD DISCUSSION

Hopefully your group is functioning smoothly at this point, but perhaps you recognize the need for improvement. In either case, you will benefit from taking the time to evaluate yourself and your group. Without evaluation, you will judge your group on subjective emotions. You may think everything is fine and miss some opportunities to improve your effectiveness. You may be discouraged by problems you are confronting when you ought to be encouraged that you are doing the right things and making progress. A healthy Bible-study group is not one without problems, but is one that recognizes its problems and deals with them the right way. At this point in the course, as you and your group are nearly halfway completed with the study of the Old Testament prophets, it is important to examine yourself and see if there are any mid-course corrections that you feel are necessary to implement. Review the evaluation questions list found on page 11 of this Leader's Guide, and jot down two or three action points to begin implementing next week. Perhaps you have made steady improvements since the first time you answered the evaluation questions at the beginning of the course. If so, your improvements should challenge you to be an even better group leader for the final seven lessons in the study.

ACTION POINTS:

1. _____

_____

2. _____

_____

3. _____

_____

6

MEMORY VERSE

"Therefore, if a man cleanses himself from these things, he will be a vessel for honor, sanctified, useful to the Master, prepared for every good work."

BEFORE THE SESSION

❑ Remember the Boy Scout motto: **BE PREPARED!** The main reason a Bible study flounders is because the leader is unprepared and tries to "shoot from the hip," so to speak.

❑ Make sure to mark down any discussion questions that come to mind as you study.

❑ If you want to do further study, look at 1 and 2 Kings and 1 and 2 Chronicles, and read about the kings who ruled while Isaiah ministered. You may also benefit from doing the lesson on Hezekiah from *Following God: Life Principles from the Kings.* The revival during Hezekiah's reign was influenced by the ministry of Isaiah.

❑ Don't forget to pray for the members of your group and for your time of studying together. You don't want to be satisfied with what **you** can do. You want to see God do what only **He** can do!

WHAT TO EXPECT

In this lesson, realize that all of us, sooner or later, will fall prey to comparing ourselves to others around us instead of to the holy standards of God.

Make sure you allow time for members of your group to share honestly about their struggles. Realize that there may be some sin God wants to deal with so that He can make each member more useable to Him in His work. Be sensitive to any questions this lesson may surface about ministry, and guard your group from applying it only to those with a "vocational" ministry.

> ### THE MAIN POINT
> The main point to be seen in this lesson is that, before God can use us, He must first make us useable.

In other words, before He can do a work **through** us, He must first do a work **in** us. Before Isaiah *"saw the Lord"* his message was *"woe"* to this person and *"woe"* to that person. But when he saw the Lord, his message changed to *"woe is me"* (Is. 6:5). His own sin had to be dealt with before he could get to the place of saying, *"Here am I, send me"* (Is. 6:8).

DURING THE SESSION

 OPENING: 5–10 MINUTES

Opening Prayer—Remember to have one of your group members open your time together in prayer.

Opening Illustration—A good way to begin your discussion time is by asking the question, "Why does a surgeon sterilize his scalpel before he operates?" This should get your group thinking. The main idea they should come to is that a surgeon sterilizes his scalpel to protect his patient from infection. Think about it. A surgeon operating with a dirty scalpel is going to do more harm than good. In fact, he may put the patient's life at risk unnecessarily. The parallel is obvious—God will not use us in someone else's life until He has first cleansed us and made us useable.

⧗ DISCUSSION: 30–40 MINUTES

Remember to pace your discussion so that you will be able to bring closure to the lesson in the time allotted. You are the one who must balance lively discussion with timely redirection to ensure that you don't end up finishing only part of the lesson.

Main Objective in Day One: In Day One, the main objective is to see what Isaiah's message was like before his encounter with the Lord. You don't necessarily need to spend a lot of time on Day One, but you want to make sure your group members make the connection that without a clear view of God, it is easy to let the sins of others cloud our view of our own sins. Check which discussion questions from Day One you find to be useful.

_____ What common denominators did you see in Isaiah's early message?

_____ Do you ever struggle with seeing the sins of others more clearly than your own? Why?

_____ Ask your group if they have any questions from their study of Day One.

Main Objective in Day Two: In Day Two, we learn some of the specifics of Isaiah's relationship with King Uzziah and the impact his death may have had on Isaiah's view of himself and of God. The main principle here is that when those around us commit great sins, it is easy to judge our own righteousness by how we "stack up" against them. We will always win such a comparison. Instead, we must realize that sin is not relative—it is not how we are compared to other sinners. Sin is how far we fall short of God. Check which discussion questions from Day Two you will use.

_____ What lessons can we learn from King Uzziah?

_____ How do you think Isaiah felt about the failings of Uzziah?

_____ What effect do you think Uzziah's sin had on Isaiah's view of himself?

_____ How do you think Uzziah's death changed how Isaiah saw himself?

Main Objective in Day Three: Day Three introduces us to the transforming experience Isaiah had when he *"saw the Lord"* (Is. 6:1). There are two key points you want to make sure your group members see from Day Three: **1)** it is God who reveals Isaiah's sin, and **2)** it is God who deals with Isaiah's sin. Isaiah did not see his own sin before, focused as he was on the sins of others. But when he saw the Lord, God revealed to him his own sinfulness. God did not leave him there, though. God only reveals sin so that He can deal with it. Check which discussion questions from Day Three you will use.

_____ Looking at the passage, what things stand out to Isaiah in this vision?

_____ How would you feel if you were in Isaiah's place?

_____ Why do you think Isaiah's lips were touched with fire from the altar?

_____ What else stands out to you from Isaiah's encounter with the Lord?

Main Objective in Day Four: In Day Four, we see the all-important principle that **after** God has dealt with our sin, then He is able to use us. It is on the heels of Isaiah's forgiveness that he receives the invitation from God, "Whom shall I send?" Check which discussion questions from Day Four you will use.

_____ What do you think about the statement, "until we see ourselves as useless, we really aren't useable"?

_____ We usually think of ministry as a "call" (as if God picked us and we had no choice), but here we see it as an "invitation," something to which we can choose to say yes. What do you think about that?

_____ We see that God's task for Isaiah was a ministry with no fruit. Have you ever experienced that?

_____ What kind of struggles did it bring?

Day Five—Key Points in Application: The most important application point out of Day Five is that we cannot use "immediate results" as a yardstick to measure whether or not we are doing what God wants us to do. It is obedience to God, and not results that measure our successes or failures in His work. Check the discussion questions from Day Five that pertain to your study group.

_____ Has a lack of results ever caused you to doubt that you were serving in the right place?

_____ What is the right way to know if you are serving rightly?

_____ Who are the Uzziah's in your life that you measure yourself against?

_____ What is the biggest application point you that you recognized this week?

CLOSING: 5–10 MINUTES

❑ **Summarize**—Highlight the key points.

❑ **Remind** those in your group that the victorious Christian life is not attained when we try hard to be like Jesus, but when we surrender our lives to God and let Him work through us.

❑ **Preview**—Take a few moments to preview next week's lesson on **"Micah: What Does the Lord Require of You."**

❑ **Pray**—Close in prayer.

TOOLS FOR GOOD DISCUSSION

As discussed earlier, there are certain people who show up in every discussion group that you will ever lead. We have already looked at "Talkative Timothy" and "Silent Sally." This week, let's talk about another person who also tends to show up. Let's call this person **"Tangent Tom."** He is the kind of guy who loves to talk even when he has nothing to say. Tangent Tom loves to "chase rabbits" regardless of where they go. When he gets the floor, you never know where the discussion will lead. You need to understand that not all tangents are bad. Sometimes, much can be gained from discussion "a little off the beaten path." But these diversions must be balanced against the purpose of the group. In the "Helpful Hints" section of **How to Lead a Small Group** (p. 6), you will find some practical ideas on managing the "Tangent Tom's" in your group. You will also get some helpful information on evaluating tangents as they arise.

7

Micah

MEMORY **Micah 12:24** VERSE

"He has told you, O man, what is good; and what does the Lord require of you but to do justice, to love kindness, and to walk humbly with your God."

Before the Session

❑ It might be a good idea for you to try to get your homework done early in the week. This will allow time for you to reflect on what you have learned. Don't succumb to the temptation to procrastinate.

❑ Keep a highlight pen handy to highlight any things you want to be sure to discuss or any questions that you think your group may have trouble understanding. Mark down any good discussion questions that come to mind as you study.

❑ If you want to do further study, look at 1 and 2 Kings and 1 and 2 Chronicles, and read about the kings who ruled while Micah ministered. You may also benefit from doing the lesson on **Hezekiah** from *Following God: Life Principles from the Kings of the Old Testament.* The revival of Hezekiah's day was influenced by the ministry of Micah.

❑ Don't think of your ministry to the members of your group as something that only takes place during your group session. Pray for each group member by name during the week. Pray that each member learns much from his or her studies. Encourage all members of your group as you have opportunity.

What to Expect

In this lesson, we are afforded a very practical opportunity to teach our group members the right and wrong ways of dealing with sin. This is one of the most important tools you can place in their spiritual toolboxes. You will make it easier for your members to be open and honest with their own struggles with sin if you come prepared to share from your own experiences and struggles. Knowing that you have not "arrived" spiritually will make it easier for them to face the fact that they have not yet "arrived" and will give them courage to address this important issue.

Our study in Micah will help us focus on what it takes to please God. Micah's message comes as the Northern Kingdom (Israel) faced total annihilation because of that nation's rebellion against Jehovah. God speaks to the Southern Kingdom (Judah) and says, "Even though you are religious, you are just as sinful as rebellious Israel."

> **THE MAIN POINT**
> What God desires from us is not religious ritual, but a heart relationship with Him that produces justice and mercy in our actions.

DURING THE SESSION

 OPENING: 5–10 MINUTES

Opening Prayer—It would be a good idea to have a different group member open your time together in prayer each week.

Opening Illustration—A good way to begin your discussion time is by asking the question, "What if someone offended you greatly, and instead of apologizing and asking forgiveness, they baked you a plate of cookies—would that make things right in your relationship?" After allowing some discussion, the point you want your group to see is that this is what we do with God when we try to deal with our sins our own way instead of His way.

 DISCUSSION: 30–40 MINUTES

A key objective in how you manage your discussion time is to keep the big picture in view. Your job is not as a school teacher, grading their papers, but as a tutor, making sure they understand the subject. Keep the main point of the lesson in view and make sure they take that point home with them.

Main Objective in Day One: In the discussion for Day One, your main objective as group leader should be to help your group understand the context in which Micah lived and ministered. Nothing is meaningful without a context, and it is impossible to fully appreciate the message and ministry of Micah without understanding the days in which he lived. Since his message is directed to Judah, we will not take the time to study the rulers of the Northern Kingdom during his ministry. Check which discussion questions for Day One that you plan to use.

_____ How do you think the people of Judah viewed the people of the Northern Kingdom (Israel)?

_____ How do you think the people of Judah saw themselves?

_____ How do you think God's judgment of Israel through the Assyrian conquest changed Judah's views?

_____ How do you think Micah's messages changed their views?

_____ What else stood out to you about the days in which Micah ministered?

Main Objective in Day Two: In Day Two, we learn some of the specifics of Micah's message of judgment and his explanations of why it would come. By looking at what he confronts in the people, and by seeing the explanations he gives, we can begin to understand why judgment had come upon Israel, why it would eventually come to Judah, and, in principle, we can see why it comes upon us today. It is important to understand that God judges the sin of His people. As Christians, our eternal destiny with Christ is never to be doubted, but that does not mean that God will not chasten us on earth for our sins. Check which discussion questions you will use from Day Two.

_____ What do you think the people of Judah thought about the idea of God judging them?

_____ On page 100, the statement is made that, "A fundamental law of the universe is that we reap what we sow." How do you think that statement applies to Christians?

_____ Why do you think God is so hard on his own people?

_____ Second Timothy 4:3 talks about an inevitable time when people will _"accumulate for themselves teachers in accordance with their own desires."_ What do you think this verse means?

Main Objective in Day Three: Day Three introduces us to the message of hope that accompanied Micah's preaching of judgment. Yes, Judah's sin would have to be addressed. But even though Israel and Judah had changed in how they followed God, Jehovah had not changed in any aspect whatsoever. He would still be faithful to fulfill all that he had promised. God was not (and is still not) finished with Israel. Check the discussion questions that you will use from Day Three.

_____ Do you ever struggle with feeling hopeless when you see your own sin?

_____ What stands out to you as you look at the promises that Micah emphasizes?

_____ Do you expect that God will fulfill all that He has promised to Israel?

_____ Were there any questions raised by your study in Day Three?

Main Objective in Day Four: In Day Four, Micah closes his message to us by drawing our eyes to God's forgiveness and how we are to experience it. Sooner or later, all believers will find themselves in need of a fresh experience of God's forgiveness. Micah shows us how to receive this forgiveness. Check the questions from Day Four that you will use in your discussion

_____ What comes to mind when you hear the word "forgiveness"?

_____ Why do you think forgiveness is still an issue for people who were forgiven at the cross (Christians)?

_____ In Micah 6:6–7, we see some of the ways Israel and Judah tried to make up for their sins. How do we try to do that today?

_____ What should we be doing?

_____ What stands out to you from these last three verses of Micah (7:18-20)?

Day Five—Key Points in Application: The most important application from Day Five is that we cannot approach God on our own terms. We must approach Him as He requires. Micah 6:8 reiterates this thought of coming to God on His terms, and, in reality, we must approach this verse from the end and work our way backward. For example, before we can love mercy with others, and expect justice of ourselves, we must walk humbly with Him. Make sure your group fully understands Micah 6:8. Check which discussion questions from Day Five you will use.

_____ What are some ways we fail to expect justice of ourselves?

_____ What stands out to you about loving mercy in your relationships with others?

_____ What things get in the way of walking humbly with God?

_____ What is the biggest application point you saw this week?

⌛ CLOSING: 5–10 MINUTES

❑ **Summarize**—You may want to read the paragraph at the beginning of the leader's notes for this lesson, called "The Main Point" of Micah.

❑ **Preview**—If time allows, preview next week's lesson on **"Jeremiah: Trusting in God When Life Looks Hopeless."**

❑ **Pray**—Close in prayer.

TOOLS FOR GOOD DISCUSSION

One of the issues you will eventually have to combat in any group Bible study is the enemy of **boredom.** This antagonist raises its ugly head from time to time, but it shouldn't. It is wrong to bore people with the Word of God! Often boredom results when leaders allow their processes to become too predictable. As small group leaders, we tend to do the same thing in the same way every single time. Yet God the Creator, who spoke everything into existence is infinitely creative! Think about it. He is the one who not only created animals in different shapes and sizes, but different colors as well. When He created food, He didn't make it all taste or feel the same. This God of creativity lives in us. We can trust Him to give us creative ideas that will keep our group times from becoming tired and mundane. In the "Helpful Hints" section of **How to Lead a Small Group** (pp. 8–9), you'll find some practical ideas on adding spice and creativity to your study time.

Jeremiah

MEMORY **Psalms 27:13** VERSE

*"I would have despaired unless I had believed that I would
see the goodness of the Lord in the land of the living."*

BEFORE THE SESSION

❏ Your own preparation is key not only to your effectiveness in leading the group-discussion time, but also to your confidence in leading. It is hard to be confident if you know you are unprepared. These discussion questions and leader's notes are meant to be a helpful addition to your own study but should never become a substitute.

❏ As you do your homework, study with an eye to your own relationship with God. Resist the temptation to bypass this self-evaluation on your way to preparing to lead the group. Nothing will minister to your group more than the testimony of your own walk with God.

❏ Look at 1 and 2 Kings and 1 and 2 Chronicles, and read about the kings who ruled while Jeremiah ministered. You may also benefit from doing the lesson on **Josiah** from *Following God: Life Principles from the Kings of the Old Testament*.

❏ Don't think of your ministry to the members of your group as something that only takes place during your group time. Pray for each group member by name during the week, and, as you pray, ask God to enlighten them while they do their homework. Encourage your group as you have opportunity.

WHAT TO EXPECT

In this lesson, we will touch on an area of life that is sometimes painful and vulnerable. It is only fitting that this idea of "trusting God when life looks hopeless" comes later in the study, when relationships have been built to the point of allowing for a certain amount of vulnerability. Be prepared for the possibility that some in your group may be living in a situation that they feel is hopeless, perhaps with an unbelieving spouse or a prodigal child. While these truths from Jeremiah should be a great comfort, they may also bring to the surface some hidden pain. Don't be afraid of some honest emotion spilling out into the group time.

> ### THE MAIN POINT
> The main point in Jeremiah is the testimony he offers of faith in God in the midst of hopeless-looking circumstances.

Jeremiah ministered not so much to his own generation, but to the future remnant who would one day return to the promised land. Though he lamented the fall of Jerusalem, he stood on the promises of Jehovah that one day the people of God would return to the land and worship in righteousness. While the story of Jeremiah may seem like ancient history, the principles from his life are just as applicable today when you and I find ourselves in hopeless situations.

DURING THE SESSION

 OPENING: 5–10 MINUTES

Opening Prayer—A good prayer with which to open your time is the prayer of David in Psalms 119:18, *"Open my eyes, that I may behold wonderful things from Thy law."* Remember, if it took the illumination of God for men to write Scripture, it will take the same for us to understand it.

Opening Illustration—A good way to begin your discussion time is by asking the question, "What is the most hopeless situation you can think of?" After allowing some discussion, ask, "Is that situation hopeless for the Christian?" You want your group to understand that usually what is defined as hopeless is based on an earthly, circumstantial set of values instead of being based on an eternal perspective.

DISCUSSION: 30–40 MINUTES

Remember to pace your discussion so that you don't run out of time to get to the application questions in Day Five. This time for application is perhaps the most important part of your Bible study. It will be helpful if you are familiar enough with the lesson to be able to prioritize the days for which you want to place more emphasis, so that you are prepared to reflect this added emphasis in the time you devote to each day's reading.

<u>**Main Objective in Day One:**</u> In Day One, the main objective is to understand the context in which Jeremiah lived and ministered. Nothing is meaningful without a context, and it is impossible to fully appreciate the message and ministry of Jeremiah without understanding the days in which he lived. Review the discussion questions for Day One below, and check the ones that you will use for your discussion time:

____ What stands out to you about the last four kings of Judah?

____ What were the three things God did to Jeremiah before He formed him in the womb?

____ How do those three things apply to us today?

____ Have you ever felt "too young" for a responsibility God has given you? What does Jeremiah have to say about that?

<u>**Main Objective in Day Two:**</u> In Day Two, we learn some of the specifics of Jeremiah's preaching. By looking at what he confronts in the people, and by seeing the response for which he calls from them, we can have a sense of what God desires from His people throughout the ages. It is important to understand that God judges the sin of His people. Though we may be Christians who are eternally saved by God's grace, He will still chasten us for our transgressions. Check which discussion questions you will use from Day Two.

____ The two sins of Judah were **a)** forsaking the fountain of living waters (God), and **b)** hewing their own cisterns that would hold no water. What are some ways people do that today?

____ In speaking of their judgment, Jeremiah 2:19 says, *"Your own wickedness will correct you."* Can you think of some examples from your life or those you know where sin was its own punishment?

____ How do we distinguish true repentance over sin from remorse over sin's consequences?

____ What else stood out to you from Day Two?

<u>**Main Objective in Day Three:**</u> Day Three introduces us to the pain of speaking truth to those who reject it. Jeremiah's was not a pleasant ministry. His example ought to remind us that we do not judge the success or failure of a ministry or task based on how people respond, but rather, based on being faithful to God's assignment. Check the questions below from Day Three that you find to be essential to your group's discussion.

____ Jeremiah was faithful to preach truth even though he had no expectation that the people would respond. How does Jeremiah's faithfulness apply to us today?

____ Have you ever experienced grief like that of Jeremiah's over someone else who vehemently refused to repent?

____ What are some modern examples of persecution to those who preach truth?

_____ Why do you think the unrepentant persecute the messenger when they hear truth?

_____ Were there any questions raised by your study in Day Three?

Main Objective in Day Four: In Day Four, our study of Jeremiah takes us to the reality that, sooner or later, God will place us in a situation where we have to act in faith instead of by sight. He will call us to step out on truth instead of allowing us to react to our circumstances. Jeremiah also shows us the necessity of keeping our future hope in view as we face the present. Check the discussion questions from Day Four that you will use in your group session.

_____ What stands out to you from this story of Jeremiah buying the farm?

_____ Have you ever experienced "buyer's remorse" after stepping out in faith?

_____ What do you learn from the future promises made to Israel?

_____ What are some ways our present life on earth requires walking by faith rather than walking by sight?

_____ What else stood out to you from Day Four?

Day Five—Key Points in Application: Among the applications introduced in Day Five, the most noteworthy concept is that we should not be as concerned with the visible results of our actions as in whether or not we are doing what God has called us to do. Make sure that your group understands that success in life always comes in doing what God says and leaving the results to Him. Check any questions that you would like to use for discussion on Day Five.

_____ Of the three things God did before He formed Jeremiah ("_knew,_" "_consecrated,_" "_appointed_" [Jeremiah 1:5]), which stands out the most to you personally?

_____ Is there a hopeless situation in your life you need to surrender to God? Do you need to accept what He has appointed for you?

_____ Out of fear, have you failed to do something that you know God has called you to?

_____ Is there anything you need to "recall to mind" about God in your present circumstances?

_____ What other applications did you come to understand from this week's lesson?

CLOSING: 5–10 MINUTES

❑ **Summarize**—Restate the key points. You may want to read the paragraph at the beginning of the leader's notes for Jeremiah called "The Main Point."

❑ **Preview**—If time allows, preview next week's lesson on **"Habakkuk: Following God in the Low Places of Life."**

❑ **Pray**—Close in prayer.

TOOLS FOR GOOD DISCUSSION

From time to time each of us can say stupid things. Some of us, however, are better at it than others. I suspect the apostle Peter fell into this category. One minute he was on the pinnacle of success saying, _"Thou art the Christ, the Son of the Living God"_ (Matthew 16:16), and the next minute he was putting his foot in his mouth, trying to talk Jesus out of going to the cross. Proverbs 10:19 states, _"When there are many words, transgression is unavoidable...."_ What do you do when someone in the group says something that is obviously wrong? First of all, remember that how you deal with a situation like this not only affects the present, but the future. In the "Helpful Hints" section of **How to Lead a Small Group Bible Study** (p. 9), you'll find some practical ideas on managing the obviously mistaken comments that may be presented in your group discussion.

9

Habakkuk

MEMORY **Habakkuk 3:18–19** VERSES

"Yet I will exult in the Lord, I will rejoice in the God of my salvation. The Lord God is my strength, And He . . . makes me walk on my high places."

BEFORE THE SESSION

❑ Pray each day for the members of your group—that they spend time in the Word, grasp the message God wants to bring to their lives, and that they surrender to what God is saying to them through their study of His Word.

❑ As you pray that your group members will grow in their study of the Scriptures, make sure you have searched the Scriptures carefully for each day's lesson as well.

❑ Walk through the discussion questions given throughout this Leader's Guide lesson, and select which questions you think might enhance your group discussion.

❑ **Suggestions for Additional Study**—To better understand the condition of Judah at this time you may want to review last week's lesson on **Jeremiah,** and look at *Following God: Life Principles from the Kings of the Old Testament,* (Lesson 9), entitled **"Josiah: The Impact of Following the Word of God."**

❑ Remain ever teachable. Look first for what God is saying to you. This will help you in understanding and relating to some of the struggles that your group members may be facing in the "low places" they are going through.

WHAT TO EXPECT

This lesson may reveal some evident struggles that one or a few members of your group may be facing. Do not feel like you have to be "The Answer Man" or "The Answer Woman." Sometimes the most faith-filled response to a question is "I don't know," followed by "but we know we can trust God. He is faithful and trustworthy." Some in your group will have some tremendous testimonies of victory or rejoicing in the midst of some very dark days. You may see and hear some wonderful testimonies of the grace of God at work. I knew a very dear man of God, Oscar Thompson, a professor of evangelism at Southwestern Seminary in Fort Worth, Texas in the 1970's. The ravaging effects of cancer plagued his body, and he faced some very rough days before his death. But he also experienced some wonderful days of grace. God allowed him to minister and counsel many people from all over the country who were facing the pains of chemotherapy or even the day of their death. He often spoke to them of the grace of God. He said, "God gives dying grace on dying days." He does not give dying grace on non-dying days. Oscar Thompson lived in that reality and died in that reality. God truly gives whatever grace and wisdom we need when we need it. Help your group members see this truth so that they may continue to follow God through the low places of their lives.

> ## THE MAIN POINT
>
> We will learn to live by faith in the "high places" of God's grace, as we walk through the "low places" of the dark circumstances in life.

DURING THE SESSION

 OPENING: 5–10 MINUTES

Opening Prayer—Remember to ask the Lord for **His** wisdom. He promised to guide us into the truth.

Opening Illustration—The following hymn, "He Giveth More Grace" was written by Annie Johnson Flint:

"He giveth more grace when the burden grows greater;
He sendeth more strength when the labors increase.
To added affliction He addeth His mercy;
to multiplied trials, His multiplied peace.

"His love has no limit; His grace has no measure;
His pow'r has no boundary known unto men.
For out of His infinite riches in Jesus,
He giveth, and giveth, and giveth again!"

The second verse says,

"When we have exhausted our store of endurance,
When our strength has failed ere the day is half done,
When we reach the end of our hoarded resources,
Our Father's full giving is only begun."

["He Giveth More Grace" © 1941, Renewed 1969 Lillenas Publishing Co. Used by permission]

How true these words are for the trials we face!

 DISCUSSION: 30–40 MINUTES

Select one or two specific questions to get the group started. Keep the group focused along the main study of Habakkuk. By this point in the course (Week 9), you know both the talkative ones and the quiet ones. Continue to encourage members in the importance of their input. Some of the greatest life lessons we ever learn may come from someone who has said very little up to this point.

Main Objective in Day One: In Day One, the main objective is to see the symptoms of being in a "low place," the darkness and distress sin has brought. Check the discussion questions for Day One that you will use.

_____ What was the condition of Judah in the days of Habakkuk, especially around 609–605 B.C.? What parallels do you see today?

_____ How does a leader affect those around him? What did you discover about King Jehoahaz?

_____ How do the sins of others bring discouragement to you personally? What can we do to encourage one another to follow the Lord and obey His Word day-by-day?

_____ How do you face the questions you have (especially the unanswered questions) about the way circumstances are turning out for you? How could you help others with their particular questions?

Main Objective in Day Two: Here we learn that the "low places" show us our hearts and our attitudes, especially the attitude of **pride**. Make sure everyone in your group sees the truth about pride in today's lesson. Check the discussion questions for Day Two that you will use.

_____ What is the difference between living by sight (feelings, emotions, human logic) and living by faith (God's logic)? You may want to read 2 Corinthians 4:16–18, the testimony of Paul in the face of the pressure of circumstances.

_____ Describe pride. What does a prideful person look like, sound like, act like?

_____ How has God dealt with you about an area of pride? Can you recall a time when God was speaking specifically to you about your pride?

_____ What are some ways we try to fix circumstances in others' lives or in our own instead of urging others to humble themselves before God or humbling ourselves before God?

_____ What are some ways God may seek to bring us to humble ourselves?

Main Objective in Day Three: In Day Three, the study concentrates on Habakkuk's new attitude toward God. Select a question or two from the list below that you think might be useful for your discussion of Day Three.

_____ Habakkuk truly heard the message that God spoke to him. What are some ways God speaks in the midst of our circumstances?

_____ How can we make sure we are "all ears" when God is speaking?

_____ How can we gain a clearer view of who God is and what He wants in our lives?

_____ What are some ways God has worked in your life, both to your benefit and to the benefit of others around you?

_____ Are there some things God has revealed about Himself that you would not have known had it not been for the rough days that God has allowed to enter your life?

Main Objective in Day Four: Here we see the triumph of Habakkuk in the midst of the coming calamities of his people. His focus was on the Lord and how the Lord would guide His people **through** the difficult days. Check a question or two from the list below that you find to be profitable to your discussion of Day Four.

_____ Habakkuk trembled when he thought about what the future held. Yet, he also rejoiced. How do the ideas of trembling and rejoicing fit together?

_____ How can a person have joy even in the midst of difficulties, including the loss of prosperity? What was Habakkuk's solution to all that he faced?

_____ How can you personally focus more fully on the Lord, and how can you help others do the same?

Day Five—Key Points in Application: The most noteworthy application point from Day Five is that we make sure that our faith is directed upon God, not on people or earthly things. Encourage your group members to discern whether the motivations for their lifestyles come from God or from the world. Review the Day Five question list below, and select the ones that you feel will enhance your group discussion.

_____ What shapes the way most people (even many Christians) look at life?

_____ What do you know for sure about God's knowledge and wisdom? What are some

world opinions that have gotten mixed in with what you see in Scripture?

_____ How has God shown His love in your life?

_____ What are some struggles you have faced, difficulties that are dark threads in the tapestry that God is weaving? What is God saying to you through Habakkuk?

⧖ CLOSING: 5–10 MINUTES

❑ **Summarize**—Restate the key points the group shared. Review the objectives for each of the days found at the beginning of these leader notes.

❑ **Focus**—Using the memory verses (Habakkuk 3:18–19), focus the group on the centrality of faith in the character and ways of God. As Psalm 119:68 says, _"Thou art good and doest good."_ We can trust Him.

❑ **Ask** them to share their thoughts concerning Day Five, especially the truths about the "gates" that all God's decisions come through.

❑ **Encourage**—We have finished nine lessons. This is no time to slack off. Encourage your group to keep up the pace. We have three more lessons full of life-changing truths. Take a few moments to preview next week's lesson on **"Daniel: Confidence in the God of Heaven."** Encourage your group members to do their homework and to space it out over the week.

❑ Close in prayer.

⚒ TOOLS FOR GOOD DISCUSSION ⚒

The Scriptures are full of examples of people who struggled with the problem of pride. Unfortunately, pride isn't a problem reserved for the history books. It shows up just as often today as it did in the days the Scriptures were written. In your group discussions, you may see traces of pride manifested in a "know-it-all" group member. **"Know-It-All Ned"** may have shown up in your group by this point. He may be an intellectual giant, or he may be a legend only in his own mind. He can be very prideful and argumentative. If you want some helpful hints on how to deal with "Know-It-All Ned," look in the "Helpful Hints" section of **How to Lead a Small Group Bible Study** (p. 7).

10

Daniel

MEMORY **Isaiah 66:2b** VERSE

*"But to this one will I look, to him who is humble and contrite
of spirit, and who trembles at My word."*

BEFORE THE SESSION

❑ Never underestimate the importance of prayer for yourself and for the members of your group. Ask the Lord to give them understanding in their time in the Word and bring them to a new level of knowing Him.

❑ Remember to mark those ideas and questions you want to discuss or ask as you go through the study.

❑ Suggestions for Additional Study: To better understand the condition of Judah at this time you may want to look at two lessons in *Following God: Life Principles from the Kings of the Old Testament*. The first lesson is titled, **"Josiah: The Impact of Following the Word of God."** To see how God worked near the end of Daniel's life you may want to look at **"Zerubbabel and Ezra: Following God's Will."**

❑ Be sensitive to the needs of your group. Be prepared to stop and pray for a member who may be facing a difficult struggle or challenge.

WHAT TO EXPECT

Some in your group may recall some things they have heard about Daniel as a youth (i.e., the story of Daniel in the Lion's Den), while others may find the study completely new. There may be some tough questions that surface in dealing with the things God allows in our lives or in facing some matters dealing with authorities in our lives. Remember that your job is not to teach the lesson, but to guide discussion so that all can learn from each other. You will want to emphasize the faithfulness of God in Daniel's life and how God is ever faithful to each member in your group. Just because God is always faithful to us does not mean that He will reveal to us all of the why's and why not's of life. God's faithfulness to us means that He will take us all the way to the finish line in the race He has set out for us. He takes us there in His way, in His timing, along His paths. Those paths are always chosen out of His covenant love for us, and He has promised to **never** leave us nor forsake us—just as we see in Daniel's life. May this lesson be a real encouragement to your group to **see God** at work in their lives and to **seek God** in the circumstances they are facing.

> ### THE MAIN POINT
> We can place our total confidence and trust in the God of Heaven who rules over all. He is **always** at work fulfilling His purposes for His people.

During the Session

⏳ **OPENING: 5–10 MINUTES**

Opening Prayer—Have one of the group members open the time with prayer.

Opening Illustration—Confidence in the Word of God. King Josiah emphasized the importance of following **all** of the Word of God (2 Kings 23:25). Apparently he made an impact on young Daniel and Daniel's family. The Babylonian army was known for its fierce and proud soldiers. Their reputation had spread far and wide. Habakkuk had talked much about them. Now Daniel faced them and was a captive in their caravan back to Babylon. As a fourteen-year-old youth he discovered that the Word of God was sufficient wherever he was and in whatever circumstance he faced. His confidence in the God of Heaven meant a confidence in the Word of the God of Heaven. We can discover the same.

⏳ **DISCUSSION: 30–40 MINUTES**

Select one or two specific questions to get the group to start talking. This lesson on Daniel covers over 70 years of his life and has application points for every stage of life. Focus on the power and reign of the Lord in our lives. Keep the group directed on the **faithfulness of God** in Daniel's life as well as on the **faith of Daniel** in God's faithfulness. Continue to encourage each member in the importance of his or her input.

Main Objective in Day One: In Day One the main objective is to see the righteous God Daniel knew and Daniel's desire to follow His righteous Word. Check which discussion questions you will use from Day One .

_____ What would it mean to have a king like Josiah leading the people (imagine you and your parents) in following all the Word of God? How would you respond if you were Daniel?

_____ What would it be like to hear about coming judgment and then see the armies of Babylon? If you were Daniel's parents, what would you say to your children when you heard Habakkuk, Jeremiah, or Zephaniah proclaiming the message God had given

him? How would you prepare yourself or your children in light of the messages of these prophets?

_____ How do you face new circumstances? Think of all the "new" things Daniel and his friends faced. Have you experienced a major move with your family or some major change in your life? What can you learn from Daniel about what's important?

_____ Sometimes we must take a stand or confront a person or group because of a personal conviction God has given us. What principles have you gleaned from the way Daniel responded to his situation?

Main Objective in Day Two: Sometimes we face situations that are beyond our own understanding or abilities, but they are not beyond God's. The Lord wants us to depend on Him and look to Him for His wisdom and grace for difficult situations. Check the discussion questions that you will use from Day Two.

_____ What stood out to you about Daniel's attitude and confidence in God in the face of this trial?

_____ What were priorities to Daniel and his three friends? What did they do first? second? third? What does that say to you about how you should face trials?

_____ Can you think of a time when you faced a trial in which you needed wisdom, and how God gave you that wisdom?

_____ Describe a time when you depended on man's wisdom, man's might or strength, or man's riches. What did God teach you (or what is He teaching you now about this) in light of Jeremiah 9:23–24?

_____ What practical lessons can you glean from Daniel's confidence in God's ability to reveal the way to go, the choices to make, and the things to do? What about the things **not** to do?

Main Objective in Day Three: The main objective is to see that "*it is Heaven that rules*" and in seeing that to also see the attitude of humility and trust that God wants in us. Check the discussion questions from Day Three that are relevant to your group.

____ Nebuchadnezzar's dream was followed by twelve months of waiting. God was waiting to see his response, then He acted to carry out the dream He had given him. How have you seen the Lord's reign in your life through His timing of some event or answer to prayer?

____ Nebuchadnezzar's view of life was filled with pride. What are some ways that **pride** fills our view of life today? What do we need to do when we see this?

____ What are some ways God has humbled you in your pride?

____ Daniel served for many years under several rulers, some of whom were very proud. How did Daniel serve under such men? Where was his focus, and how did that focus get him through those years of service?

Main Objective in Day Four: Daniel's relationship with the Lord impacted all that he did—his job and his home life, not just his spiritual life. The same can be true of us. Place a check mark near the questions that are best suited for your discussion.

____ Daniel was marked by integrity on the job. How important is integrity? What difference did Daniel's integrity make to Darius or to Daniel's co-workers?

____ How can our relationship to God affect our relationships to those in authority over us? How can our relationships with those in authority over us affect our fellowship with God?

____ How important is the Word of God in our lives? In Daniel 9, we find that Daniel was reading the prophecy of Jeremiah. How do you think that affected how he prayed and what he prayed?

____ Where was Daniel focused as he thought of and prayed for Jerusalem and the people of Israel? How does that speak to you about your focus in life or your focus in prayer?

Day Five—Key Points in Application: The most important application point seen in the life of Daniel is this: we should make sure that we see life and its many circumstances from **God's point of view** rather than seeing life only from the level of our cir-

cumstances. Check which discussion questions you will use from Day Five.

____ In God's scheme of things, how we finish the race is far more important than how we start the race. How did Daniel finish his race? What can you do to insure a good finish in your life?

____ Daniel served under a variety of authorities—some idolatrous, some proud, some unpredictable. Paul the Apostle wrote Romans 13 (about authorities) during the reign of Nero, a very wicked ruler.

____ Where was the focus of Daniel or Paul? How did they deal with authorities in their lives? What can we learn from them?

____ What has God shown you about the "kingdom" where you are "ruling" or, in most cases, serving?

____ Daniel has some things to say about facing surprises in life. What do we know for sure about the surprises of life, things like sudden changes in our jobs, schools, locations, finances, relationships, friends or family?

⌛ CLOSING: 5–10 MINUTES

❑ **Summarize.**

❑ **Ask** your group to express their thoughts about the key applications from Day Five.

❑ **Preview**—Take time to preview next week's lesson on **"Haggai: A Call to Consider Your Ways."**

❑ **Pray**—Close in prayer.

TOOLS FOR GOOD DISCUSSION

So, group leaders, how have the first nine weeks of this study been for you? Have you dealt with anyone in your group called **"Agenda Alice"**? She is the type that is focused on a Christian "hot-button" issue instead of the Bible study. If not managed properly, she (or he) will either sidetrack the group from its main study objective, or create a hostile environment in the group if she fails to bring people to her way of thinking. For help with "Agenda Alice," see the "Helpful Hints" section of **How to Lead a Small Group Bible Study** (pp. 7–8).

11

MEMORY **2 Corinthians 6:16** VERSE

"For we are the temple of the living God; just as God said, 'I will dwell in them and walk among them; and I will be their God, and they shall by My people.'"

BEFORE THE SESSION

❑ Pray for your group as they walk through this week's lesson.

❑ Spread your study time over the week. Think of the lesson as a large meal. You need time to chew each truth and digest it fully.

❑ Remember to mark those ideas and questions you want to discuss or ask as you go.

❑ Suggestions for Additional Study: To better understand the condition of Jerusalem at this time you may want to look at the lesson on **"Zerubbabel and Ezra: Following God's Will"** (Lesson 10) in *Following God: Life Principles from the Kings of the Old Testament*.

WHAT TO EXPECT

Haggai will be a new name for some (perhaps for all) in your group. He appears only for a brief moment on the stage of the Old Testament, but what He said lingers throughout time into eternity. Along with the newness of Haggai, some will find the discussion about the Tabernacle or Temple to be new or at least unfamiliar. There may be a few questions about Zerubbabel or the "signet ring" or God's promises for the future that are not easily answered.

Be patient. Study diligently in your preparation time. You may want to consult a Bible dictionary about some of these things. As you tread through the lesson, seek to keep the main point the main point. Emphasize what you clearly know and understand. Then you can move on to the things that are not as clear as the Lord gives time and insight.

> ### THE MAIN POINT
> God continually calls us to "consider" our "ways" in our walk with Him, and He calls us to adjust our ways to His ways through following His Word.

DURING THE SESSION

⌛ **OPENING: 5–10 MINUTES**

Opening Prayer—Have one of the group members open the time with prayer.

Opening Illustration—It's the Little Things That Count. Often we are tempted to think that only the big things in life, or the big events, or the "big name" people are what is really important. But a small rudder turns the greatest of ships, and the tongue, though it is one of the smallest members of our bodies, is often the most powerful. How many times we have found that it is not a whole book or a whole chapter of the Bible that impacts—but a small verse or part of a verse or phrase empowered by the Spirit of God that pierces us in soul and spirit. This little book of Haggai (only two chapters, 38 verses) has this powerful potential. In this small book, the call to consider our ways rings clear with the promise that obedience will bring the blessing of God.

⏳ DISCUSSION: 30–40 MINUTES

This lesson on Haggai covers only a year of his life but looks at God's plans for the ages. Focus on the Lord's call to consider our ways in the light of His plans in our lives. Keep the group directed at the mercy and faithfulness of God. Help them see His "never give up" attitude with His people and with His plans. Every **call** for us to consider our ways is a **promise** that His mercy and grace are available to the obedient heart.

Main Objective in Day One: The main point here is to discover the preeminence of God's priorities and the importance of making those priorities ours. Check which discussion questions you will use from Day One.

_____ Do you find it easy to focus on "taking care of business" (i.e., your own "business") and forgetting the things of God?

_____ What things got in the way of building the Temple in Haggai's day? What things can get in the way of what God wants to do in and through our lives?

_____ How can we follow the command to "set your heart on your ways"? How do we "set" our hearts or "consider" our ways?

_____ God got their attention through their economy (the dew, the crops, and their expenses). How does the Lord get our attention today? How has he gotten your attention about your walk?

Main Objective in Day Two: In Day Two, we learn the importance of God's presence and what it means to walk practicing His presence. Check the discussion questions for Day Two that you will use.

_____ How have you seen the difference between "existing" and "living" in your life or perhaps in your family's life?

_____ What does it mean to you that God wants to "dwell with" **you**?

_____ What does "fearing the Lord" mean to you? What are some ways you can (or do) show reverence for the Lord?

_____ We see that the people of Jerusalem were energized by their obedience to the Word of the Lord. What does it mean to be "energized" by your obedience? What does that look like?

Main Objective in Day Three: Day Three focuses on the promise of the presence and provision of the Lord as the people obeyed. Decide which discussion questions for Day Three you will use from the list below:

_____ What would the promise of the Lord's presence and provision mean to people walking out of Egypt into the Wilderness of Sinai? What would it mean to people rebuilding a temple from the rubble in a city with no walls and a depressed economy?

_____ What is the one thing someone wants when they are really thirsty? What kind of thirst did Jesus talk about in John 7? Name some ways you have experienced thirst—physically or spiritually.

_____ Name some ways Jesus has quenched your soul's thirst. What is the difference between the **"living water"** Jesus gives and the "waters" of the world?

_____ Haggai's messages were meant to bring the people into a much greater understanding and experience of the presence and provision of God in daily life. What do the promises of God mean in your life today? How do the promises of God give you comfort or encouragement?

Main Objective in Day Four: Day Four looks at how the Lord treated Israel to bring them back to a full experience of His presence and power. Check which discussion questions you will use from Day Four.

_____ **Whatever It Takes**—That is what we see again and again as Haggai speaks (Haggai 2:16–17) about how God uses different means to get our attention, to cause us to look up to Him in a fresh way, to come to a new day of full obedience. What does this tell you about the Lord?

____ The Lord not only used circumstances to speak to His people, He also sent His prophets with a clear message from His heart. God speaks through His Word to us today. What hinders us from obeying what is clear in His Word?

____ All that God did and said was meant to encourage and energize His people in their walk and for the tasks they would face in the days ahead. How can you be an encouragement and an energizer to others as opposed to a "discourager" and an "energy-drainer"?

____ The Lord did not stop His words of encouragement to Haggai. He had more to say through Zechariah. What does this tell you about the Lord's love and care for His people? What does this say about His care for you today? How can this encourage you and others in following God?

Day Five—Key Points in Application: The most important application point seen in the ministry of Haggai is found in the statement: *"consider your ways"* (Haggai 1:5). Is He real in the everyday affairs of your life, or do you just give Him a little attention on Sunday? Check which discussion questions from Day Five you will use.

____ We don't go to a Temple to acknowledge the presence of the Lord, we are the Temple of His Spirit. Everywhere we go, God and His Temple goes. How can the recognition of the truth that we are the Temple of God's Spirit affect your daily life?

____ What has this lesson said to you about your priorities? Are they the priorities that a disciple of Jesus Christ should have?

____ On page 179 in the workbook, the statement is made: "He wants us to walk—not **ahead** of Him, trying to control our own lives; not **behind** Him, rebelling against Him and His ways; but **with** Him, cooperating and enjoying the fellowship of the journey." What are some application points in that statement that touch your life?

____ God speaks in a language we understand. He uses the image of a tent to speak of dwelling with His people, of living with them like a family. Think of some pictures that describe the kind of relationship God wants with you (for example, a Father to a child).

⧗ CLOSING: 5–10 MINUTES

❑ **Summarize**—Restate the key points.

❑ **Ask** the group members to share their thoughts about the key applications from Day Five.

❑ **Preview**—Take time to preview next week's lesson on **"Christ the Prophet: Worshiping in Spirit and Truth."** Encourage them to do their homework for this final lesson in the study of the Old Testament prophets.

❑ **Pray**—Close in prayer.

⚒ TOOLS FOR GOOD DISCUSSION ⚒

Well, it is evaluation time again! You may be saying to yourself, "Why bother evaluating at the end? If I did a bad job, it is too late to do anything about it now!" Well, it may be too late to change how you did on this course, but it is never too late to learn from this course what will help you on the next. Howard Hendricks, that peerless communicator from Dallas Theological Seminary, puts it this way: "The good teacher's greatest threat is satisfaction—the failure to keep asking, 'How can I improve?' The greatest threat to your ministry is **your ministry.**" Any self-examination should be an accounting of your own strengths and weaknesses. As you consider your strengths and weaknesses, take some time to read through the evaluation questions list found in the **How to Lead a Small Group Bible Study** section on pages 11–12 of this leader's guide. Make it your aim to continue growing as a discussion leader. Below, jot down two or three action points for you to implement in future classes.

ACTION POINTS:

1. _____

_____

2. _____

_____

3. _____

_____

12

Christ the Prophet

MEMORY **John 5:24** VERSE

"Truly, truly, I say to you, he who hears My word, and believes Him who sent Me, has eternal life, and does not come into judgment, but has passed out of death into life."

BEFORE THE SESSION

❑ Never underestimate the importance of prayer for yourself and for the members of your group. Pray for each group member by name.

❑ Spread your study time over the week.

❑ Remember to mark those ideas and questions you want to discuss or ask as you go through the study. Add to those some of the questions listed below.

❑ Be sensitive to the working of the Spirit in your group meeting, ever watchful for ways to help one another truly follow God.

WHAT TO EXPECT

Like seeing the facets of a diamond or emerald from several angles, seeing Christ as The Prophet will hopefully give fresh perspective to the members in your group. Hopefully, all will experience a deeper level of obedience to the Lord and His Word, and with that, discover the reward of receiving a prophet (The Prophet) of the Lord. When we focus on Jesus Christ we often discover answers to the deepest cries of our heart. We also face new questions and desire greater understanding. Some questions may arise that you may not be able to answer

or to answer as fully as you would like. Remember that you do not need to be "The Answer Man" or "The Answer Woman" for all the things that come up. Rejoice in the new insights and challenge the group to deeper study with the unknowns. As you move through the lesson, seek to keep the main focus the main focus. Emphasize what you clearly know and understand. Then you can move on to the things that are not as clear as the Lord gives time and insight.

> ### THE MAIN POINT
>
> As we study the life and ministry of Christ Jesus the Prophet, we will learn the necessity of honoring Him and His Word with a life of worship in spirit (heart) and truth.

DURING THE SESSION

⌛ **OPENING: 5–10 MINUTES**

Opening Prayer—Psalm 119:18 says, *"Open my eyes, that I may behold wonderful things from Thy law."* Ask the Lord to open your eyes as you meet together. Have one of the group members open the time with prayer.

Opening Illustration—It has been said of George Whitefield, the great evangelist of the First Great

Awakening (1740s), that he could be clearly heard in a crowd of 20,000 with no means of amplification. More than that, his message thundered with the conviction of the Holy Spirit through the hearts of thousands. Imagine what it was like to hear the Lord Jesus when He spoke His Sermon on the Mount or when He spoke at the feeding of the 5,000. Matthew 7:28–29 says *"the multitudes were amazed at His teaching; for He was teaching them as one having authority, and not as their scribes."* As you look at Christ the Prophet, may He speak with authority and conviction to each one in your group.

⏳ DISCUSSION: 30–40 MINUTES

This lesson on Christ the Prophet focuses on Christ's clear grasp of the Word of His Father, how He faithfully proclaimed that Word, and the reward for an obedient response on the part of His hearers. For today, through this lesson, **we** are each His hearers. The admonition of Hebrews 12:1–2 cries out to all of us, *". . . let us run with endurance the race that is set before us,* **fixing our eyes on Jesus,** *the author and perfecter of faith. . . ."* As you and your group set your eyes on Christ the Prophet, hearing and heeding His Word will result in a greater walk of faith and a deeper experience of His joy.

Main Objective in Day One: The main point here is to see how the Lord raises up those who speak the truth because He longs for His people to walk in that truth. Ultimately, He sent His Son, the Lord Jesus. Choose one or more discussion questions from Day One that is relevant to your group.

_____ God warned about deception and lies in the Canaanite culture. What are some of the sources of falsehood, lies, and deception we face in our lives today?

_____ How does the fact that God wants you to know the truth bring encouragement to you? What are some of His sources of truth for us today?

_____ How important is it to come to the Lord and His Word with an open, listening heart? How can we do that more consistently?

_____ Have you ever heard someone speak "straw" as opposed to "grain," like Jeremiah talked about? How have you seen the difference in your life or in what you have heard?

Main Objective in Day Two: In Day Two, the main objective is to see how Christ fulfilled the promise given to Moses—God would raise up a prophet like Moses who would speak **all** the Word He gave Him to speak. Check the questions that you might consider using for your group discussion for Day Two.

_____ What would it be like to know that the one teaching you was absolutely true in everything he said? What do you think the people thought as they heard Jesus?

_____ What is it like when you learn that someone has told you something that was deceptive in any way?

_____ Jesus spoke with authority. How does your confidence in the Lord Jesus and His Word bring comfort or encouragement to you?

_____ Jesus had an open, honest relationship with His Father. He walked in the freedom of the truth. How has His truth given you freedom in some area?

Main Objective in Day Three: Day Three focuses on **the focus** of the Lord Jesus—a right relationship with God the Father and right worship. Check the discussion questions that you will use for Day Three.

_____ What are some things that get in the way of people seeing God as He really is? Or to put it another way: What are some of the substitutes for true worship? With what do people try to replace true worship?

_____ How do Christians sometimes fail to worship in spirit and truth? What gets in the way in their relationship with God the Father?

_____ Why does the Lord want us to deal honestly with our sin? What good is that? How important is that?

_____ What is the result of dealing with sin and focusing on pure worship in spirit and truth?

Main Objective in Day Four: Day Four looks at the importance of receiving The Prophet and the message He brings. Check which discussion questions from Day Four you will use.

_____ Many believed Jesus to be a prophet, but refused to heed what He said. What does it mean to receive Him and His Word?

_____ A personal relationship with Jesus Christ involves walking with Him in the truth. What should we do when we do not fully understand Him or His Word?

_____ Practically speaking, how do we continue receiving His Word?

_____ What has it meant to you to receive Jesus Christ as your Lord and Savior, as the Prophet, the Way, the Truth, and the Life?

Day Five—Key Points in Application: The most important application point in the study of Christ the Prophet is the practical application of His Word to our lives. Place a checkmark next to the questions for Day Two that you will use in your discussion time.

_____ What can you do to insure that you are continuing to hear Christ the Prophet?

_____ Is there an area where you are struggling, where there is little or no freedom, where you don't know the truth that deals with that struggle?

_____ What are you doing to prepare for His prophesied return?

_____ What has the Lord showed you about your worship and obedience of Him?

⏳ CLOSING: 5–10 MINUTES

❑ **Summarize**—Restate the key points.

❑ **Focus**—Using the memory verse (John 5:24), focus the group on what it means to truly hear and believe His Word.

❑ **Ask** some of your group members to share their thoughts about the key applications from Day Five.

❑ **Pray**—Close your time in prayer by thanking the Lord for the journey of learning on which He has led you over the past 12 weeks.

 **TOOLS FOR GOOD DISCUSSION**

Congratulations! You have successfully navigated the waters of small group discussion. You have finished all 12 lessons in _Following God: Life Principles from the Prophets of the Old Testament_, but there is so much more to learn, so many more paths to take on our journey with the Lord, so much more to discover about what it means to follow Him. Now What? It may be wise for you and your group to continue with another study. In the front portion of this leader's guide (in the "Helpful Hints" section of **How to Lead a Small Group Bible Study,** pp. 9–10), there is information on how you can transition to the next study and share those insights with your group. Encourage your group to continue in some sort of consistent Bible study. Time in the Word is much like time at the dinner table. If we are to stay healthy, we will never get far from physical food, and if we are to stay nourished on "sound" or "healthy" doctrine, then we must stay close to the Lord's "dinner table" found in His Word. Job said it well, _"I have not departed from the command of His lips; I have treasured the words of His mouth more than my necessary food"_ (Job 23:12).

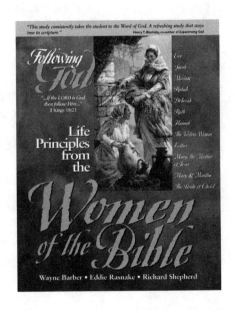

LIFE PRINCIPLES

FROM THE

WOMEN OF THE BIBLE

Table of Contents

Eve 141

Sarah 144

Miriam 147

Rahab 150

Deborah 153

Ruth 156

Hannah 159

Esther 162

The Virtuous
Woman (Proverbs 31) 165

Mary and
Martha 168

Mary, Mother
of Jesus 171

The Bride
of Christ 174

Eve

MEMORY **2 Corinthians 11:3** VERSE

"But I am afraid, lest as the serpent deceived Eve by his craftiness, that your minds should be led astray from the simplicity and purity of devotion to Christ."

BEFORE THE SESSION

☐ Be sure to familiarize yourself with the chart showing where Eve fits in the chronology of the week of creation.

☐ Spread out your homework instead of trying to cram everything into one afternoon or night. Perhaps use this as your daily quiet time.

☐ Always look for those personal applications, some of which the Lord may have you share with the group. The more impact the Word makes in your heart the more enthusiasm you will communicate to others

☐ As you study, write down any good discussion questions as they come to mind.

☐ Additional Study: For a good companion to this study you can look at **"Adam: Following God's Design"** in *Following God: Life Principles from the Old Testament.*

☐ A good Bible dictionary article on Eve will give you more background information. Reference works often help you see the historical or cultural setting in which the man or woman lived.

☐ Be transparent before the Lord and before your group. We are all learners—that is the meaning of the word "disciple."

WHAT TO EXPECT

Many in your group may have experienced new insights or rich applications from their study this week. Some will understand for the first time the process of temptation and what happens when we give in to sin. Expect the Lord to do a fresh work in you as well as in the members of your group. He waits to show Himself strong toward *"those whose heart is fully His."* (See 1 Chronicles 16:9a.) Some may have questions about the study or even about the validity of some portions of the Word of God. You can help them see the Bible as God's Word written in love. They can discover that this Book is eternal wisdom and is ever able to teach, reprove, correct, and train in righteousness (2 Timothy 3:16–17).

> ### THE MAIN POINT
> Temptation will from time to time draw us into sin, but we can always return to following God when we do sin.

DURING THE SESSION

 OPENING: 5–10 MINUTES

Opening Prayer—You or one of your group members should open in prayer. Remember that if it took the inspiration of God for people to write Scripture, it will also take His illumination for us to understand it.

Opening Illustration—Peter was a man of great passion. He boasted to the Lord, *"with you I am ready to go both to prison and to death!"* (Luke 22:33). Yet when push came to shove, he denied he even knew the Lord. When the realization of what he had done "sank in," he went out and wept bitterly. Even after the resurrection, he was not the same, and he tried to return to his old life of fishing. It was not that he had lost faith in Christ. His failure had caused him to lose faith in himself. He doubted that he had what it took to follow the Lord. Fortunately for him and for us, the Lord didn't leave him there in his failure. After an unsuccessful night of fishing, Jesus came to Peter and did the same miracle He had done when He first called Peter to follow Him. Then Jesus asked Peter three times, "Do you love Me?"—once for each of the three times Peter denied Him. Graciously the Lord restored him. As we see in Peter, and as we will see this week with Eve, failure doesn't have to be final. We can always come back to following Him.

⏳ DISCUSSION: 30–40 MINUTES

Main Objective in Day One: The main objective for Day One is to see the purpose God originally intended for Adam and Eve—His original design. Below, check the discussion questions for Day One that you will use.

_____ Describe your feelings about God's purposes for mankind.

_____ What role did God intend for Adam and Eve in the rest of creation?

_____ Can you see any ways our world has digressed from God's original plan for mankind?

_____ What was Eve's unique role in creation?

_____ What stands out to you from the marriage principles of Day One?

Main Objective in Day Two: In Day Two, our study looks closely into the process of temptation to find the common denominators of the types of temptation we face today. Check any discussion questions for Day Two that you find to be useful.

_____ Why do you think Eve was willing to enter into a conversation with the serpent?

_____ What stands out most to you from what you observed about Satan's activities?

_____ What did you see in the differences between what God had said, and how Eve quoted Him?

_____ Where do you think those differences came from?

Main Objective in Day Three: Day Three continues our analysis of the temptation, and how Eve succumbed to that temptation. Below, examine the discussion questions list for Day Three and choose one or two questions for your group session.

_____ How did Satan cast doubt on God and what He had said?

_____ Did you see any principles in how Satan tried to tempt Eve that relate to us today?

_____ What did you learn from 1 John 2:16?

_____ State your opinion as to why Adam didn't play a more prominent role in Eve's battle with temptation.

Main Objective in Day Four: Day Four focuses on the fact that our failures are not as important in God's eyes as to how we respond to them. In Adam and Eve we learn much about the wrong way to deal with failure. Some good discussion questions for Day Four might include. . . .

_____ What does Adam and Eve's hiding say to you concerning how you deal with sin?

_____ Can you relate with Adam and Eve in trying to blame others for their choices?

_____ What stood out to you from the consequences of sin we looked at in Genesis 3:14–24?

_____ What observations did you make about the difference between how Adam and Eve tried to deal with their sin, and how God dealt with it?

_____ What other aspects of this lesson grabbed your attention?

Day Five—Key Points in Application: The most important application point to be gained from studying Eve is that we learn to avoid falling to temptation, and learn to deal with it the right way when we do fall. Check any questions for Day Five that you might consider using in your discussion time.

_____ What are some ways that you are tempted to doubt the truthfulness of what God has said in the Bible?

_____ What are some ways you are tempted to doubt the goodness of God's motives toward you?

_____ What are some consequences of sin that you have seen in your life or those around you?

_____ Have you made some of the mistakes that Adam and Eve made in dealing with sin by hiding it or blaming others?

⌛ CLOSING: 5–10 MINUTES

❑ **Summarize**—Restate the key points highlighted in the class.

❑ **Preview**—Take a few moments to preview next week's lesson on **"Sarah: A Woman of Faith."**

❑ **Encourage** the group to be sure to do their homework.

❑ **Pray**—Close in prayer.

TOOLS FOR GOOD DISCUSSION

Some who are reading this have led small group Bible studies many times. Here is an important word of warning: experience alone does not make you a more effective discussion leader. In fact, experience can make you **less effective**. You see, the more experience you have, the more comfortable you will be at the task. Unfortunately, for some that means becoming increasingly comfortable in doing a bad job. Taking satisfaction with mediocrity translates into taking the task less seriously. It is easy to wrongly assert that just because one is experienced, he or she can successfully "shoot from the hip," so to speak. If you really want your members to get the most out of this study, you need to be dissatisfied with simply doing an adequate job and make it your aim to do an excellent job. A key to excellence is to regularly evaluate yourself to see that you are still doing all that you want to be doing. We have prepared a list of over thirty evaluation questions for you to review from time to time. This list of questions can be found on page 11 in this Leader's Guide. The examination questions will help to jog your memory and hopefully will become an effective aid in improving the quality of your group discussion. Review the evaluation questions list, and jot down below two or three action points for you to begin implementing next week.

ACTION POINTS:

1. _____

_____

2. _____

_____

3. _____

_____

MEMORY **Hebrews 11:11** VERSE

"By faith even Sarah herself received ability to conceive, even beyond the proper time of life, since she considered Him faithful who had promised."

BEFORE THE SESSION

❑ Remember that your goal is not to teach the lesson, but to facilitate discussion.

❑ You should benefit greatly from reading the New Testament commentary on Sarah's life found in the passages of Hebrews 11:11, 1 Peter 3:6, and Romans 9:9.

❑ Make sure your own heart is right with God. Be willing to be transparent with the group about your own life experiences and mistakes. This will make it easier for them to open up.

❑ Don't be afraid of chasing tangents for a while if the diversions capture the interest of the group as a whole. However, don't sacrifice the rest of the group to belabor the questions of one member. Trust God to lead you.

❑ You may want to keep a highlight pen handy as you study to mark key statements that stood out to you.

❑ As a supplement to your study of Sarah, you may want to take a close look at the Following God lesson **"Abraham: Following God at Any Cost"** (Lesson 4) in *Following God: Life Principles of the Old Testament*.

WHAT TO EXPECT

Someone once said, "Behind every great man there is a great woman." One cannot look at the prominent role Abraham played in Judaism and the Old Testament without also recognizing his helpmate, Sarah. Although we do not know all that we would like to know about her, she is one of the most mentioned women in the Bible and was the grandmother of the nation of Israel. Her story is a very human one, replete with her own mistakes as well as the mistakes of others. Expect that your group will find much in her that they will be able to emulate and apply to their own walk with God.

> ### THE MAIN POINT
> The essence of faith is a willingness to take God at His word and live accordingly.

DURING THE SESSION

 OPENING: 5–10 MINUTES

Opening Prayer—Ask someone in your group to open the session with prayer.

Opening Illustration—The great hymn, "Have Thine Own Way" was written in 1902 by Adelaide

Pollard during a time she referred to as suffering "a great distress of soul." Shortly before, she had tried unsuccessfully to raise funds for a missionary trip to Africa. God met with her in a prayer meeting, and the result was these words to this powerful hymn:

"Have Thine own way, Lord! Have Thine own way!
Thou art the Potter; I am the clay.
Mould me and make me after Thy will,
While I am waiting, yielded and still."

Adelaide had learned that true ministry is **received**, not achieved. Sarah had to learn this lesson the hard way. Ishmael was an ever-present reminder that when we try to help God, we usually make a mess.

⌛ DISCUSSION: 30–40 MINUTES

Once your group gets talking, you will find that all you need to do is keep the group directed and flowing with a question or two or a pointed observation. You are the gatekeeper of discussion. Don't be afraid to ask someone to elaborate further or to ask a quiet member of the group what they think of someone else's comments. Time will not allow you to discuss every single question in the lesson one at a time. Instead, make it your goal to cover the main ideas of each day, and help the group to personally share what they learned. You don't have to use all the discussion questions. They are there for your choosing. Use your own judgment as to which questions are applicable to your group.

Main Objective in Day One: In Day One the central objective is to paint a portrait of what Sarah's early relationship with Abraham was like and how God worked through that. Select a question or two from the list below as a discussion starter.

_____ How does Sarah's relationship with Abraham relate to marital relationships today?

_____ Do you ever struggle with submitting to your husband or to those God has placed as your authorities?

_____ How do obedient Christians stand out in our culture today?

_____ Do you have any questions about Day One?

Main Objective in Day Two: In Day Two, we learn an important principle about walking with God: He doesn't need our help—He only needs our submis-sion to Him and His plan. Check the questions that you will use for discussion starters for Day Two.

_____ Talk about the impact of Sarah's idea.

_____ What kind of struggles do you have with waiting on God?

_____ Why do you think Sarah's relationship with Hagar changed after Hagar became pregnant?

_____ Why do you think the Lord planned for Sarah to have to live with Hagar and Ishmael?

Main Objective in Day Three: When God revisited Abraham and Sarah, their struggle was in believing Him. In the Day Three study, we see God deal with their struggles and help them in their unbelief. Check which discussion questions you will use for Day Three.

_____ Why do you think Abraham and Sarah strug-gled with the promise that God would give them a son?

_____ Why do you think Sarah laughed (Genesis 18:12)?

_____ How do you reconcile Sarah's laughter with this week's memory verse (Hebrews 11:11)?

_____ What do you think about the phrase, _"at the appointed time"_ (Genesis 18:14; 21:2; etc.)?

_____ What conclusions can we draw from Sarah's experience about the nature of faith?

Main Objective in Day Four: Although Sarah was godly and used by the Lord, she was not perfect. Our study in Day Four shows us where she stum-bled and gives us the opportunity to learn from her mistakes. Choose a discussion question or two from the list below.

_____ Why do you think the Bible records Abraham and Sarah's failures?

_____ Have you ever experienced a fall after a spir-itual high point?

_____ What speaks to you most from Sarah's failure?

_____ What else from Day Four do you find inter-esting?

Day Five—Key Points in Application: The single most important application point from Sarah's life is that our faith in God is reflected in our willingness to take Him at His word and respond accordingly. Good discussion questions for Day Five include. . . .

_____ Where in life do you find your greatest struggles with trusting God?

_____ Are you submissive to authorities?

_____ Do you struggle with trying to help God?

_____ Did God show you anything you need to do differently through this lesson?

⌛ CLOSING: 5–10 MINUTES

❑ **Summarize**—Restate the key points.

❑ **Remind** your group that the Christian life is not exemplified in our trying hard to be like Jesus, but in our daily surrender to God and in allowing Him work through us.

❑ **Preview**—Take a few moments to preview next week's lesson on **"Miriam: Trusting God with Your Position in Life."**

❑ **Pray**—Close in prayer.

TOOLS FOR GOOD DISCUSSION

Bill Donahue, in his book, _Leading Life-Changing Small Groups_ (Grand Rapids: Zondervan Publishing House, 1996), lists four facilitator actions that will produce dynamic discussion. These four actions are easy to remember because they are linked through the acrostic method to the word, **ACTS.** You will profit from taking time to review this information in the "Helpful Hints" section of **How to Lead a Small Group Bible Study,** which is on page 5 of this Leader's Guide book.

Miriam

MEMORY **I Corinthians 12:18** VERSE

"But now God has placed the members, each one of them, in the body, just as He desired."

BEFORE THE SESSION

❑ Pray each day for the members of your group—that they spend time in the Word, grasp the message God wants to bring to their lives, and that they surrender to what God is saying.

❑ Do your homework—don't procrastinate.

❑ Mark those ideas and questions you want to discuss as you go through the study. Those, along with the questions listed below, can personalize the discussion to fit your group. Think of the needs of your group, and look for applicable questions and discussion starters.

❑ Remain ever teachable. Look first for what God is saying to you.

❑ Be prepared to be transparent and open about what God is teaching you. Nothing is quite as contagious as the joy at discovering new treasures in the Word.

WHAT TO EXPECT

For everyone in your group, the issue of God's sovereignty over the opportunities He gives and does not give in our lives will strike a chord. Sooner or later, everyone goes through the struggle of desiring a position or a relationship or an opportunity that God has not given. As we see in Miriam, dissatisfaction with our place in God's plan and with what we do not have can rob us of the joy God offers in what we do have. As women in different arenas dominated by men, many of your group members will be able to relate with the character of this week's lesson on a very personal basis. You will need to guide them away from simply sharing common frustrations, although that will probably come up. When this happens, be prepared to point your group to God and the truths of His word this lesson puts forward.

> **THE MAIN POINT**
> We are to trust God with where He places us as well as with the opportunities He chooses not to give us.

DURING THE SESSION

 OPENING: 5–10 MINUTES

Opening Prayer—Remember that the Lord is the Teacher, and He wants us to depend on Him as we open the Scriptures.

Opening Illustration—Noted author and speaker, Ron Dunn tells the story of a young man who came up to him after he had just finished speaking to a gathering of Christian leaders. The young man had just graduated from seminary and he said, "Brother Dunn, I am ready to be used by God." After a bit of reflection, Ron Dunn replied, "But are you ready to not be used by God?" His point was a simple but important one—being used by God is His choice, not ours, and is based on His timing, not ours. The young man wrongly assumed that since he was finished with his training, God had to use him as he desired. Like a water faucet, our value is determined not by our output, but by our availability to fulfill our master's purposes as He sees fit. A faucet that runs when and where it is not needed is not a blessing but a problem. God chose to use Miriam in some great ways, but in the process she struggled with some of the ways He chose not to use her. All of us will benefit from studying her life.

 DISCUSSION: 30–40 MINUTES

Keep the group directed along the main theme of trusting God with your position in life. You may have a pointed observation that helps sharpen the focus of the group. Encourage some to elaborate further on a key point, or ask a quiet member of the group what he or she thinks of someone else's comments. Watch the time, knowing you can't cover every single question in the lesson. Seek to cover the main ideas of each day, and help the group to personally share what they learned.

Main Objective in Day One: The main objective of Day One is to set a background for Miriam's life by looking at how she was used by the Lord in protecting Moses as an infant. Review the discussion questions from the Day One list below, and select one or two for your group session.

_____ Describe the days in which Miriam and Moses lived.

_____ Why do you think God allowed Israel to be in slavery to Pharaoh?

_____ What effect do you think the deliverance of Moses had on Miriam's faith?

_____ What else stood out to you from Day One?

Main Objective in Day Two: Here we learn a little of Miriam's role in the leadership of the newborn nation, when Israel was finally released from Egyptian slavery. Check which discussion questions you will use from Day Two.

_____ What role did Miriam play in Israel's leadership during the Exodus?

_____ Did anything in particular intrigue you about Miriam's song of deliverance?

_____ How do you think Miriam functioned in the overall leadership of Israel?

_____ Do you think Miriam's role was affected by the cultural views of women during her day?

_____ Do you think God's design for women is limiting or demeaning?

Main Objective in Day Three: Day Three introduces us to the danger of pride and its affect on how we view ourselves as well as others. Check any discussion questions from Day Three that are applicable to your group time.

_____ Why do you think Miriam chose to deal with her concerns about Moses' wife in such a public way?

_____ What do you think was the root motive of Miriam's complaints?

_____ Have you ever expressed concerns about one thing, when the real problem was a hidden negative attitude? What was the result?

_____ What role do you think the appointment of the seventy elders played in Miriam's discontentedness?

Main Objective in Day Four: The main idea for your group to grasp from Day Four is that sin has consequences, especially the public sins of a leader. Choose a question from the list below that you feel might enhance your group's discussion on Miriam.

_____ How did God deal with Miriam's sin?

_____ Why do you think God dealt less harshly with Aaron's sin?

_____ What do you see of repentance in the way Aaron's perspective changed?

_____ Are there any leaders with whom you have struggled as Miriam did with Moses?

_____ Has this lesson raised any questions for you?

<u>**Day Five—Key Points in Application**</u>: The most important application point is the truth that we must trust God with where He places us and with whatever role He chooses to give us. In addition to any discussion starters you might have in mind, the following questions may also prove to be worthy of mention.

_____ Can you think of a time when wrong attitudes in your heart made you overly critical of another person? What was the outcome?

_____ What is the right way to deal with the concerns that we have with others (Matthew 18:15)?

_____ What authorities in your life do you struggle with the most?

_____ Have you ever struggled with coveting another's position?

 CLOSING: 5–10 MINUTES

Summarize—Restate the key points the group shared. Review the objectives for each of the days found in these leader notes.

❏ **Ask** the group to express their thoughts about the key applications from Day Five.

❏ **Preview**—Take a few moments to preview next week's lesson on **"Rahab: A Fresh Start with Faith."** Encourage your group to be sure to properly manage their homework by spacing it out over the week.

❏ **Pray**—Close in prayer.

 **TOOLS FOR GOOD DISCUSSION**

One of the people who show up in every group is a person we call **"Talkative Timothy."** Talkative Timothy tends to talk too much and dominates the discussion time by giving less opportunity for others to share. What do you do with a group member who talks too much? In the "Helpful Hints" section of **How to Lead a Small Group Bible Study** (p. 5), you'll find some practical ideas on managing the "Talkative Timothy's" in your group.

MEMORY **Hebrews 11:31** VERSE

*"...by faith Rahab the harlot did not perish along
with those who were disobedient, after she had welcomed
the spies in peace."*

BEFORE THE SESSION

❑ Be sure to do your own study far enough in advance so as not to be rushed. You want to allow God time to speak to you personally.

❑ Don't feel that you have to use all of the discussion questions listed below. You may have come up with others on your own, or you may find that time will not allow you to use them all. These questions are to serve you, not for you to serve.

❑ You are the gatekeeper of the discussion. Do not be afraid to "reel the group back in" if they get too far away from the lesson.

❑ Remember to keep a highlight pen ready as you study to mark any points you want to be sure to discuss.

WHAT TO EXPECT

The story of Rahab is perhaps not as familiar as other characters we have studied. Yet, as you can see, there are some very practical lessons to be learned from her life—the main one being that it is never too late to start following God. One of the most exciting realities of the Christian life is that when we place our trust in Christ, not only do we

get a new future, but we also get a new past. We become a new creation—the old things pass away. (See 2 Corinthians 5:17.) Rahab is a beautiful picture of what God's grace can do in transforming a life when accessed by simple faith. Be aware that there will be some in your group who, like Rahab, lived their lives deeply embedded in a quagmire of sin long before they ever decided to follow God. Allow time for pertinent sharing, yet guide the conversation so that Christ is the One who is lifted up.

THE MAIN POINT
When we choose to trust God, we have the opportunity to make a fresh start. There is no past that cannot become a glorious future with faith.

DURING THE SESSION

⏳ **OPENING: 5–10 MINUTES**

Opening Prayer—Remember that if it took the inspiration of God for people to write Scripture, it will also take His illumination for us to understand it. Have one of the more serious minded members of your group open your time together in prayer.

Opening Illustration—Corrie Ten Boom was a powerful voice after World War II, testifying to the sustaining grace of God that she experienced in the German concentration camps. It was there that she watched her sister die, and barely survived herself. In 1947, she was speaking in Munich, when afterward, a man came forward from the crowd. Immediately, Corrie recognized him. He was one of the cruelest Nazi guards she had known at the Ravensbruck concentration camp. To her surprise, he exclaimed, "I have become a Christian." He went on to say, "I know that God has forgiven me for the cruel things I did there. . . .Will you forgive me?" Though her emotions rebelled, by faith she stuck her hand in his, and then was overwhelmed with love and forgiveness for this former enemy. Corrie then responded, "I forgive you, brother. . . .with all my heart!" She realized that Christ had changed the man into a new creation. This week we want to look at another life transformed by the grace of God—Rahab.

⌛ DISCUSSION: 30–40 MINUTES

Once your group gets talking, you will find that all you need to do is keep the group directed and flowing with a question or two or a pointed observation. You are the gatekeeper of discussion. Don't be afraid to ask someone to elaborate further ("Explain what you mean, Barbara.") or to ask a quiet member of the group what they think of someone else's comments ("What do you think, Dave?"). Time will not allow you to discuss every single question in the lesson one at a time. Instead, make it your goal to cover the main ideas of each day, and help the group to share what they personally learned. You don't have to use all the discussion questions below. They are there for your choosing.

Main Objective in Day One: In our Day One study, we should see the way faith was revealed by Rahab's actions. True faith always gives evidence in actions. Check which discussion questions you will use from Day One.

_____ Why do you think God chose to use this immoral woman to protect the spies sent into Canaan?

_____ Was Rahab wrong to lie to protect the spies?

_____ What evidences of faith do you see in Rahab?

_____ Where do you think Rahab had heard all that she heard of the Lord?

_____ What does her story say to you about God's dealings with those who receive no regular witness?

Main Objective in Day Two: In Day Two, we learn the key principle that there is no place safer than being in God's will. Because Rahab cast her lot with God's people, she would enjoy His protection. Place a checkmark next to the questions that will work for your discussion time. Or you can rank the questions in order of your preference.

_____ Do you think the spies had any doubts about Rahab's faith?

_____ What is your assessment about the agreement between Rahab and the spies?

_____ Why do you think the spies had her tie a "scarlet cord" in her window?

Main Objective in Day Three: Day Three introduces us to the results of Israel's conquest of Jericho. By faith, they were able to see God's deliverance just like Rahab! Examine the question list below, and select one or two for your discussion time.

_____ What are your thoughts on the conquest of Israel?

_____ Why do you think God had the army march around the city with the ark?

_____ What insecurities do you think Rahab would have had after Jericho was destroyed?

_____ What do you think her life was like with Israel?

Main Objective in Day Four: In Day Four, we look at all the New Testament tells us of Rahab. The best commentary on the Old Testament is always the New Testament. Check which discussion questions you will use from Day Four.

_____ Why do you think the Lord had Rahab be part of the ancestry of Jesus?

_____ What about the other women mentioned?

_____ Would someone like to comment on Hebrews 11, the "Hall of Faith" chapter, and its inclusion of Rahab?

_____ What does James say about Rahab's faith?

_____ What do James' comments about Rahab tell you about the nature of faith?

Day Five—Key Points in Application: The single most important application point from the life of Rahab is that through faith, anyone can have a fresh start. Choose any questions from Day Five that are essential to your group discussion.

_____ Have you ever mistakenly assumed that your past determines that you can never be close to God or used by Him?

_____ What encouraged you most from Rahab's story?

_____ What are some things from which God has saved and changed you that you appreciate most?

_____ What other applications did you see this week?

⌛ CLOSING: 5–10 MINUTES

❏ **Summarize**—Restate the key points that were highlighted in the class. You may want to briefly review the objectives for each of the days found in these leader notes for Rahab.

❏ **Remind** the group that the victorious Christian life is not attained when we try hard to be like Jesus, but only when we totally surrender to God and allow Him to work through us.

❏ **Ask** your group what they thought were the key applications from Day Five.

❏ **Preview**—Take a few moments to preview next week's lesson on **"Deborah: the Battle Is Not Yours, but the Lord's."** Encourage them to be sure to do their homework.

❏ **Pray**—Close in prayer.

 ## TOOLS FOR GOOD DISCUSSION

As mentioned earlier, there are certain people who show up in every discussion group. Last week we looked at "Talkative Timothy." Another person who is likely to show up is "Silent Sally." She doesn't readily speak up. Sometimes her silence is because she doesn't yet feel comfortable enough with the group to share her thoughts. Other times, it is simply because she fears being rejected. Often, her silence is because she is too polite to interrupt and thus is headed off at the pass each time she wants to speak by more aggressive (and less sensitive) members of the group. In the "Helpful Hints" section of **How to Lead a Small Group** (p. 6), you'll find some practical ideas on managing the "Silent Sally's" in your group.

5

Deborah

MEMORY **2 Chronicles 20:15b** VERSE

*"...thus says the LORD to you, 'Do not fear
or be dismayed because of this great multitude,
for the battle is not yours but God's."*

BEFORE THE SESSION

❑ Resist the temptation to do all your homework in one sitting or to put it off until the last minute. You will not be as prepared if you study this way.

❑ Make sure to mark down any discussion questions that come to mind as you study. Don't feel that you have to use all of the suggested discussion questions included in this leader's guide. Feel free to pick and choose based on your group and the time frame with which you are working.

❑ For further study on Deborah, you may want to consult a Bible dictionary.

❑ Remember your need to trust God with your study. The Holy Spirit is always the best teacher, so stay sensitive to Him!

WHAT TO EXPECT

In this lesson, expect that all your group members need to better understand the key principle that the battle is not ours, but the Lord's. In Deborah we see a powerful example of God delivering in a mighty way. We also see in her a beautiful reminder that being used greatly by God is not something reserved just for men. Not only did Deborah have a fruitful ministry as a judge, but also through working with

Barak, she was used greatly as a deliverer of her people. Some in your group will need the encouragement that women are of equal importance in the plans and inner workings of God. All will benefit from the reminder that God fights our battles for us when we are rightly related to Him.

> ### THE MAIN POINT
> God will fight our battles for us if we will trust Him and walk with Him.

DURING THE SESSION

⏳ **OPENING: 5–10 MINUTES**

Opening Prayer—Remember to have one of your group members open your time together in prayer.

Opening Illustration—In 2 Chronicles 20, King Jehoshaphat finds himself in an impossible circumstance. Judah was surrounded and vastly outnumbered by the armies of Moab and Ammon, who were set on its destruction. Fear was Jehoshaphat's first response. But he immediately turned his attention to seek the Lord. He saw the approaching armies, but he didn't let his focus stay there. He led the people in fasting and seeking God. Then the Spirit of the Lord came upon Jahaziel, and he began to prophesy,

"Listen, all Judah and the inhabitants of Jerusalem and King Jehoshaphat: thus says the LORD to you, 'Do not fear or be dismayed because of this great multitude, for the battle is not yours but God's. . . . You need not fight in this battle; station yourselves, stand and see the salvation of the LORD on your behalf" (2 Chronicles 20:15, 17). The people of Judah obeyed, and instead of fighting, sang praises to God, resulting in the Lord giving them a mighty deliverance. This week's lesson on Deborah is another powerful example of what can happen when we let God fight our battles for us.

⏳ DISCUSSION: 30–40 MINUTES

Remember that your job is not to teach this lesson, but to facilitate discussion. Do your best to guide the group to the right answers, but don't elaborate on a point someone else in the group could make.

Main Objective in Day One: The main point here is to gain a feel for the days in which Deborah lived and ministered, and to see what God was doing through the difficulties He sent to Israel. Check which discussion questions you will use from Day One.

_____ What are your thoughts about the "sin cycle" of the book of Judges?

_____ What does God's giving Israel *"into the hand of Jabin king of Canaan"* (Judges 4:2) say to you? Have you ever experienced anything like that?

_____ Why do you think the Lord picked someone like Deborah through whom to work?

_____ Did anything else grab your attention in the Day One study?

Main Objective in Day Two: In Day Two, we identify Deborah as the person with whom God chooses to work, and we look at some of the reasons why God chose Deborah. Decide which questions you will use for your discussion on Day Two.

_____ What is significant about Deborah's character and home life?

_____ What about Deborah's patriotic feelings for her nation?

_____ Why do you think God chose to use her as a judge?

_____ Why do you think God chose to use a woman in this instance instead of a man?

Main Objective in Day Three: Day Three introduces us to the plan God gave to Deborah of how He wanted to deliver Israel. We see clearly that the glory belongs to God, not Deborah, nor Barak. Below are some ideas for discussion starter questions for Day Three.

_____ Would someone like to describe the plan God revealed to Deborah?

_____ Why do you think Barak insisted on Deborah accompanying the army?

_____ What are your feelings about Sisera's foolish decision to move his troops out into the open?

_____ Have you ever seen God use someone's pride against them? Have you ever experienced that yourself?

Main Objective in Day Four: In Day Four, we see the results of God's plan as He delivered Israel from Jabin and Sisera. In addition to any ideas you have for discussion questions, the following questions may also be helpful:

_____ What does Deborah's presence at the battle say to you about hearing from God in the midst of trials?

_____ Why do you think God chose to vanquish Sisera's army in the way He did?

_____ What role does faith play in this deliverance?

_____ What do you think God is saying by using another woman to kill Sisera?

_____ Did this lesson raise any questions for you?

Day Five—Key Points in Application: The important thing to notice out of Day Five is God's desire for us to depend on Him and let Him fight our battles for us. Place a checkmark next to the questions below that might enhance your group's discussion.

_____ Has God placed you in any difficult situations recently?

_____ What are some ways of "warring in your own power" in which you are tempted?

_____ What do we need to do to make sure that we are in a position to hear from God in the midst of our difficulties?

_____ Is there anything else in this study of Deborah that left an impression on you?

⌛ CLOSING: 5–10 MINUTES

❑ **Summarize**—Restate the key points.

❑ **Ask** the group to comment on what they thought were the key applications from Day Five.

❑ **Preview**—Take a few moments to preview next week's lesson on **"Ruth: Following Our Kinsman-Redeemer."**

❑ **Pray**—Close in prayer.

 ## TOOLS FOR GOOD DISCUSSION

Hopefully your group is functioning smoothly at this point, but perhaps you recognize a need for improvement. In either case, you will benefit from taking the time to evaluate yourself and your group. Without evaluation, you will judge your group on subjective emotions. You may think everything is fine and miss some opportunities to improve your effectiveness. You may be discouraged by problems you are confronting when you ought to be encouraged that you are doing the right things and making progress. A healthy Bible-study group is not one without problems, but is one that recognizes its problems and deals with them the right way. At this point in the course, as you and your group are nearly halfway completed with your study of the women of the Bible, it is important to examine yourself and see if there are any mid-course corrections that you feel are necessary to implement. Review the evaluation questions list found on page 11, and jot down two or three action points for you to begin implementing next week. Perhaps you have made steady improvements since the first time you answered the evaluation questions at the beginning of the course. If so, your improvements should challenge you to be an even better group leader for the final seven lessons in the study.

ACTION POINTS:

1. _____

_____

2. _____

_____

3. _____

_____

6

Ruth

MEMORY **I Peter 1:17-19** VERSES

". . . conduct yourselves in fear during the time of your stay upon earth; knowing that you were not redeemed with perishable things, . . . but with precious blood . . . the blood of Christ."

BEFORE THE SESSION

❑ Remember the Boy Scout motto: BE PREPARED! The main reason a Bible study flounders is because the leader comes in unprepared and tries to "shoot from the hip."

❑ Don't forget to pray for the members of your group and for your time studying together. You don't want to be satisfied with what **you** can do— you want to see God do what only **He** can do!

❑ Familiarize yourself with the chart at the end of this lesson, "The Life of Ruth the Moabitess" (Workbook pp. 86–87). This will help you as you and your group discuss her life.

❑ Make sure to mark down any discussion questions that come to mind as you study.

❑ **Suggestions for Additional Study**—The events surrounding Ruth occurred during the time of the judges in Israel. To better understand this period you may want to read the book of Judges first. You may also want to look at the lessons on **Gideon** and on **Samson** in *Following God: Life Principles from the Old Testament* or on **Samuel** in *Following God: Life Principles from the Prophets of the Old Testament.* You may gain additional insights by looking in a Bible dictionary for articles on "Ruth," "Moab," or "The Moabites."

WHAT TO EXPECT

For some, this lesson will reveal new truths from Scripture and new facts about the cultures of the Bible. Ruth was from Moab, a country marked by idolatry and the worship of the god, Chemosh. In this lesson on Ruth, we see how the Lord worked to bring someone into the family of God from outside Israel. We also see many truths about a kinsman-redeemer. Those truths are at the heart of what happened in Ruth's life. A companion theme at the heart of this study is the sovereign hand of God working, not only in the life of Ruth, but in the lives of Naomi and Boaz as well. These currents running through the book of Ruth provide many points of application. Help guide the group in seeing these main points as well as any other applications. In addition, look for those truths that proved especially meaningful to the members of your group.

THE MAIN POINT

In the story of Ruth and Boaz, we are introduced to the concept of the "Kinsman-Redeemer." The New Testament reveals our Kinsman-Redeemer to be Jesus Christ.

DURING THE SESSION

 OPENING: 5–10 MINUTES

Opening Prayer—As you begin your group session, have one of the group members open the meeting with prayer.

Opening Illustration—A story is told of a gentleman in England who died, leaving a vast fortune—with no surviving family members. On an appointed day, all his fortune was to be auctioned. As the estate lawyer opened the auction, he declared that the will stipulated that the first item to be auctioned was a painting of his only son. This man had dearly loved his son who bravely served in the Royal Air Force during the war and gave his life in battle. The painting was a simple portrait with no unique artistic value. As the bidding began, no one spoke up. They were waiting for the treasures to come. A longtime servant of the family was there who affectionately remembered the son. He bid on the painting and quickly redeemed it. With that the lawyer said to a shocked crowd that the auction was over. The will also stipulated that whoever received the painting of the son also received the entire estate.

In the story of Ruth, we find that she gave up her life in Moab, receiving Israel's God as her God and His people as her people. In so doing, she also received "the entire estate" of what the Lord God could give. She received far more than she could have ever imagined, not only through her kinsman-redeemer Boaz, but also through the family the Lord would give her. So we have received much in our Kinsman-Redeemer, the Lord Jesus, who has redeemed us—purchased us—promising us that we are joint heirs with Him in His estate. Allow these truths to sink deep into your mind and heart as you and your group members walk through the life of Ruth the Moabitess.

 DISCUSSION: 30–40 MINUTES

Remember to pace your discussion so that you will be able to bring closure to the lesson at the designated time. You are the one who must balance lively discussion with timely redirection to ensure that you don't end up finishing only part of the lesson.

<u>Main Objective in Day One</u>: Day One introduces the situation surrounding Elimelech, Naomi, their two sons, and the wives they married in Moab. Those circumstances set the stage for what God wanted to do in the lives of Naomi and Ruth. Here are some good questions that you can use for your discussion:

_____ How would you describe the period of the judges in Israel?

_____ Imagine that you have recently met the family of Elimelech and Naomi. How would you introduce them to the group?

_____ What strikes you about Naomi as you watch her face these difficult days?

_____ What practical applications about following God have you seen in Day One?

<u>Main Objective in Day Two</u>: In Day Two, we begin to see "the rest of the story." God is not finished with Naomi or Ruth. The main objective is to see how the Lord works to care for His own. Some discussion questions for Day Two might be. . . .

_____ What characteristics of Ruth did you notice as they prepared to leave Moab for Bethlehem? How was she different from Orpah?

_____ What are some ways we can "seek refuge" under the "wings" of the Lord?

_____ What are some substitutes to which we run instead of running to the Lord?

_____ What are some of the applications you saw in the "Stop and Apply" section at the end of Day Two (Workbook p. 76)?

<u>Main Objective in Day Three</u>: In Day Three, we see how Boaz, the Kinsman-Redeemer, worked on behalf of Ruth. In addition to any discussion-starter questions that you might have, the following questions may also prove to be useful:

_____ What does it mean to you when someone else stands up for you or seeks to help you in some way?

_____ What are some ways we can help others and encourage others in the Body of Christ?

_____ Ruth said to Naomi, _"All that you say, I will do"_ (Ruth 3:5). What applications to how we act toward one another do you see in her statement?

_____ Imagine you are writing a letter to a friend. Describe Boaz from what you have learned in Day Three, and tell any way his example spoke specifically to you.

Main Objective in Day Four: Day Four's main objective is to show how the Lord fulfills His purposes not only in Ruth and those around her but also in our lives. Check which questions you will use for your group discussion.

_____ What do you see about the care of the Lord in all that occurred between Boaz, the other relative, the city elders, Ruth, and Naomi?

_____ What other characteristics of the Lord did you see in the events that take place in Ruth 4?

_____ How did the truths found in the genealogy of Jesus speak to you personally?

_____ From looking at all God did in and through Ruth, what encouragement do you find for your life?

Day Five—Key Points in Application: The main application point in our study of Ruth is the overarching hand of God at work in the lives of Ruth, Naomi and Boaz. Some good discussion questions to help focus the applications from Day Five might include. . . .

_____ What have you seen about the Lord and His ways that has a direct application to your circumstances?

_____ What is God teaching you about security through this lesson (or through personal circumstances combined with this lesson)?

_____ What does it mean to leave behind the idols of our past [or present]? How is it worth it to leave it behind in order to receive what the Lord wants to give?

_____ Why do we "struggle" so much to find "rest"? What is the answer according to the testimony of the life of Ruth?

⌛ CLOSING: 5–10 MINUTES

❑ **Summarize**—Restate the key points the group shared. Review the Main Objectives for each of the days.

❑ **Remind**—Using the memory verses (1 Peter 1:17–19), remind the group of how we have been redeemed by our Kinsman-Redeemer, Jesus, and what the concept of redemption means.

❑ **Ask** some of your group members to reveal their thoughts about the key applications from Day Five.

❑ **Preview**—We have finished the first 6 lessons in _Following God: Life Principles from the Women of the Bible_. Take a few moments to preview next week's lesson on **"Hannah: Bringing Our Barrenness to the Lord,"** and encourage your group members to do their homework.

❑ **Pray**—Close your time in prayer.

 TOOLS FOR GOOD DISCUSSION

As discussed earlier, there are certain people who show up in every discussion group that you will ever lead. We have already looked at "Talkative Timothy" and "Silent Sally." This week, let's talk about another person who also tends to show up. He is known as **"Tangent Tom."** He is the kind of guy who loves to talk even when he has nothing to say. Tangent Tom loves to "chase rabbits" regardless of where they go. When he gets the floor, you never know where the discussion will lead. You need to understand that not all tangents are bad. Sometimes, much can be gained from discussion "a little off the beaten path." But these diversions must be balanced against the purpose of the group. In the "Helpful Hints" section of **How to Lead a Small Group** (p. 6), you will find some practical ideas on managing the "Tangent Tom's" in your group. You will also get some helpful information on evaluating tangents as they arise.

7

Hannah

MEMORY **I Samuel 2:2–3** VERSES

"There is no one holy like the Lord, Indeed, there is no one besides Thee, . . . Boast no more so very proudly, do not let arrogance come out of your mouth; for the Lord is a God of knowledge, and with Him actions are weighed."

BEFORE THE SESSION

❑ Try to get your lesson plans and homework done early this week. This gives time for you to reflect on what you have learned and process it mentally. Don't succumb to the temptation to procrastinate.

❑ Make sure you keep a highlight pen handy to highlight any things that you intend to discuss, including any questions you think your group may have trouble comprehending. Jot down any good discussion questions that come to your mind as you study.

❑ For further insights on the time in which Hannah lived you may want to read the book of **Judges**. You may glean some additional insights on Hannah in the lesson on **"Samuel: Hearing God—Following His Word,"** (Lesson 1) in *Following God: Life Principles from the Prophets of the Old Testament.*

❑ Don't think of your ministry to the members of your group as something that only takes place during your group time. Pray for your group members by name during the week that they would receive spiritual enrichment from doing their daily homework. Encourage them as you have opportunity.

WHAT TO EXPECT

Everyone in your group has experienced some kind of emptiness in life—some difficulty that left them bewildered. Some called on the Lord. Others sought answers somewhere else. Some may still be in a time of drought or despair, emptiness or bewilderment. The life of Hannah will provide a testimony of the way of escape. Hannah learned what it means to call on the Lord, and she found Him to be faithful and true in every way. Look for ways to focus on the Lord's faithfulness and His full knowledge of each person's situation. This lesson may be the starting point for some to bring their "barrenness" to the Lord. Be sensitive to the Lord and to needs that surface in your group time. There may be opportunity to pray for someone or to encourage him or her at a low point. This could become a significant turning point in a group member's life.

> ### THE MAIN POINT
> God alone is the answer to our barrenness in life. Coming to Him means coming to the source of all life and all fruitfulness.

DURING THE SESSION

 OPENING: 5–10 MINUTES

Opening Prayer—It would be a good idea to have a different group member open your time together in prayer each week.

Opening Illustration—Paul had a problem! In 2 Corinthians 12:7–10, Paul tells us about this problem and how he prayed diligently. He came before the Lord three specific times asking Him to take away this *"thorn in the flesh."* We do not know what the problem was, and it is probably best that we don't know, for the lesson we learn from Paul can quickly be applied to our own lives. Paul was weak. He could not fix his problem. He was helpless, but he discovered that God was neither weak nor helpless. As a matter of fact he discovered that God uses weak things, broken things, barren things in our lives. That was certainly true in Hannah's life and is doubtless true of some in your group. As you journey through the life of Hannah keep in mind this truth, that God uses the weak and broken and barren things in our lives to reveal His strength and wholeness and fruitfulness. This can give new hope and assurance to your group members that God is not finished with any of us yet. He is still at work and wants to work even as you walk through this lesson.

DISCUSSION: 30–40 MINUTES

A key objective in how you manage your discussion time is to keep the big picture in view. Your job is not like a schoolteacher's job, grading papers and tests and the like, but more like a tutor's job, making sure your group understands the subject. Keep the main point of the lesson in view, and make sure they take that main point home with them.

Main Objective in Day One: In Day One, we discover the situation in which Hannah lived and the anguish and bitterness of soul that she experienced. Some good discussion questions from Day One might be. . . .

_____ What was Elkanah doing right in this family?

_____ What do you think Hannah's barrenness meant to her?

_____ What is the main problem we face when we focus on our circumstances? How would you

counsel Hannah about all she faced in her home?

_____ God uses circumstances and relationships to get our attention. What applications about the ways of God in our lives have you seen so far in Day One?

Main Objective in Day Two: In Day Two, the main objective is to see how Hannah focused on the Lord in the midst of her circumstances. Below, decide which discussion questions you will use for your group session for the Hannah lesson.

_____ How does honesty in prayer make a difference in how we pray and how God hears?

_____ How important is humility in coming to the Lord. How does He view a broken and contrite heart? (See Psalms 34:18; 51:17; Isaiah 61:1.)

_____ What does the name *"the LORD of Hosts"* mean to you? Could praying to the Lord of Hosts apply to any of your circumstances or relationships?

_____ What difference does true prayer make in bringing peace of heart and soul? What is the key to peace for Hannah?

Main Objective in Day Three: Day Three reveals the blessedness of surrender to the Lord—His ways and His will. Possible discussion questions for Day Three include. . . .

_____ How does answered prayer encourage you in your walk with the Lord?

_____ What does it mean to others when you share an answer to prayer for which they also have been praying?

_____ The essence of worship is surrender to the Lord. How do you see surrender to the Lord in the lives of Hannah and Elkanah?

_____ How has your view of worship changed (if at all) in looking at Hannah and Elkanah?

Main Objective in Day Four: Day Four focuses on Hannah's heart—her celebration song of worship. Check which questions you intend to use in your discussion time.

_____ Describe Hannah's view of the Lord.

_____ How important was it that Hannah humble herself before the Lord? How important is it for us to humble ourselves before the Lord?

_____ What blessings came out of Hannah's brokenness and humility?

_____ What has the Lord shown you personally in looking at the path down which the Lord led Hannah?

Day Five—Key Points in Application: The most important application point seen in Hannah is the choice to humble ourselves before the Lord in brokenness rather than walking in the bitterness of pride. Some good discussion questions to help focus the applications from Day Five are. . . .

_____ What personal applications about barrenness have you experienced in your life?

_____ What encouragement have you received from the life of Hannah?

_____ What encouragement would you give a friend from the life and example of Hannah?

_____ What have you seen about the character, power, and purposes of God that is most meaningful to you?

⌛ CLOSING: 5–10 MINUTES

❑ **Summarize**—Restate the key points the group shared. Review the main objectives for Hannah.

❑ **Focus**—Using the memory verses (1 Samuel 2:2–3), focus the group on the character of the Lord and His call for us to humble ourselves before Him in our words and in our actions.

❑ **Ask** the group members to express their thoughts on the key applications from Day Five.

❑ **Preview**—Take a few moments to preview next week's lesson titled: **"Esther: Useable to God Wherever He Places Us."** Encourage your group members to do their homework.

❑ **Pray**—Close your time in prayer.

  ## TOOLS FOR GOOD DISCUSSION

One of the issues you will eventually have to combat in any group Bible study is the enemy of **boredom.** This enemy raises its ugly head from time to time, but it shouldn't. It is wrong to bore people with the Word of God! Often boredom results when leaders allow their processes to become too predictable. As small group leaders, we tend to do the same thing in the same way every single time. Yet God the Creator, who spoke everything into existence is infinitely creative! Think about it. He is the one who not only created animals in different shapes and sizes, but different colors as well. When He created food, He didn't make it all taste or feel the same. This God of creativity lives in us. We can trust Him to give us creative ideas that will keep our group times from becoming tired and mundane. In the "Helpful Hints" section of **How to Lead a Small Group** (pp. 8–9), you'll find some practical ideas on adding spice and creativity to your study time.

Esther

MEMORY **Esther 4:14** VERSE

"...if you remain silent at this time, relief and deliverance will arise for the Jews from another place and you and your father's house will perish. And who knows whether you have not attained royalty for such a time as this?"

BEFORE THE SESSION

☐ Your own preparation is key not only to your effectiveness in leading the group session, but also in your confidence in leading. It is hard to be confident if you know you are unprepared. These discussion questions and leader's notes are meant to be a helpful addition to your own study, but should never become a substitute.

☐ As you do your homework, study with a view to your own relationship with God. Resist the temptation to bypass this on your way to preparing to lead the group. Nothing will minister to your group more than the overflow of your own walk with God.

☐ For further study, look at **"Zerubbabel and Ezra"** in *Following God: Life Principles from the Kings of the Old Testament.*

☐ Don't think of your ministry to the members of your group as something that only takes place during your group time. Pray for your group members by name during the week that they would receive spiritual enrichment from doing their daily homework. Encourage them as you have opportunity.

WHAT TO EXPECT

In this lesson, we are touching on an area of life that is rather easy to comprehend. Everyone needs to understand that we are useable to God wherever He places us as long as we are willing to surrender to Him. Hopefully from this lesson your group will begin to look at where God has placed them in a fresh light. Instead of seeing their positions as being for their own benefit and comfort, perhaps from Esther they will gain a sense of what God wants to do through them for the benefit of others. Don't be afraid to challenge your group to examine their own lives to look for points of application.

> **THE MAIN POINT**
> From Esther's testimony, we learn that as we surrender to God, He is able to use us to benefit those around us.

DURING THE SESSION

 OPENING: 5–10 MINUTES

Opening Prayer—A good prayer with which to open your time is the prayer of David in Psalm 119:18, *"Open my eyes, that I may behold Wonderful things from Thy law."* Remember, if it took the illumination of

God for men to write Scripture, it will take the same for us to understand it.

Opening Illustration—Joseph, the son of Jacob had a hard life. As a young man, his brothers betrayed him by selling him as a slave to a caravan headed for Egypt. As a slave, he worked hard but wound up being thrown in prison on false charges. It is there that he interpreted the dreams of Pharaoh's baker and a cupbearer, who eventually mentioned him to Pharaoh. Through interpreting a dream of Pharaoh, he ended up being placed as prime minister over all of Egypt, guiding the people of that nation to store the surplus grain in years of plenty so that they were well prepared when famine came. In God's providence, Joseph's brothers were eventually forced to come to him for food. When they worried that he would seek revenge, he comforted them, asking, *"Am I in God's place?"* He went on to explain, *"And as for you, you meant evil against me, but God meant it for good in order to bring about this present result, to preserve many people alive"* (Genesis 50:19–20). Joseph understood that it was God who had placed him in Egypt, and that God had a purpose in him being there. If we are able to trust God with where He has placed us, then we become useable to Him in that place. We see that this week with Esther.

⌛ DISCUSSION: 30–40 MINUTES

Remember to pace your discussion so that you don't run out of time to get to the application questions in Day Five. This time for application is perhaps the most important part of your Bible study. It will be helpful if you are familiar enough with the lesson to be able to prioritize the days for which you want to place more emphasis, so that you are prepared to reflect this added emphasis in the time you devote to that particular day's reading.

Main Objective in Day One: The main objective in Day One is to introduce the different characters in the dramatic account of Esther as well as to see how God placed each where they were. Check which discussion questions from Day One you will use.

_____ What process led to a new queen for Persia?

_____ What role do you think Esther's upbringing played in the formation of her character?

_____ Why do you think Esther found favor with the king and his eunuch?

_____ What do you think is significant regarding Mordecai's actions toward the king?

Main Objective in Day Two: In Day Two, we begin to investigate the problem of Haman and his vendetta against Mordecai and the Jews. God has placed everyone so that He can do what He desires. Check which discussion questions you will use from Day Two.

_____ Describe your opinion of Haman.

_____ Why did Mordecai not bow to Haman, and what was Haman's response?

_____ Has your faith ever resulted in alienating an unbeliever?

_____ What do you think was behind Haman's plan, and what does it reveal of his character?

_____ What else stood out to you from Day Two?

Main Objective in Day Three: Day Three introduces us to the implementation of Haman's plan, and how it drove God's people to seek the Lord. Check which discussion questions you will use from Day Three.

_____ What role do you think faith plays in the response of the Jews?

_____ Mordecai clearly sought God as he fasted and mourned. What does that say about the plan of action he suggested?

_____ What do you think about Mordecai's plan?

_____ We see Esther's actions with the advantage of hindsight. What do you think was running through her mind as she made her choice?

_____ Were there any questions raised by your study in Day Three?

Main Objective in Day Four: In Day Four, our study of Esther takes us to the results of God's working through Mordecai and Esther. Choose a couple of questions for your discussion time.

_____ What stands out to you from the king's response to Esther?

_____ How did Haman's pride set him up for failure?

_____ How do you see God's providence in the king's inability to sleep?

_____ What are some ways our present life on earth requires walking by faith and trusting God's sovereign placement of us?

_____ What other aspects of Day Four would you like to discuss?

Day Five—Key Points in Application: The most important application point from Day Five is that God in His sovereign will is constantly involved in placing us exactly where we are for His purposes. Check any discussion questions that you might consider using for Day Five.

_____ Why do you think God picked Esther?

_____ Where has God placed you?

_____ Are there any "Mordecai's" in your life who serve as models for you?

_____ Are there any places in your life where your devotion to God has offended the ungodly?

_____ Is there any evidence of revenge taking place in your life?

_____ What other applications did you see this week?

⏳ CLOSING: 5–10 MINUTES

❑ **Summarize**—Restate the key points. You may want to read the paragraph at the beginning of the leader notes on "The Main Point of Esther."

❑ **Remind** the group that the victorious Christian life is not attained when we try hard to be like Jesus, but only when we totally surrender our lives to God and let Him work through us.

❑ **Preview**—If time allows, preview next week's lesson on **"The Virtuous Woman."** Encourage your group to be sure to complete their homework.

❑ **Pray**—Close in prayer.

TOOLS FOR GOOD DISCUSSION

From time to time, each of us can say stupid things. Some of us, however, are better at it than others. The apostle Peter certainly had his share of embarrassing moments. One minute, he was on the pinnacle of success, saying, _"Thou art the Christ, the Son of the Living God"_ (Matthew 16:16), and the next minute, he was putting his foot in his mouth, trying to talk Jesus out of going to the cross. Proverbs 10:19 states, _"When there are many words, transgression is unavoidable. . . ."_ What do you do when someone in the group says something that is obviously wrong? First of all, remember that how you deal with a situation like this not only affects the present, but the future. In the "Helpful Hints" section of **How to Lead a Small Group** (p. 9), you'll find some practical ideas on managing the obviously wrong comments that show up in your group.

The Virtuous Woman

9

MEMORY **Proverbs 31:30** VERSE

*"Charm is deceitful and beauty is vain, but a woman who
fears the Lord, she shall be praised."*

BEFORE THE SESSION

❑ Pray each day for the members of your group—
that they spend time in the Word, grasp the
message God wants to bring to their lives, and
that they surrender to what God is saying.

❑ Be sure you have searched the Scriptures carefully for each day's lesson.

❑ Walk through the discussion questions below,
looking at your lesson, and select which questions you will use.

❑ Remain ever teachable. Look first for what God
is saying to you. This will help you in understanding and relating to some of the struggles
your group members may be facing.

WHAT TO EXPECT

Proverbs 31 is a very familiar passage, especially to
women, but often it has been presented as the yardstick by which a woman of God is measured instead
of as the goal toward which all women should be
moving. This leaves many who study it frustrated,
overwhelmed, guilty, or angry. Expect that some in
your group may arrive showing evidence of that
struggle. You need to do everything you can to com-

municate the message that success is measured in
progress, not perfection. You also want to make sure
that your group sees the "being" of Proverbs 31 and
not just the "doing." It is only as God works in our
lives that He can create this character in us. **He**, not
she, must be our focus. Do all you can to keep this
message before your group.

> ### THE MAIN POINT
> Proverbs 31 tells us what a woman can be
> by the grace and working of God and
> what a man should value in a woman.

DURING THE SESSION

⧗ **OPENING: 5–10 MINUTES**

Opening Prayer—Remember to ask the Lord for
His wisdom. He promised to guide us into the truth.

Opening Illustration—Recently the Christian world
has been awash in all sorts of paraphernalia sporting
the initials WWJD. Of course that stands for "What
Would Jesus Do?" and was born out of a youth group
impacted by the classic book by Charles Sheldon, *In
His Steps*. It involves regularly aiming yourself toward
the right direction by approaching each situation with
the question, "What Would Jesus Do?" But as many

Christians have discovered, it is easier to wear the bracelet than to live the life. In fact, no one consistently does what Jesus did. That is because there is only one Jesus. If we could do what He did, we wouldn't need a savior (Galatians 2:21). The Christian life is not exemplified in our trying hard to be like Jesus, but in our walking with God, yielding our lives to His control, and letting Jesus be Jesus in us. That same reality stands clear when we look at Proverbs 31. This is not a message of what we should try to do and be for God, but rather, what God desires and is able to do and be through us.

⧗ DISCUSSION: 30–40 MINUTES

Select one or two specific questions to get the group started. Keep the group directed along the main highway of Proverbs 31. By this point in the course (Week 9), you know the talkative and the quiet ones. Continue to encourage each member in the importance of his or her input. Some of the greatest life lessons we ever learn may come from someone who has said very little up to this point.

Main Objective in Day One: As authors, our goal for Day One is to get you and your group to understand the main objectives of the book of Proverbs—particularly the context of chapter 31. Check which discussion questions you will use from Day One.

_____ What role has the book of Proverbs played in your Christian life?

_____ What do the eight action verbs in Proverbs 2:1–4 say to you?

_____ Have you experienced any of the results of pursuing wisdom?

_____ What other aspects of Day One would you like to discuss?

Main Objective in Day Two: Here we begin to focus on all that Proverbs 31 puts forward of the character of the virtuous woman. Possible discussion starters for Day Two include. . . .

_____ For what purpose do you think Proverbs 31 was written?

_____ Express your sentiments on the idea of being "clothed" with strength and dignity.

_____ What are your comments regarding the words of a virtuous woman?

_____ Did you see the contrast between what the world does to earn praise and what the believer does? What does that say to us today?

Main Objective in Day Three: Day Three introduces us to the labor of the Virtuous Woman—what she "does." Below, check any questions that have the potential of enhancing your group discussion for Day Three.

_____ Name some of the cultural differences between a "working woman" in Solomon's day and one of today.

_____ Have you ever felt ostracized for your career choices?

_____ What stands out to you about the virtuous woman's provision for her family?

_____ What did you learn from looking at the virtuous woman's income-producing activities? What does that say to you?

Main Objective in Day Four: Here we look at what Proverbs 31 teaches about the Virtuous Woman in the arena of relationships. Check which discussion questions you will use for your discussion on Day Four.

_____ What kind of things do you think build trust in a husband or friend?

_____ What kind of things destroy trust?

_____ Give a description of the "ministry heart" that exists in a virtuous woman.

_____ Did this lesson raise any questions for you or leave any questions unanswered?

Day Five—Key Points in Application: The most important application point you and your group can learn from the study of the Virtuous Woman is that our progress can only come from walking with God and letting Him make us into the people He wants us to be. In addition to any other discussion questions that you may have prepared, the questions below may also prove to be useful.

_____ As you look at the three main areas we saw addressed in Proverbs 31, which would you say needs the most work in you?

_____ What do you want to see God do in your character, labors, and relationships?

⌛ CLOSING: 5–10 MINUTES

❑ **Summarize**—Restate the key points the group shared. Review the objectives for each of the days found in these leader notes.

❑ **Ask** your group to convey their thoughts about the key applications from Day Five.

❑ **Encourage**—We have finished nine lessons. This is no time to slack off. Encourage your group to keep up the pace. We have three more lessons full of life-changing truths. Take a few moments to preview next week's lesson on **"Mary and Martha: Seeing What is Eternal."** Encourage them to do their homework, spacing it out over the week.

❑ **Pray**—Close in prayer.

TOOLS FOR GOOD DISCUSSION

The Scriptures are full of examples of people who struggled with the problem of pride. Unfortunately, pride isn't a problem reserved for the history books. It shows up just as often today as it did in the days the Scriptures were written. In your group discussions, you may see traces of pride manifested in a "know-it-all" group member. **"Know-It-All Ned"** may have shown up in your group by this point. He may be an intellectual giant, or he may be a legend only in his own mind. He can be very prideful and argumentative. If you want some helpful hints on how to deal with "Know-It-All Ned," look in the "Helpful Hints" section of **How to Lead a Small Group Bible Study** (p. 7).

10

Mary and Martha

MEMORY **John 11:25–26** VERSES

"Jesus said to her, I am the resurrection and the life; he who believes in Me shall live even if he dies and everyone who lives and believes in Me shall never die. Do you believe this?"

BEFORE THE SESSION

❑ Never underestimate the importance of prayer for yourself and for the members of your group. Ask the Lord to give your group members understanding and bring them to a new level of knowing Him as they study the Word.

❑ Spread your study time evenly over the week.

❑ Remember to mark those ideas and questions you want to discuss or ask as you go through the study.

❑ To grasp the big picture, you may want to familiarize yourself with the Chart, *"A Chronology of the Activities and Events of Mary and Martha,"* found at the end of this lesson.

❑ Suggestions for Additional Study: To better understand Mary and Martha, you may want to read some of the articles in a good Bible dictionary on "Mary of Bethany," "Mary and Martha," "Lazarus," or "Bethany." You may also want to look at some of the lessons on the disciples in *Following God: Life Principles from the New Testament Men of Faith*. (These lessons include **Peter, John,** and **Thomas.**)

❑ Be sensitive to the needs of your group. Be prepared to stop to pray for a member who may be facing a difficult struggle or challenge.

WHAT TO EXPECT

Often when we have a surface understanding of a Bible passage or of a person in Scripture, we miss the many other truths God wants us to see and obey. That is often true when it comes to our understanding of Mary and Martha. Some in your group will remember Martha from the statement of Jesus, *"Martha, Martha,"* when He confronted her busy-ness while she was preparing a meal for Him and the disciples. Mary, on the other hand, is often remembered for her attentive listening to the Lord's words or for the incident of anointing the body of Jesus with the precious perfume the week before His crucifixion. Others will think of both Mary and Martha in relationship to the death and resurrection of Lazarus.

All of the incidents involving Mary and Martha help us gain a clearer picture of two people who were learning to follow God. Though not perfect, they were certainly pursuing a living and loving relationship with the Lord Jesus. The members of your group can learn from these two and can begin to see what is eternal at a new depth. As you guide the discussion, seek to keep the focus on how Jesus continually redirected the focus of both of these women on Him, His Word, and the Father's will. That is ever the call to each one in your group.

THE MAIN POINT

Seek what is eternal! Eternal gain comes from embracing Jesus' Word, seeking His will, and learning to worship Him.

DURING THE SESSION

 OPENING: 5–10 MINUTES

Opening Prayer—Have one of the group members open the time with prayer.

Opening Illustration—While still in college, Jim Elliott wrote in his journal, "He is no fool who gives up what he cannot keep to gain what he cannot lose." In a few short years, he would demonstrate that truth with his very life. In 1956, he and four other missionaries to the Auca Indians in South America came near the village to further establish contact with the members of that tribe. There on a sandy beach they were shot through with arrows and became martyrs for the gospel of Christ. However, the massacre of these missionaries did not stop the gospel witness to the Aucas. That witness only continued, and today there are many Aucas who know Jesus Christ as their Lord and Savior. As for Jim Elliott and the four who "gave up what they could not keep," they have begun the joy of what they will "never lose"—eternal life in the presence of Christ forever. Mary and Martha can help the members of your group better understand what is of eternal worth and what is eternally insignificant. Be looking for those touch points of practical application as you walk through the lesson.

 DISCUSSION: 30–40 MINUTES

Select one or two specific questions to get the group started in discussion. This lesson on Mary and Martha covers the main events in the lives of these two sisters and their brother Lazarus. Remember to look at the central truth in each of these incidents to help the members of your group see the applications God has for each one of them. Continue to encourage each member in the importance of his or her insights and input.

Main Objective in Day One: Day One looks at the visit of Jesus to the home of Mary and Martha in the autumn of 29 AD (about six months before Jesus'

crucifixion). What Jesus taught these women that day was eternally significant. Some good discussion questions from Day One might be . . .

_____ What are the marks of someone who is spiritually hungry for the Word of God?

_____ How can you tell what a person is hungering for?

_____ How did Jesus show His love for both Mary and Martha? How do His words to each of them speak to you about how He will show you His love?

_____ We never get beyond being a "learner." What does this incident tell you about how you are as a "learner/disciple" in listening or learning?

Main Objective in Day Two: In Day Two, the main objective is to see how the Lord puts us in His "waiting room" to accomplish His will. Some good discussion questions for Day Two might be . . .

_____ Why do you think God makes us wait when difficulties arise?

_____ What does it mean to know that God loves us in all that He does or allows in our lives?

_____ Jesus followed His Father in every detail of life. How did He show His Father's love to Mary and Martha?

_____ Jesus wanted the Father's will for Mary, Martha, and Lazarus. They wanted to see Lazarus healed. The Father wanted to see Lazarus raised from the dead. Therefore, Jesus waited. It was a matter of **time** versus **timing**. What does this say to you about the ways of God in your life or the life of someone close to you?

Main Objective in Day Three: In Day Three, the main objective is to see how Jesus followed and fulfilled His Father's will in the lives of Mary, Martha, and Lazarus and how they responded. Possible discussion questions for Day Three include . . .

_____ Jesus is the "I AM." ("I will always be Who I have always been.") What personal applications do you see? What difference does that make in your life?

_____ What are some of the struggles you face in knowing what the will of God is in your life?

_____ What does it mean to you that Jesus' work in you will be carried through to the end?

_____ Mary and Martha moved to a new level of trust, surrender, and worship. What does that mean to you? How would that new level look in your life or in the life of someone close to you?

Main Objective in Day Four: Through Mary, we see a beautiful picture in Day Four of a worshiping heart. Place a checkmark next to the questions that you feel are relevant to your group. Or you can rank the questions in the order of your preference.

_____ Mary gave much in breaking the alabaster vial. How are worship and giving related?

_____ What can prevent us from having a worshiping heart? What robs us of truly worshiping the Lord?

_____ What are some substitutes for true worship? What was Judas' substitute for Mary's act of worship?

_____ What are the indelible marks of a ministry worth remembering, such as we see in Mary's act of devotion?

Day Five—Key Points in Application: The most important concept to grasp in our study of Mary and Martha is to learn to differentiate between the **eternal** and the **eternally insignificant** and then live in the light of that concept by yearning for things eternal. Some questions to help focus the applications from Day Five are as follows:

_____ How would a right view of eternity affect the way a person related to other Christians in the local church?

_____ How would a right view of eternity affect how we spend our time during the week?

_____ How can you encourage someone who is in God's "waiting room"? What encouragement have you found in waiting on God?

_____ How can we encourage one another to wholeheartedly worship God? How can we deal with the opinions of others who think we are wasting our time, money, or lives in our worship of the Lord Jesus?

⧗ CLOSING: 5–10 MINUTES

❑ **Summarize**—Restate the key points the group shared. You may want to review the statement at the beginning of the leader notes, called **"The Main Point"** of Mary and Martha. Also, ask them to give their thoughts about the key applications from Day Five.

❑ **Focus**—Using this lesson's memory verse (John 11:25–26), focus the group on the relationship of faith to which Jesus called Martha and to which He calls us.

❑ **Remind** them that the same Lord who fellowshipped with Mary and Martha and walked them through many trials has promised to be with us and to never forsake us. Whether in life or in death, He is our Resurrection and Life.

❑ **Preview**—Take a few moments to preview next week's lesson on **"Mary, Mother of Jesus: The Journey of a Bondservant."** Encourage your group members to do their homework.

❑ **Pray**—Close in prayer.

TOOLS FOR GOOD DISCUSSION

So, group leaders, how have the first nine weeks of this study been for you? Have you dealt with anyone in your group called **"Agenda Alice"**? She is the type that is focused on a Christian "hot-button" issue instead of the Bible study. If not managed properly, she (or he) will either sidetrack the group from its main study objective, or create a hostile environment in the group if she fails to bring people to her way of thinking. For help with Agenda Alice, see the "Helpful Hints" section of **How to Lead a Small Group Bible Study** (pp. 7–8).

11

Mary, Mother of Jesus

MEMORY **Luke 1:46–49** VERSES

"And Mary said: My soul exalts the Lord, and my spirit has rejoiced in God my Savior for He has regard for the humble state of his bondslaves.... for the Mighty One has done great things for me; and holy is His name."

BEFORE THE SESSION

❑ Pray for your group as they walk through this week's lesson.

❑ Spread your study time over the week. Think of the lesson as a large meal. You need time to chew each truth and digest it fully.

❑ Be sure to familiarize yourself with the chart, "The Life of Mary the Mother of Jesus," at the end of this lesson. This will help you put in perspective the various seasons of her life.

❑ Remember to mark those ideas and questions you want to discuss or ask as you go.

❑ **Suggestions for Additional Study**—To better understand the life of Mary you may want to look at the lesson on **"James"** (the son of Mary and Joseph and one of Jesus' brothers), in *Following God: Life Principles from the New Testament Men of Faith* (Lesson 6). Another **Following God** lesson, **"Christ the Prophet"** (Lesson 12 of *Following God: Life Principles from the Prophets of the Old Testament*), may also give you some added insights about Mary's journey through life. Additional information may be gleaned from any article on "Mary" that you find in a Bible dictionary.

WHAT TO EXPECT

Most in your group will be familiar with Mary, especially her part in the Christmas story. Over the years, countless opinions have been expressed about Mary, the mother of Jesus. Many of these ideas and teachings have surfaced in the years since Mary lived. Some in your group may have one opinion while others have opposing opinions. The important thing on which to focus is the truth of Scripture.

What does the Scripture say about Mary and how she followed the Lord? We know from the Scriptures that she was not perfect, nor did she understand all that was taking place. We also know she had the heart of a bondservant and reflected that even as a young woman about to give birth to the Lord Jesus. Mary can teach each of the members of your group some valuable lessons on faith including some practical insights on flexibility to the Lord's will and the Lord's plans for our lives. The Lord certainly took Mary on a faith adventure, and this lesson can be that for your group.

THE MAIN POINT

Having the heart of a bondservant and trusting our Master through all seasons of life is essential to following God.

During the Session

OPENING: 5–10 MINUTES

Opening Prayer—Open your session with prayer.

Opening Illustration—The Old Testament picture of a bondservant is a beautiful portrait of a loving, trusting relationship. A bondservant loves his or her master. Read Deuteronomy 15:12–17. Verse 16 speaks of this kind of relationship. When the servant in that passage had the opportunity to go free, he made a unique choice stating, *"I will not go out from you."* Why? Verse 16 continues to explain that he did that *"because he loves you [the master] and your household, since he fares well with you."* At that point the Lord instructed through Moses to mark that servant because *"he shall be your servant forever"* (15:17). We see that love and devotion in the heart of Mary. It comes through in her responses to the angel and to the Lord and in her words of praise for what He has done. Look for the attitudes, actions, and words of a bondservant as you walk with Mary, and compare her heart and her choices with your own.

DISCUSSION: 30–40 MINUTES

Mary will be a very familiar name for some, perhaps for all, in your group. There may be some questions raised that are not answered in this lesson. Be patient. Study diligently in your preparation time. You may want to consult a Bible dictionary for more information. As you pace through the lesson, seek to keep the main focus the main focus. Emphasize what you clearly know and understand. Then you can move on to the things that are not as clear as the Lord gives you time and insight.

Main Objective in Day One: In Day One, the main objective is to see the trusting relationship between the Lord and His bondservant Mary. That trust is first seen in her response to the angel's announcement. Some good discussions for Day One may be . . .

_____ Mary had questions. What is the difference between questions of faith and questions of unbelief?

_____ When you think of the plan and promise of God going all the way back to the Garden of Eden, how do you see God at work and Mary fitting into that plan?

_____ What are some of the marks of a bondservant evident in Mary's words and actions?

_____ Mary had knowledge of the Scriptures as seen in her song of praise. What does that have to do with living with the heart of a bondservant?

Main Objective in Day Two: Day Two looks at the journeys the Lord planned for Mary, Joseph, and Jesus in the early years. The main objective is to see and trust the ways of God in placing us according to His will. Here are some discussion starter possibilities:

_____ What comfort do you find in the fact that a bondservant enters into the plans and places of his or her master? What challenges do you find?

_____ Mary continually pondered the things that had happened and the things being said by others. What is the value of pondering the various occurrences in your journey of faith?

_____ Simeon's prophetic message of the Messiah was also **personal** to Mary. Our Master uses many means to get His personal messages to us. How can we maintain the teachable, listening heart of a bondservant?

_____ Every place God had purposed for Joseph, Mary, and Jesus fit His plan. The time factor and the timing factor were part of His watchful care. How does this give you confidence in the Lord's plans and place for you?

Main Objective in Day Three: Day Three focuses on the purposes of the Father and His Son and how Mary began learning how to trust the Lord with those purposes. Some good discussion questions from Day Three include these:

_____ How could you help someone better understand the purposes of God in his or her life through what happened with Mary at the Temple when Jesus was twelve years old?

_____ What help can you find in dealing with personal struggles over the purposes of God in your life as you look at the life of Mary and Joseph?

_____ How does understanding that the Father has purposeful plans help you deal with the surprises in life?

_____ The most important plan and purpose of the Father is for us to have a personal relationship of faith and obedience with Him. What applications do you see for your life?

Main Objective in Day Four: In Day Four, the main objective is to see how the Lord Jesus revealed His power and brought men and women, including His family, to believe in Him. Check which questions you intend to use for your group discussion on Day Five.

_____ How do the early responses of Jesus' brothers show the necessity of the convincing work of the Holy Spirit to follow Jesus?

_____ Mary and all the followers of Jesus faced personal struggles over Jesus' death. What does this say about the struggles we face today?

_____ After His resurrection, Jesus appeared to His brother James. What does that say about Jesus' care and concern?

_____ What did Mary learn about the power of her son, the Lord Jesus, in all she saw and experienced?

Day Five—Key Points in Application: The most important application point in the study of Mary, the Mother of Jesus is the confidence a bondservant of the Lord can know and experience in the journeys our Master and Savior has for us. Some questions to help focus the applications from Day Five are . . .

_____ A bondservant yields to the Master's purposes, places, promises, and power. What does that mean to you now—where you are in the journey?

_____ What is your greatest struggle in being a bondservant?

_____ Seeing things from the end of the journey, like seeing the valley from the mountain top, helps us to see things in proper perspective. How does this apply to being a bondservant?

_____ In what ways can you see that your Master, the Lord Jesus, has shown Himself faithful in your journey?

⧗ CLOSING: 5–10 MINUTES

❑ **Summarize**—Review the key points.

❑ **Focus**—Using the memory verse (Luke 1:46–49), focus the group again on what it means to have the heart of a bondservant.

❑ **Ask** your group members to reveal their thoughts about the key applications from Day Five.

❑ **Preview**—Take a few moments to preview next week's lesson on **"The Bride of Christ: Walking in the Beauty of Holiness."** Encourage the members in your group to do their homework in proper fashion by spacing it out over the course of the week.

❑ **Pray**—Close in prayer.

TOOLS FOR GOOD DISCUSSION

Well, it is evaluation time again! You may be saying to yourself, "Why bother evaluating at the end? If I did a bad job, it is too late to do anything about it!" Well, it may be too late to change how you did on this course, but it is never too late to learn from this course what will help you on the next. Howard Hendricks, that peerless communicator from Dallas Theological Seminary, puts it this way: "The good teacher's greatest threat is satisfaction—the failure to keep asking, 'How can I improve?' The greatest threat to your ministry is **your ministry**." Any self-examination should be an accounting of your own strengths and weaknesses. As you consider your strengths and weaknesses, take some time to read through the evaluation questions list found in **How to Lead a Small Group Bible Study** on pages 11–12 of this leader's guide. Make it your aim to continue growing as a discussion leader. Jot down below two or three action points for you to implement in future classes.

ACTION POINTS:

1. _____

_____

2. _____

_____

3. _____

_____

The Bride of Christ

12

MEMORY **2 Corinthians 11:2** VERSE

*"For I am jealous for you with a godly jealousy;
for I betrothed you to one husband, that to Christ I might
present you as a pure virgin."*

BEFORE THE SESSION

❏ You will certainly need to pray for your group as they work through this last lesson in *Following God: Life Principles from the Women of the Bible.* Ask the Lord to give you clear insight into what the Scripture teaches about the Bride of Christ. Never underestimate the importance of prayer for yourself and for the members of your group. Pray for each of them by name.

❏ Remember to mark those ideas and questions you want to discuss or ask as you go through the study. Add to those some of the questions listed below.

❏ As an added tool for discussion, you may want to familiarize yourself with the poem, "A Bride to Be," at the end of this lesson (Workbook p. 200). The poem captures the panorama of redemption in Christ calling His Bride.

❏ **Suggestions for Additional Study**—To better see the Bride of Christ you may want to look at the lessons that refer to Christ in other Following God studies. These lessons include: **"Adam: Following God's Design"** (Lesson 1) in *Following God: Life Principles from the Old Testament,* **"The True King in Israel: Following the King of Kings"** (Lesson 12) in *Following God: Life*

Principles from the Kings of the Old Testament, **"Christ the Prophet: Worshiping in Spirit and Truth"** (Lesson 12) in *Following God: Life Principles from Prophets of the Old Testament,* and **"The Son of Man: Following His Father"** (Lesson 12) in *Following God: Life Principles from the New Testament Men of Faith.* You may also want to look in a Bible dictionary for articles on "the Bride of Christ."

❏ Be sensitive to the working of the Spirit in your group meeting, ever watching for ways to help one another truly follow God.

WHAT TO EXPECT

This lesson is unique in a study of women of the Bible. The Lord chose to use the imagery of a woman, a bride, to convey His call to salvation and His work of redemption. Because this is not a common topic of study, there may be many new truths that you and the members of your group will discover in this lesson. Certainly the statement that the Bride *"has made herself ready"* (Revelation 19:7) stands as a challenge to examine our lives. Are we following the counsel of 1 John 3:3, *"and everyone who has this hope* [of His appearing] *fixed on Him purifies himself, just as He is pure"?* It is vital for your group to see the personal applications of the truths about the Bride of Christ found in Scripture. Many new insights may surface as you progress through this study, and some questions may not be answered to the fullest extent. That is OK! Unanswered questions simply mean we have more ground to plow in the Word of God and can expect a greater harvest of truth in the days ahead. As you study through the lesson, seek to keep the main point the main point. Emphasize what you clearly know and understand. Then you can move on to the things that are not as clear as the Lord gives you time and insight.

> ### THE MAIN POINT
> As Christians, it is important that we walk in the beauty of holiness and prepare for our Bridegroom's imminent return and The Wedding to follow.

DURING THE SESSION

 ### OPENING: 5–10 MINUTES

Opening Prayer—Psalm 119:18 says, *"Open my eyes, that I may behold wonderful things from Thy law."* Ask the Lord to open your eyes as you meet together. Have one of the group members open the time with prayer.

Opening Illustration—Every culture in the world loves the celebration of a wedding. All wedding celebrations seem to have common elements. There is the involvement of the parents of the bride and the bridegroom as they pass on their blessing (and financial investments) to the couple. There is also a recognition of the seriousness of the commitment between a husband and a wife. It is often referred to as *holy* matrimony. The ritual is sealed with solemn vows, promising undying faithfulness and love. Often rings are exchanged as tokens or reminders of what has stood as a most honored relationship through the centuries and across the continents. Those vows and the giving of rings is solemnized by one who, under the authority of the moral and civil laws of the land, gives official pronouncement of a couple as husband and wife.

The seriousness into which this ceremony is entered must speak to us as believers in Christ. We are His Bride, and our relationship with Him must be treated with even greater seriousness, for it is an eternal union. May the members of your group recognize

these truths as you walk through this lesson on the Bride of Christ.

 ### DISCUSSION: 30–40 MINUTES

Select one or two specific questions to get the group started. This final lesson focuses on the relationship between Christ and His Bride, the Church. Look for those "velcro" points where members can see something that applies to their own lives. The admonition of Hebrews 12:1–2 cries out to all of us, *". . . let us run with endurance the race that is set before us,* **fixing our eyes on Jesus,** *the author and perfecter of faith. . . ."* As you and your group set your eyes on Christ, looking to His return as your Bridegroom, you can experience a greater endurance in the race and a deeper joy in looking forward to The Wedding.

Main Objective in Day One: In Day One, the main objective is to see how the Lord proposes to His Bride and what that means for our walk with Him today. Some good discussion questions from Day One include these . . .

_____ What does it mean to you that Jesus came to seek you as His Bride?

_____ In what practical ways should we look for His return? How should we live in light of His return?

_____ What does it mean to you that we have the security of His Holy Spirit (like an engagement ring in an unbreakable engagement) as our guarantee of The Wedding to come?

Main Objective in Day Two: In Day Two, the main objective is to see how Christ is preparing a place for His Bride and preparing His Bride for that place. Possible discussion questions for Day Two could be . . .

_____ What expectation do you have about the place Christ is preparing for you as His Bride?

_____ How can we walk in oneness with the Lord now?

_____ How can we grow in our oneness with the Lord until He returns?

_____ What expectation do you have about personally standing by Christ's side *"cleansed"* as a bride *"in all her glory"*?

Main Objective in Day Three: Day Three focuses on the purity of the Bride of Christ, especially the responsibility the Bride has to walk in purity in preparation for the Wedding Day. Here are some suggested discussion starters for your group session:

_____ What are some characteristics of a person who lives in submission to Christ?

_____ What are some practical ways of not being *"led astray from the simplicity and purity of devotion to Christ"* (2 Corinthians 11:2–3)? How do we maintain a pure focus on Christ?

_____ How does the hope of seeing Christ just as He is and being made like Him help us purify ourselves *"just as He is pure"* (1 John 3:1–3)?

_____ What does holiness mean? Or, to put it another way, how are we to walk set apart to Christ?

Main Objective in Day Four: Day Four looks at the presentation of the Bride to her Bridegroom, the Lord Jesus. Check which questions you are considering using in your discussion time.

_____ What do you most anticipate at the return of the Lord for His Bride?

_____ What is it like to find yourself dressed in a way that does not fit the occasion?

_____ We cannot lose our status as part of the Bride of Christ. That is secure. But we can lessen our status by not diligently obeying and following the Lord. How are you doing putting together your "fine linen" garments?

_____ What applications have you seen in how you are preparing for the Lord's return?

Day Five—Key Points in Application: The most important application point seen in this study of The Bride of Christ is the call for Christians to live in holiness and purity, awaiting the imminent return of our Bridegroom, Jesus Christ. Some good questions to help focus the applications from Day Five are . . .

_____ To *"glorify"* (1 Corinthians 6:20) is to help form a good opinion about someone. How can we help others form a good opinion of our Bridegroom?

_____ What should be in the heart of a bride or a bridegroom?

_____ Name at least one thing about your heavenly Bridegroom (Jesus Christ) for which you are thankful.

_____ What is the most important application you have seen in studying the Bride of Christ?

⏳ CLOSING: 5–10 MINUTES

❑ **Summarize**—Restate the key points the group shared. Review the main objectives for each of the days found in these leader notes.

❑ **Focus**—Using the memory verse (2 Corinthians 11:2), direct the group's focus on the importance of purity in heart, mind, deed, and word as they look to the coming of Christ.

❑ **Ask** your group members to share their thoughts about the key applications from Day Five.

❑ **Pray**—Close your time in prayer by thanking the Lord for the journey on which He has led you over the past twelve weeks.

TOOLS FOR GOOD DISCUSSION

Congratulations! You have successfully navigated the waters of small group discussion. You have finished all 12 lessons in *Following God: Life Principles from the Women of the Bible*, but there is so much more to learn, so many more paths to take on our journey with the Lord, so much more to discover about what it means to follow Him. Now what? It may be wise for you and your group to continue with another study. In the front portion of this leader's guide (in the "Helpful Hints" section of **How to Lead a Small Group Bible Study**, pp. 9–10), there is information on how you can transition to the next study and share those insights with your group. Encourage your group to continue in some sort of consistent Bible study. Time in the Word is much like time at the dinner table. If we are to stay healthy, we will never get far from physical food, and if we are to stay nourished on "sound" or "healthy" doctrine, then we must stay close to the Lord's "dinner table" found in His Word. Job said it well, *"I have not departed from the command of His lips; I have treasured the words of His mouth more than my necessary food"* (Job 23:12).

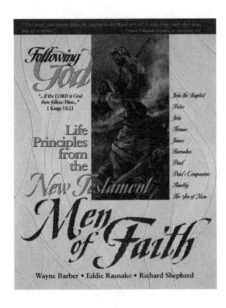

LIFE PRINCIPLES

FROM THE

NEW TESTAMENT

MEN OF FAITH

Table of Contents

John the Baptist 181

Peter 184

Peter 187

John 190

Thomas 193

James 196

Barnabas 199

Paul 202

Paul 205

Paul's Companions 208

Timothy 211

The Son of Man 214

John the Baptist

MEMORY **John 3:27, 28, 30** VERSES

"...A man can receive nothing, unless it has been given him from heaven. You yourselves bear me witness, that I said, 'I am not the Christ,' but, 'I have been sent before Him.'... He must increase, but I must decrease."

BEFORE THE SESSION

❑ Always look for those personal applications, some of which the Lord may have you share with the group. The more impact the Word makes in your heart, the more enthusiasm you will communicate.

❑ One of the most important parts of leading your group is the time you spend in prayer for your session. Ask the Lord to give each member clear insight into the Scriptures. Never underestimate the importance of prayer for yourself and for the members of your group.

❑ Part of this study looks at the relationship between John the Baptist and Jesus, as well as some of the prophecies of His coming. To better see the Person and Ministry of Christ, you may want to look at the following lessons in other Following God studies: **"The True King in Israel: Following the King of Kings"** (Lesson 12) in *Following God: Life Principles from the Kings of the Old Testament,* **"Christ the Prophet: Worshiping in Spirit and Truth"** (Lesson 12) in *Following God: Life Principles from the Prophets of the Old Testament,* **"The Bride of Christ: Walking in the Beauty of Holiness"** (Lesson 12) in *Following God: Life Principles from Women of the Bible,* and the last lesson in this book, **"The**

Son of Man: Following His Father." You may also want to look at a Bible dictionary article on John the Baptist to glean added insights about his background or his ministry.

❑ Remember to mark those ideas and questions you want to discuss or ask as you go through the study. Add to those some of the suggested questions listed throughout these Leader's Guide notes on John the Baptist.

WHAT TO EXPECT

As we open the pages of the New Testament, one of the first people to greet us is John the Baptist, the fiery preacher in the wilderness calling men and women to *"repent, for the kingdom of heaven is at hand"* (Matthew 3:2). Most who have read some of the Scripture know something of John the Baptist, but few realize the full picture of the journey on which the Lord took him. This lesson will open new windows of truth and let in more light on this mysterious prophet who bridged the Old and New Testaments. We will look at some of the ways of John the Baptist, but more importantly we will see some of **the ways of God** with John as well as with his mother and father, Zacharias and Elizabeth. As we begin to understand the ways of God with these followers, we can better see His ways with us. You can be a great encouragement to the members of your group as you point them to these truths about the ways of God. The Lord Jesus continues to work in and through believers today. We don't always understand His ways, and this lesson can be an encouragement to help in that understanding—not only for ourselves, but also for those around us.

> ## THE MAIN POINT
>
> We need to learn to trust God's ways and to do God's will God's way. What John the Baptist learned about God's ways can guide us in following the Lord.

During the Session

 OPENING: 5–10 MINUTES

Opening Prayer—Have one of the group members begin the time with prayer.

Opening Illustration—The following maritime story illustrates the need for us to accurately assess our situations. A naval ship sent a radio message for a nearby vessel to change course 15 degrees north to avoid a collision. A response came back with a call for the naval ship to divert its course 15 degrees south. Then the captain of the naval ship demanded that the mysterious vessel divert its course, to which came the identical response—a demand for the naval ship to alter its course. The naval ship quickly radioed that it was part of a fleet with a number of destroyers, cruisers, and support vessels. Since all necessary measures would be taken to assure the safe passage of this fleet, therefore, the captain ordered the vessel one final time to divert its course. The response came back, "This is a lighthouse. You make the call." **That was the way it was.**

No one can change the placement or the course of a lighthouse anymore than we can change the wise and loving ways of God. The naval ship simply had to deal with things as they were. As God worked in the lives of Zacharias, Elizabeth, and John the Baptist, they had to adjust to His ways. It was not always easy, and at times they wanted to do things according to the way they saw them, but God continued to show them Himself and His ways. He does the same with us.

⧗ **DISCUSSION: 30–40 MINUTES**

Select one or two specific questions to get the group started. This lesson on John the Baptist focuses on the ways of God in the life of this forerunner of the Messiah. Remember to look for those "velcro" points where members can see something that applies to their own lives. This lesson helps focus our attention on God's ways not only in John's life but in our lives as well. As you discuss his life, listen for the insights God has given your group members as well as the insights that will come up in discussion.

Main Objective in Day One: In Day One, the main objective is to see how God prophesied and prepared for the coming of His "Messenger," announcing the Messiah. Below are some suggested discussion questions for you to use in your group time.

_____ Think of the many barren years of Zacharias and Elizabeth. Why do you think Zacharias responded to the angel Gabriel as he did? How do God's ways enter into the picture?

_____ From what you have read, how would you describe Elizabeth? Also, describe the relationship between her and Mary.

_____ Zacharias changed over the months. What do you think he learned about the ways of God as he and Elizabeth awaited John's miraculous birth?

Main Objective in Day Two: In Day Two, the main objective is to see what it means to be sent and to have the attitudes of humility and submission we need. Check which discussion questions you will use from Day Two.

_____ What does it mean to be "sent" in ministry— whether in vocational ministry or in being sent to witness, to encourage a brother or sister, or to serve in some way?

_____ How does grace apply to service in the Body of Christ? What does it mean that each of us have a different part to play in this Body?

_____ John's focus was Jesus. How does that apply to us as we minister in and through the Body of Christ?

Main Objective in Day Three: Day Three focuses on how others sometimes do not understand God's ways in what He has called us to do. The following questions below are only suggested discussion starters for your group session. Check the ones that appeal to you.

_____ How do we sometimes face rejection or opposition from certain religious leaders today?

_____ Why do believers sometimes face rejection, interrogation, or even opposition from political leaders or governments today?

_____ How can we remain faithful to follow the call of God, and to help others do the same?

Main Objective in Day Four: In Day Four, the main objective is to see how to deal with those times when we ourselves do not understand God's ways. Check which discussion questions you will use for Day Four.

_____ What insights do you glean from the fact that John had questions about the way Jesus was doing things?

_____ Why do we sometimes question God's ways, especially in our own lives or in the life of someone close to us?

_____ What encourages you most as you run? What discourages you most?

Day Five—Key Points in Application: The most important application point seen in **John the Baptist** is the importance of running our race as God has set it out for us, trusting His ways along life's journey. Check which discussion questions you will use to help focus the applications from Day Five.

_____ How has the Christian life been like a race to you?

_____ How can we prepare for the unexpected in the race God has set out for us?

_____ How can we encourage others to run more consistently and with sharper focus?

⌛ CLOSING: 5–10 MINUTES

❑ **Summarize**—Restate the key points the group shared. Review the main objectives for each of the days found at the beginning of these leader notes.

❑ **Focus**—Using the memory verses (John 3:27–30), focus the group on the ways of God—how John learned to trust God in His ways and how the Lord wants to teach us those same things.

❑ **Preview**—Take a few moments to preview next week's lesson, **"Peter: Too Much Confidence in Self."** Encourage your group members to do their homework.

❑ **Pray**—Close your time in prayer thanking the Lord for the journey you have begun.

✂ TOOLS FOR GOOD DISCUSSION 🔨

Some who are reading this have led small-group Bible studies many times. Here is an important word of warning: experience alone does not make you a more effective discussion leader. In fact, experience can make you **less effective**. You see, the more experience you have, the more comfortable you will be at the task. Unfortunately, for some that means becoming increasingly comfortable in doing a bad job. Taking satisfaction with mediocrity translates into taking the task less seriously. It is easy to wrongly assert that just because one is experienced, he or she can successfully "shoot from the hip," so to speak. If you really want your members to get the most out of this study, you need to be dissatisfied with simply doing an adequate job and make it your aim to do an excellent job. A key to excellence is to regularly evaluate yourself to see that you are still doing all that you want to be doing. We have prepared a list of over thirty evaluation questions for you to review from time to time. The list of questions can be found on page 11 in this Leader's Guide. The examination questions will help to jog your memory and, hopefully, will become an effective aid in improving the quality of your group discussion. Review the evaluation questions list, and jot down below two or three action points for you to begin implementing next week.

ACTION POINTS:

1. _____

_____

2. _____

_____

3. _____

_____

TOO MUCH CONFIDENCE IN SELF

MEMORY **I Corinthians 10:12** VERSE

"Therefore let him who thinks he stands take heed lest he fall."

BEFORE THE SESSION

❑ Remember that your goal is not to teach the lesson, but to facilitate discussion. Think of open-ended questions that will engender dialogue.

❑ Make sure your own heart is right with God. Be willing to be transparent with the group about your own life experiences and mistakes. This will make it easier for them to open up.

❑ Don't be afraid to chase tangents for a while if they capture the interest of the group as a whole, but don't sacrifice the rest of the group to belabor the questions of one member. Trust God to lead you.

❑ As you study, you may want to keep a highlight pen handy to mark any key statements that stand out to you from the lesson.

WHAT TO EXPECT

The danger of dealing with such a familiar character as Peter is that although most everyone will have some knowledge of certain events in his life, few will have seriously studied him. Many have never studied the New Testament passages that relate to Peter in detail. What they know of Peter is woven from the snippets they have heard of him in sermons and the like. Many will find it easy to relate to Peter in this problem of placing too much confidence in self. Make sure that, if nothing else, everyone comes away seeing this main point

THE MAIN POINT
Peter had to learn that the victorious Christian life is not based on how strong of a commitment we have, but on our level of surrender.

DURING THE SESSION

⌛ **OPENING: 5–10 MINUTES**

Opening Prayer—Ask someone in your group to open your session in prayer.

Opening Illustration—Psychologist David Myers, in his article, "The Inflated Self" (*The Christian Century*, 1 December 1982, p. 1226-8), reveals some startling evidence regarding man's perception of himself. Unlike the "New Age" identification of man's problem as ignorance of his potential and divineness, Myers's evidence point out that man's real problem is an inflated view of self. His research reveals that almost all people see themselves as better than average. Most American business people see themselves as more ethical than most; most community residents view themselves as less prejudiced than others; and most drivers assume that they are better-than-average drivers. When asked to rate themselves, **zero percent** of the 829,000 students who answered the poll thought themselves below average, sixty percent saw themselves in the top ten percent, and twenty-five percent rated themselves in the top one percent. As we see in this week's lesson, Peter had a problem with thinking too highly of himself and what he could do.

⌛ DISCUSSION: 30–40 MINUTES

Once your group gets talking you will find that all you need to do is keep the group directed and flowing with a question or two or a pointed observation. You are the gatekeeper of discussion. Don't be afraid to ask someone to elaborate further or to ask a quiet member of the group what they think of someone else's comments. Time will not allow you to discuss every single question in the lesson one at a time. Instead, make it your goal to cover the main ideas of each day and help the group to share what they learned personally. You don't have to use all the discussion questions. They are there for you to pick and choose from.

Main Objective in Day One: The main objective here is to look closely at Peter's boasting and see what is revealed there of Peter placing too much confidence in himself. Check which discussion questions you will use from Day One.

_____ What stands out to you most from Peter's boast in Luke 22:33?

_____ What do you think Peter's motive was in the things he had to say?

_____ What grabbed you from what James has to say about boasting?

_____ Why do you think Satan had to get "permission" to sift Peter like wheat?

_____ Why didn't Jesus protect Peter from Satan's attack?

Main Objective in Day Two: Here we see that one of the ways Peter's confidence in himself instead of in Christ was manifested was in his prayerlessness. We pray as much as we see our need for God to work. Make sure they catch that one point. Some good discussion questions you may want to consider for Day Two are . . .

_____ What do you see in Jesus' model of the importance of prayer?

_____ Why do you think Peter struggled with making prayer his priority that night?

_____ What is your assessment of Jesus' rebuke of the disciples?

_____ What difference do you think it would have made if Peter had been more watchful in prayer?

Main Objective in Day Three: Day Three introduces us to how Peter's confidence in himself moved him to action before he had heard from God. Decide on some discussion starters for Day Three. Below are some suggestions.

_____ What lessons do you see in one of the disciples asking Jesus what to do and in Peter not asking?

_____ What do you think this says about Peter and his self-confidence?

_____ How did Peter's actions affect Jesus' arrest?

_____ What is the message of Jesus' point about the twelve legions of angels?

_____ What stands out to you from what James 1:20 reveals about anger?

Main Objective in Day Four: In Day Four, we see the potential pitfall that into which each of us can stumble: following the Lord at a "safe" distance. It is this action by Peter that sets the stage for his big failure. In addition to any questions you may have in mind for your Day Four discussion, the following questions may also prove to be useful in enhancing your group session.

_____ Why do you think Peter was following "at a distance"?

_____ What happened to John who followed more closely?

_____ What do you think contributed to Peter's weak faith here?

_____ Did anything else stand out to you from Day Four?

Day Five—Key Points in Application: The most important application point from this lesson on Peter is to not place our confidence in ourselves and what we think we can do for God. Check which application questions you will use for your Day Five discussions.

_____ Can you see any examples in your own life or those around you of boasting of what you would or wouldn't do, only to fail later?

_____ What does your prayer life say about your awareness of your day-by-day need for God?

_____ Are there any areas where you struggle with placing too much confidence in self?

⌛ CLOSING: 5–10 MINUTES

❑ **Summarize**—Restate the key points.

❑ **Remind** those in your group that living a victorious Christian life is not attained when we try hard to be like Jesus, but only when we surrender our lives to God and let Him work through us.

❑ **Preview**—Take just a few moments to preview next week's lesson on **"Peter: Coming Back to Walking with God."**

❑ **Pray**—Close in prayer.

 **TOOLS FOR GOOD DISCUSSION**

Bill Donahue, in his book, *Leading Life-Changing Small Groups* (Grand Rapids: Zondervan Publishing House, 1996), lists four facilitator actions that will produce dynamic discussion. These four actions are easy to remember because they are linked through the acrostic method to the word, **ACTS.** You will profit from taking time to review this information in the "Helpful Hints" section of **How to Lead a Small Group Bible Study,** which is on page 5 of this Leader's Guide book.

3

Peter

COMING BACK TO WALKING WITH GOD

MEMORY **Psalm 130:3–4** VERSES

*"If Thou, LORD, shouldst mark iniquities, O Lord,
who could stand? But there is forgiveness with Thee,
That Thou mayest be feared."*

BEFORE THE SESSION

❑ Pray each day for the members of your group—
that they spend time in the Word, grasp the
message God wants to bring to their lives, and
that they surrender to what God is saying.

❑ Do your homework. Don't procrastinate.

❑ Mark those ideas and questions you want to discuss as you go through the study. Those, along
with the questions listed below, can personalize
the discussion to fit your group. Think of the
needs of your group and be looking for applicable questions and discussion starters.

❑ Remain ever teachable. Look first for what God
is saying to you.

❑ Be prepared to be transparent and open about
what God is teaching you. Nothing is quite as
contagious as the joy of discovering new treasures in the Word.

WHAT TO EXPECT

For everyone in your group, the issue of failure will
strike a cord. Everyone sooner or later has blown it.
Each of us will need forgiveness. The all-important
question that surfaces in the midst of stumbling is
"Can God ever use me again?" This lesson on Peter

is a message of hope to all who have ever longed for
a second chance. You will find that this week's lesson, perhaps more than any of the others, will bring
the personal struggles of your group members out
into the open. When this happens, be prepared to
point them to God and the truths of His word this
lesson puts forward.

> ### THE MAIN POINT
> Failure doesn't have to be final. If we are
> willing to repent, the Lord is able to
> restore us to usefulness.

DURING THE SESSION

⧗ **OPENING: 5–10 MINUTES**

Opening Prayer—Remember the Lord is the Teacher
and wants us to depend on Him as we open the
Scriptures.

Opening Illustration—Abraham Lincoln has been
considered by many Americans to be a most successful president. However, the years that preceded his
time in The White House might lead one to believe
that he was a man marked for failure. Mr. Lincoln
suffered from melancholia and endured long periods
of depression throughout his life. He could barely see

out of one eye. He suffered quite frequently from nervous attacks, severe headaches, indigestion and nausea. When Lincoln was 10 years old, he was kicked in the head by a horse, and experts now believe that his skull was severely fractured, leaving him with lifelong problems.

"Honest Abe" experienced many setbacks throughout his life, including failure in business in 1831 and political defeat for a seat in the Illinois Legislature in 1832. Despite being elected to the Illinois Legislature in 1834 and being reelected to three consecutive terms thereafter, Lincoln failed in his attempts to become Speaker in 1838 and Elector in 1840. During his time in the state legislature, Lincoln courted Mary Todd, a woman of much more genteel origins than he. A brief postponement of their engagement plummeted Lincoln into a deep spell of melancholy, though they were eventually married in 1842. But more political setbacks soon followed. Though Lincoln did win a seat in the United States House of Representatives in 1846, he only served one term. He aborted his brief attempt to win a U.S. Senate seat in 1855 and failed to garner enough support to win the Republican Vice-Presidential nomination in 1856. He ran for the Senate again in 1860 against Stephen Douglas. Despite his strong performances in the much-heralded "Lincoln-Douglas" debates, Abe came up short in the vote count once again. However, after being elected President of the United States in 1860, he could afford all his prior difficulties. Abraham Lincoln was truly a "successful failure." The one lesson we learn from his life is that failure doesn't have to be final. Through repentance, even our spiritual failures can be reversed. We see this reversal of fortunes illustrated beautifully in the apostle Peter.

⏳ DISCUSSION: 30–40 MINUTES

Keep the group directed along the main highway of God's grace. You may have a pointed observation that will help sharpen the focus of the group. Encourage some to elaborate further on a key point or ask a quiet member of the group what he or she thinks of someone's comments. Watch the time, knowing you can't cover every single question in the lesson.

Main Objective in Day One: The main objective of Day One is to study Peter's ill-fated attempt to return to fishing and look at what motivated it. The princi-

ple to be seen is that when we return to our old life, we find it has nothing to offer us. Place a checkmark next to the suggested questions that appeal to you. Or you may want to rank each question according to your preference.

_____ Why do you think Peter would go back to his old occupation of fishing, knowing that Christ was risen from the dead?

_____ What application is there for us in his lack of success?

_____ Why do you think Jesus repeated the miracle He performed when He first called Peter?

_____ What do you see in Peter's response as he recognizes Jesus?

Main Objective in Day Two: Here we learn a little of the process of restoration through which Jesus took Peter. In Peter, we find a glimpse of ourselves and our own walk with Christ. Check the discussion questions that you will use for Day Two.

_____ What do you see as the point of the charcoal fire and what Jesus is doing with Peter?

_____ Why do you think Jesus already had fish on the fire? Why do you think He included some of their fish?

_____ What do you think Jesus was referring to when He asked "Do you love Me more than these?"

_____ What other aspects of Jesus' questioning of Peter would you like to discuss?

Main Objective in Day Three: Day Three introduces us to the danger of focusing on God's call for others instead of on our own call. Some good discussion questions for Day Three include . . .

_____ Why do you think Jesus told Peter how he would die?

_____ What do you see in Peter's struggle with Jesus' calling for John?

_____ How does Jesus deal with Peter's concerns?

_____ How do you think that principle applies to us today?

Main Objective in Day Four: The main thing for your group to catch from Day Four is that Peter is a different man on the other side of his repentance.

Check which discussion questions you will use for Day Four.

_____ What lessons did Peter learn from his failure?

_____ What differences do you see in Peter after his repentance?

_____ What other aspects of Day Four grabbed your attention?

_____ Has this lesson raised any questions for you?

Day Five—Key Points in Application: The single most important application point is the truth that failure doesn't have to be final. If we repent, God will turn our failures around and restore us to usefulness. Think of some good application questions for your Day Five discussion. Consider some of the suggested questions below.

_____ Are there any failures from your past that still haunt you?

_____ In what ways have you seen the difference between the conviction of the Lord and the condemnation of the enemy?

_____ Is there any one specific application that stood out to you most from this lesson?

_____ What did this lesson change the most in your thinking about God?

 CLOSING: 5–10 MINUTES

❑ **Summarize**—Restate the key points the group shared. Review the objectives for each of the days found at the beginning of these leader notes.

❑ **Ask** your group members to share their thoughts about the key applications from Day Five.

❑ **Preview**—Take a few moments to preview next week's lesson on **"John: Walking in the Love of God."** Encourage your group to be sure to complete their homework and to space it out over the week.

❑ **Pray**—Close in prayer.

 TOOLS FOR GOOD DISCUSSION

One of the people who show up in every group is a person we call **"Talkative Timothy."** Talkative Timothy tends to talk too much and dominates the discussion time by giving less opportunity for others to share. What do you do with a group member who talks too much? In the "Helpful Hints" section of **How to Lead a Small Group Bible Study** (p. 5), you'll find some practical ideas on managing the "Talkative Timothy's" in your group.

John

MEMORY **1 John 4:9–11** VERSES

"By this the love of God was manifested in us, that God has sent His only begotten son into the world so that we might live through Him. In this is love, not that we loved God, but that He loved us and sent His Son to be the propitiation for our sins. Beloved, if God so loved us, we also ought to love one another."

BEFORE THE SESSION

❑ Be sure to do your own study far enough in advance so you will not be rushed. You want to allow God time to speak to you personally.

❑ Familiarize yourself with the small chart on *The Life of John the Apostle* at the beginning of this lesson. It shows some of the main points in his life.

❑ Don't feel that you have to use all of the discussion questions listed below. You may have come up with others on your own, or you may find that time will not allow you to use them all. These questions are to serve you, not for you to serve.

❑ You are the gatekeeper of the discussion. Do not be afraid to "reel the group back in" if they get too far away from the lesson.

❑ Remember to keep a highlight pen ready as you study to mark any points you want to be sure and discuss.

❑ Pray each day for the members of your group— that they spend time in the Word, grasp the message God wants to bring to their lives, and surrender to what God is saying.

WHAT TO EXPECT

Most people know the name John very well. There are buildings and churches and schools all over the world named after the apostle John. He was one of the three more noteworthy apostles alongside Peter and James. Some will know of him as "the Apostle of love" because he speaks so much about the love of God and love for one another. Many will recognize him as the author of the *Gospel of John*, the three epistles of John (*1 John, 2 John,* and *3 John*) and the book of *Revelation*. Needless to say, there is much we can learn from him and this lesson is a start. Expect the members of your group to acquire some new insights into the life of John, the meaning of the love of God, and what it means to walk in the love of God.

> ### THE MAIN POINT
> As Christians, we are to walk in the love of God, personally experience His love, and show that love to others.

DURING THE SESSION

 OPENING: 5–10 MINUTES

Opening Prayer—Remember that if it took the inspiration of God for people to write Scripture, it will also take His illumination for us to understand it. Have one of the members of your group open your time together in prayer.

Opening Illustration—The story is told of a little boy whose sister had need of a blood transfusion. The boy's blood type matched perfectly, so he agreed to give his blood for her and bravely went to the hospital where they were to draw the needed blood. As they began the procedure, the boy calmly watched. After a moment, he asked his mother, "How soon will I die?" In that moment his mom realized that her son thought he would have to give all of his blood—and thus give his life in order to save the life of his sister. Jesus said (and the apostle John recorded), *"Greater love has no one than this, that one lay down his life for his friends"* (John 15:13). The little boy was prepared to do that for the life of his sister. Jesus **did do that** to save our lives and to give us eternal life and a home with Him in heaven forever. He continues to show us His love, and we are continual recipients of that love. As you journey through this lesson, think of the depth of His love for you and the members of your group. Look for ways to apply what you are seeing in the Scriptures and in the questions and comments of this lesson.

⌛ DISCUSSION: 30–40 MINUTES

Once your group gets talking, you will find that all you need to do to keep the group focused and the discussion flowing is to ask a question or two or make a pointed observation. Don't be afraid to ask someone to elaborate further ("Explain what you mean, Barbara.") or to ask a quiet member of the group what they think of someone else's comments ("What do you think, Dave?"). Time will not allow you to discuss every single aspect of the lesson. Instead, make it your goal to cover the main ideas of each day, and help the group to personally share what they have learned. You don't have to use all the discussion questions above. They are there for your choosing.

Main Objective in Day One: Day One focuses on the call of John to come and follow Jesus. That was the beginning of John's journey into the love of God. Some good discussion questions for Day One are:

_____ What part does prayer play in our lives or in the lives of those we are seeking to lead?

_____ What do you see about the spiritual hunger of John and the others disciples as they began to follow Christ? What applications do you see for your life?

_____ Can our spiritual hunger increase? What are some things that may increase our spiritual hunger?

_____ Jesus called James and John the *"sons of thunder."* (See Mark 3:17.) They were not fully where Jesus wanted them in their growth. What encouragement could this be for you as you follow Christ?

Main Objective in Day Two: Day Two focuses on the lessons Jesus continued to teach His disciples. He accepted them as they were, but He did not leave them in that same condition. Check which discussion questions you will use for Day Two.

_____ Jesus exhibited patience while teaching His disciples. What encouragement do you find for your life in the way He dealt with James, John, and the other disciples?

_____ How should we deal with our greed for greatness? What would Jesus say to us?

_____ How do love and serving go together? Name a practical example in today's world.

_____ We are always learning about love and how to love. Romans 13:8 says we always owe a debt of love to one another. What applications of this truth do you see for your life?

Main Objective in Day Three: The main thing to learn from Day Three is that John's life and writings bear credible witness to who Jesus Christ is. Through John's example, we too can learn how to be effective witnesses for Christ. Select a discussion starter or two from the list below.

_____ Describe the apostle John as though you were writing a letter to a friend who knew nothing about him. What stands out most about him in your viewpoint?

_____ In looking at John, what do you see about how the Lord can change a man and use him in His work?

_____ John shows us how to be witnesses for Christ. Name some attributes of a Christian witness.

_____ How do truth and love relate to one another? What happens when you have truth without love or love without truth?

Main Objective in Day Four: In Day Four, the main objective is to see the revelation John received and how the Lord's reign and His love are clearly seen. Check which discussion questions you will use for Day Four.

_____ Past the age of ninety, John had more to see and learn about the Lord Jesus. How does this truth apply to your relationship to the Lord?

_____ Judging solely upon what we know from the leadership of Paul, Timothy, and John at the church at Ephesus, what can we learn from this body of believers?

_____ From what you have studied, what do you think it will be like to live in the New Jerusalem? How will love be evident?

_____ How can we walk more consistently in the love of God? How can we help others do likewise?

Day Five—Key Points in Application: The most important application point in the lesson on John is learning to walk in the love of God, knowing we are loved by Him and showing His love to others by the power of His Spirit. Check any application questions from the list below that appeal to you.

_____ First Corinthians 13 describes love. Where do you have the greatest struggles in showing true love? Which characteristics (for example, patience or kindness, etc.) are less evident in your life?

_____ What would life be like if every one practiced the kind of love described in 1 Corinthians 13 and Galatians 5?

_____ What keeps you from practicing the kind of love described in the Bible?

_____ God, our Father, teaches us how to love others. How is God's teaching an encouragement to you?

⌛ CLOSING: 5–10 MINUTES

❑ **Summarize**—Restate the key points that were highlighted in the class. You may want to briefly review the objectives for each of the days found at the beginning of these leader notes.

❑ **Focus**—Using the memory verses (1 John 4:9–11), focus on the reality of God's love **for us,** God's love **in us,** and the power of the Spirit to show God's love **through us.**

❑ **Ask** those in your group to share their thoughts about the key applications from Day Five.

❑ **Preview**—Take a few moments to preview next week's lesson on **"Thomas: A Faith Founded on Fact."** Stress the importance of the lesson's homework.

❑ **Pray**—Close in prayer.

TOOLS FOR GOOD DISCUSSION

As mentioned earlier, there are certain people who show up in every discussion group. Last week we looked at "Talkative Timothy." Another person who is likely to show up is **"Silent Sally."** She does not readily speak up. Sometimes, her silence is because she doesn't yet feel comfortable enough with the group to share her thoughts. Other times, it is simply because she fears being rejected. Often, her silence is because she is too polite to interrupt and thus is headed off at the pass each time she wants to speak by more aggressive (and less sensitive) members of the group. In the "Helpful Hints" section of **How to Lead a Small Group Bible Study** (p. 6), you'll find some practical ideas on managing the "Silent Sally's" in your group.

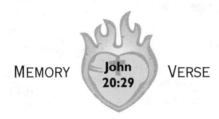

5

MEMORY **John 20:29** VERSE

*"Because you have seen Me, have you believed? Blessed are
they who did not see, and yet believed."*

BEFORE THE SESSION

❑ Resist the temptation to do all your homework
in one sitting or to put it off until the last
minute. You will not be as prepared if you study
this way.

❑ Make sure to jot down any discussion questions
that come to your mind as you study.

❑ For further study, you may want to see what you
can learn of Thomas from a Bible dictionary.

❑ Remember your need to trust God with your
study—the Holy Spirit is always the best teacher,
so stay sensitive to Him!

WHAT TO EXPECT

In this lesson, you should anticipate that all your
group members need a better understanding of the
concept of doubt. Your group needs to realize that
even a child of God can have doubts. Mentioning the
many evidences of God's grace in Thomas' story is of
utmost importance. Thomas will be a unique study
because of this issue of doubt. You should expect some
in your group to take great personal encouragement
from this particular lesson because of their own struggles with doubt. Help the members of your group to

see the benefit of helping others even if they have
never struggled with doubts. They will take special
comfort from seeing God's patience and the gracious
way He deals with us when we experience misgivings
as we follow Him.

> ### THE MAIN POINT
> Through God's grace and power, we will
> emerge from our doubts with stronger
> faith—built upon facts.

DURING THE SESSION

⏳ **OPENING: 5–10 MINUTES**

Opening Prayer—Remember to have one of your
group members open your time together in prayer.

Opening Illustration—Frank Morrison was an
English journalist who set out to prove that the story
of Christ's resurrection was nothing but a myth.
However, his efforts led him to the point where he
placed his faith in the risen Christ. Morrison went
on to write a book on his findings titled, *Who Moved
the Stone?* One of the chapters in the book is entitled
"The Book That Refused to be Written." Morrison
discovered, like so many before him and since, that
the Christian faith does not call one to ignore the
facts. One does not have to disengage his brain to

believe. Often, as with Frank Morrison, it is doubt that drives us to investigate, and the faith found on the other side is a stronger faith. This is the lesson we see this week as we study the disciple Thomas.

⏳ DISCUSSION: 30–40 MINUTES

Remember that your job is not to teach this lesson, but to facilitate discussion. Do your best to guide the group to the right answers, but don't be guilty of making a point someone else in the group could just as easily make.

Main Objective in Day One: The main objective in Day One is to see where Thomas fits in with the rest of the disciples and what background information we can find on him. Good discussion questions for Day One include . . .

_____ Where does Thomas fit in the different lists of the disciples?

_____ When you look at the list of disciples, what is your first impression of Thomas being paired with the former tax collector, Matthew?

_____ What are your thoughts concerning the final list of disciples in Acts 1:13?

_____ Were there any questions raised by your study in Day One?

Main Objective in Day Two: In Day Two, we investigate the narrative of Jesus' desire to go to Judea amid threats of death. We also see Thomas' role in encouraging the disciples to go to Judea with Christ. Below, check any discussion starters that you find to be useful.

_____ Why were the disciples afraid to go back to Judea?

_____ What are your thoughts concerning Thomas' statement?

_____ What was the attitude behind Thomas' statement to his comrades?

_____ What were the results of the trip back to Judea?

Main Objective in Day Three: Day Three introduces us to the honest questions Thomas asked when Jesus spoke of going away. Again, we see his heart reflected in his words. What discussion starters do you have in mind for Day Three? Here are some suggestions:

_____ Why do you think Jesus waited so long to talk with the disciples about his leaving?

_____ What is the point of Thomas' question?

_____ What do you think is the meaning of Jesus' answer?

_____ What does the fact that Thomas asked this question personally say to you?

Main Objective in Day Four: In Day Four, we look at the account of Thomas' post-resurrection doubts and how the Lord dealt with him. Check which discussion questions you will use for Day Four.

_____ Why do you think Thomas wasn't present when the Lord appeared to the other disciples?

_____ Do you see any particular differences in the doubts of Thomas compared to those of the other disciples?

_____ What was Thomas' response after he had his questions answered?

Day Five—Key Points in Application: The important thing to see out of Day Five is that God is willing and able to deal with our doubts if we bring them to Him. In addition to any of your own application-based questions that you may want to use, the following suggested questions may also be of help.

_____ Can you think of a time when you struggled with doubts about your faith?

_____ How did you deal with those doubts?

_____ When have you struggled most with doubts?

⏳ CLOSING: 5-10 MINUTES

❑ **Summarize**—Highlight the key points.

❑ **Remind** those in your group that living a victorious Christian life is not attained when we try hard to be like Jesus, but only when we surrender our lives to God and let Him work through us.

❑ **Ask** the members of your group to convey their thoughts on the key applications from Day Five.

❑ **Preview**—Take a few moments to preview next week's lesson on **"James: Growing in Genuine Faith."** Encourage them to be sure to complete their homework.

❑ **Pray**—Close in prayer.

Tools for Good Discussion

Hopefully your group is functioning smoothly at this point, but perhaps you recognize the need for improvement. In either case, you will benefit from taking the time to evaluate yourself and your group. Without evaluation, you will judge your group on subjective emotions. You may think everything is fine and miss some opportunities to improve your effectiveness. You may be discouraged by problems you are confronting when you ought to be encouraged that you are doing the right things and making progress. A healthy Bible-study group is not one without problems, but is one that recognizes its problems and deals with them the right way. At this point in the course, as you and your group are nearly halfway completed with the study of the men of the New Testament, it is important to examine yourself and see if there are any mid-course corrections that you feel are necessary to implement. Review the evaluation questions list found on page 11 of this Leader's Guide, and jot down two or three action points for you to begin implementing next week. Perhaps you have made steady improvements since the first time you answered the evaluation questions at the beginning of the course. If so, your improvements should challenge you to be an even better group leader for the final seven lessons in the study.

ACTION POINTS:

1. _____

_____

2. _____

_____

3. _____

_____

6

MEMORY 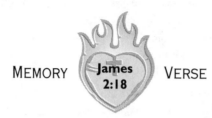 VERSE

*"But someone may well say, 'You have faith,
and I have works; show me your faith without the works, and I
will show you my faith by my works.'"*

BEFORE THE SESSION

❑ Remember the Boy Scout motto: **BE PRE-PARED!** The main reason a Bible study flounders is because the leader comes in unprepared and tries to "shoot from the hip."

❑ Make sure to jot down any discussion questions that may come to mind as you study.

❑ Don't forget to pray for the members of your group and for your time studying together. You don't want to be satisfied with what you can do—you want to see God do what only He can do!

WHAT TO EXPECT

In this lesson, realize that all of us have to be able to distinguish between what is genuine faith and what is simply lip service. Differentiating between real faith and pseudo-faith was something very important to James, for he had seen both in others and in his own life as well. He started out as a skeptic, yet ended up as a bondservant of Christ. There should be much in this lesson that will register with your group. Be sensitive to any questions that may surface in the discussion on James.

> ### THE MAIN POINT
> Real faith is not just a philosophy or intellectual pursuit, but is the result of being rightly related to Christ.

DURING THE SESSION

⏳ **OPENING: 5–10 MINUTES**

Opening Prayer—Remember to have one of your group members open your time together in prayer.

Opening Illustration—Our society is full of imitations. We have imitation butter, imitation sugar, eggs, and flavorings. Some eat hamburger made from seaweed or soybeans, ham made from turkey, and crabmeat and lobster made from fish. There are imitation products like imitation leather, "faux" diamonds and jewels, and even imitation perfumes. It seems like almost everything can be imitated, but the imitation is usually not quite as special as the real thing. We will see this week in James that there is a difference between imitation faith that is just play acting, and the real thing that flows from a life of surrender to Christ.

⏳ **DISCUSSION: 30–40 MINUTES**

Remember to pace your discussion so that you will be able to bring closure to the lesson at the designated time. You are the one who must balance lively discussion with timely redirection to ensure that you don't end up finishing only part of the lesson.

Main Objective in Day One: In Day One, the main objective is to see what we can learn of James' lack of belief during the earthly ministry of Jesus. Understanding his initial skepticism is important to setting a context for his later faith and surrender. Select a discussion question or two from the list below.

_____ What do you think it was like growing up with Jesus?

_____ Why do you think it was hard for Jesus' family to believe in Him?

_____ What was Jesus' response to His family's unbelief?

_____ Were there any questions raised by your study in Day One?

Main Objective in Day Two: In Day Two, we learn some of the specifics of how James' view of Christ changed after the resurrection. Check which discussion questions you will use for Day Two.

_____ Why do you think James was not given the responsibility of caring for Mary when Jesus died?

_____ Why do you think Jesus chose to appear specifically to James (1 Corinthians 15:7)?

_____ What else spoke to you from Day Two?

Main Objective in Day Three: Day Three introduces us to the role James assumed in leadership of the church at Jerusalem. Early Church leadership of this magnitude was a significant responsibility and speaks volumes of James' character. Place a checkmark next to the suggested questions that you like the most. Or rank them in order of your preference.

_____ Looking at Acts 12:17, compare Peter's role in the early Church to that of James.

_____ What do you think is the significance of James' role in the Jerusalem Council of Acts 15?

_____ Why do you think Paul and Barnabas were running things by James?

_____ What are your thoughts on James' role in the early Church?

Main Objective in Day Four: In Day Four, we see the all-important principle that James saw his identity not as the brother of Jesus but as a servant of Jesus. This relationship models what it means for Christ to be Lord. Check which discussion questions you will use for Day Four.

_____ Why do you think James did not choose to identify himself as the brother of Jesus?

_____ What does it say to you that James called Jesus both Lord and Christ?

_____ What stands out to you of the Old Testament concept of a "bondservant"?

_____ How do you think that applies to us today?

Day Five—Key Points in Application: The most important application point out of Day Five is that good works do not earn salvation, but they always accompany it. The deeds of the Christian flow out of his surrender to Christ. Below are some suggested application-based discussion questions.

_____ What do your deeds say about the state of your faith?

_____ Have you ever come to the place where you surrendered control of every area of your life to Christ as a bondservant?

_____ What would you say to someone who was struggling with the choice of surrender?

_____ What is the biggest application point you saw this week?

CLOSING: 5–10 MINUTES

❑ **Summarize**—Restate the key points.

❑ **Preview**—Take a few moments to preview next week's lesson on Barnabas. Encourage your group members to be sure to do their homework.

❑ **Pray**—Close in prayer.

 TOOLS FOR GOOD DISCUSSION

As discussed earlier, there are certain people who show up in every discussion group that you will ever lead. We have already looked at "Talkative Timothy" and "Silent Sally." This week, let's talk about another person who also tends to show up. Let's call this person **"Tangent Tom."** He is the kind of guy who loves to talk even when he has nothing to say. Tangent Tom loves to "chase rabbits" regardless of where they go. When he gets the floor, you never know where the discussion will lead. You need to understand that not all tangents are bad. Sometimes, much can be gained from discussion "a little off the beaten path." But these diversions must be balanced against the purpose of the group. In the "Helpful Hints" section of **How to Lead a Small Group** (p. 6), you will find some practical ideas on managing the "Tangent Tom's" in your group. You will also get some helpful information on evaluating tangents as they arise.

7

Barnabas

MEMORY **Hebrews 3:13** VERSE

"Encourage one another day after day, as long as it is still called 'Today,' lest any one of you be hardened by the deceitfulness of sin."

BEFORE THE SESSION

❑ Make every effort to get your lesson plans and homework done early this week. This gives time for you to reflect on what you have learned and process it mentally. Don't succumb to the temptation to procrastinate.

❑ Make sure you keep a highlight pen handy to mark any things you want to be sure to discuss or any questions that you think your group may have trouble with. Mark down any good discussion questions that come to mind as you study.

❑ Don't think of your ministry to the members of your group as something that only takes place during your group time. Pray for your group members by name during the week that they would receive spiritual enrichment from doing their daily homework. Encourage them as you have opportunity.

WHAT TO EXPECT

In this lesson we are afforded a very practical opportunity to teach our group members the significance of the ministry of encouragement. This is one of the most important tools you can place in their spiritual toolbox. One way that may make it easier for you to emphasize the impact of this ministry is to come prepared to share from your own experiences and to highlight those God has used as an encouragement in your life and walk with God. Make sure your group leaves with the motivation to look for those in their lives that they can encourage.

> ### THE MAIN POINT
> Recognizing the impact and value of encouragement is essential as we motivate others to follow God.

DURING THE SESSION

⏳ OPENING: 5–10 MINUTES

Opening Prayer—It would be a good idea to have a different group member each week open your time together in prayer.

Opening Illustration—When someone asked St. Francis of Assisi why and how he could accomplish so much, he replied: "This may be why. The Lord looked down from heaven upon the earth and said, 'Where can I find the weakest, the littlest, the meanest man on the face of the earth?' Then He saw me and said, 'Now I've found him, and I will work through him. He won't be proud of it. He'll see that I'm only using him because of his littleness and insignificance.'" Barnabas was a man like that. Because of his humility, God was able to do great things through him.

⧗ DISCUSSION: 30–40 MINUTES

A key objective in how you manage your discussion time is to keep the big picture in view. Your job is not like a schoolteacher's job, grading papers and tests and the like, but more like a tutor's job, making sure that your group understands the subject. Keep the main point of the lesson in view, and make sure they take that main point home with them.

Main Objective in Day One: Day One's main objective is to look at the first mention of Barnabas in Scripture and see what it reveals of his character and ministry. We want to highlight how he earned his nickname, "Son of Encouragement." Jot down some discussion question ideas. Below are some suggested questions for your discussion time.

_____ Do you have a nickname? How did you get it?

_____ How do you see encouragement in the actions of Barnabas?

_____ Why do you think Luke used Barnabas as an example?

_____ What else stood out to you from Day One?

Main Objective in Day Two: In Day Two, we learn some of the specifics of the partnership God formed between Barnabas and the apostle Paul. We begin to see the great impact Barnabas had in shaping the man that Paul eventually became. Select a discussion starter or two from the list below.

_____ What was Barnabas' role in Saul's (Paul) conversion? What was Barnabas' relationship to the church in Jerusalem?

_____ How do you think Barnabas' position in the early Church affected how Paul felt toward Barnabas?

_____ Why was Barnabas a good choice for the Jerusalem church to send to Antioch?

_____ Why do you think Barnabas wanted to include Saul in the work there?

Main Objective in Day Three: Day Three introduces us to Barnabas' role on the first missionary journey.

Even though he was in charge, with characteristic humility he did not bristle when Paul stepped to the forefront. Check which discussion questions you will use from Day Three.

_____ From what you have seen so far, would you call Barnabas Paul's co-worker, his subordinate, or his superior?

_____ How did Barnabas handle his leadership role?

_____ How do you think you would have dealt with having your disciple become the main leader?

_____ Were there any other questions raised by your study in Day Three?

Main Objective in Day Four: In Day Four, we look at some of Barnabas' failings and humanness. Even though he was used greatly by God, he was not perfect. It is his imperfection that helps us to be able to relate with him. In addition to any discussion questions that you may have decided to use, the following suggested questions may also prove to be useful:

_____ Describe the conflict that led to Paul and Barnabas separating.

_____ What do you think the Lord was doing through that?

_____ Why do you think Paul was so surprised that Barnabas fell prey to prejudice?

_____ What do Barnabas' mistakes reveal of his character?

Day Five—Key Points in Application: The most important application point out of Day Five is that encouragement has tremendous impact, and nothing is more encouraging than walking in humility. Barnabas models that trait beautifully. Check which discussion questions you will use from Day Five.

_____ Who has been the greatest encouragement in your life?

_____ Can you think of a situation where worrying about whose position was higher got in the way of your encouraging a brother?

_____ What are some ways you can encourage someone by letting them join you in your work?

_____ What is the biggest application point you saw this week?

⧗ CLOSING: 5–10 MINUTES

- ❏ **Summarize**—restate the key points. You can read the paragraph at the beginning of these leader's notes on "The Main Point" of Barnabas.

- ❏ **Remind** your group that the victorious Christian life is not attained when we try hard to be like Jesus, but when we surrender our lives to God and let Him work through us.

- ❏ **Preview** next week's lesson on **"Paul: Learning to Draw from the Right Source."**

- ❏ **Pray**—Close in prayer.

TOOLS FOR GOOD DISCUSSION

One of the issues you will eventually have to combat in any group Bible study is the enemy of **boredom.**

This antagonist raises its ugly head from time to time, but it shouldn't. It is wrong to bore people with the Word of God! Often boredom results when leaders allow their processes to become too predictable. As small group leaders, we tend to do the same thing in the same way every single time. Yet God the Creator, who spoke everything into existence, is infinitely creative! Think about it. He is the one who not only created animals in different shapes and sizes, but different colors as well. When He created food, He didn't make it all taste or feel the same. This God of creativity lives in us. We can trust Him to give us creative ideas that will keep our group times from becoming tired and mundane. In the "Helpful Hints" section of **How to Lead a Small Group** (pp. 8–9), you'll find some practical ideas on adding spice and creativity to your study time.

8

LEARNING TO DRAW FROM THE RIGHT SOURCE

MEMORY  VERSES

"...I count all things to be loss in view of the surpassing value of knowing Christ Jesus my Lord ... and count them but rubbish in order that I may gain Christ, and may be found in Him, not having a righteousness of my own derived from the Law, but that which is through faith in Christ...."

BEFORE THE SESSION

❏ Your own preparation is key not only to your effectiveness in leading the group time, but also in your confidence in leading. It is hard to be confident if you know you are unprepared. These discussion questions and leader's notes are meant to be a helpful addition to your own study, but should never become a substitute.

❏ As you do your homework, study with a view to your own relationship with God. Resist the temptation to bypass this self-evaluation on your way to preparing to lead the group. Nothing will minister to your group more than the testimony of your own walk with God.

❏ Pray that each group member would be responsive to the principles that they study while doing their homework.

WHAT TO EXPECT

The apostle Paul is the most prominent figure in the New Testament other than Jesus. In fact, he wrote nearly half of the New Testament. Much more could be said about him than we will ever be able to cover. Therefore, we have chosen to focus on his switch from a self-made man to a Christ-made man. We will

look at how he laid aside his old identity as a Pharisee and found a new identity in Christ. Expect that there may be some in your group who have a religious identity but have never really had a personal relationship with Christ. This lesson has the potential of being a real life-changer.

> ### THE MAIN POINT
> Seeing the difference between working **for** God and walking **with** God is a step in the right direction when it comes to following God.

DURING THE SESSION

 OPENING: 5–10 MINUTES

Opening Prayer—A good prayer with which to open your session is the prayer of David in Psalm 119:18, *"Open my eyes, that I may behold Wonderful things from Thy law."* Remember, if it took the illumination of God for men to write Scripture, it will take the same for us to understand it.

Opening Illustration—Hudson Taylor, founder of China Inland Mission was a missionary pioneer and innovator. Yet he endured much hardship and difficulty. In 1867, Taylor's oldest child, Gracie, died, as did his wife Maria just three years later. Not long after Maria's death, Hudson was involved in an accident that damaged his spine. But what sustained him was a lesson learned early from one of his fellow missionaries who wrote the following words of a discovered secret: "To let my loving Savior work in me His will. . . . Abiding, not striving or struggling." Like scales falling from his eyes, Hudson Taylor finally understood that the victorious Christian life was not attained through his vain attempts to **do things for God,** but through his walking with God and letting Christ work **through him.** He later testified, "As I read, I saw it all. 'If we believe not, He abideth faithful.' And I looked to Jesus and saw (and when I saw, oh, how the joy flowed). I have striven in vain to abide in Him. I'll strive no more." Taylor had moved from merely being religious, to walking in a relationship with God. We see this same powerful testimony modeled this week in our study of the apostle Paul.

⌛ DISCUSSION: 30–40 MINUTES

Remember to pace your discussion so that you don't run out of time to get to the application questions in Day Five. This time for application is perhaps the most important part of your Bible study. It will be helpful if you are familiar enough with the lesson to be able to prioritize the days for which you want to place more emphasis, so that you are prepared to reflect this added emphasis in the time you devote to that particular day's reading.

Main Objective in Day One: Day One's main objective is to take a close look at the apostle Paul's conversion, examining the kind of man he was and the change Christ made in him. Possible Day One discussion starters include . . .

____ What stands out to you about Paul's role in the stoning death of Stephen?

____ What do you think was going through Paul's mind when he realized that Jesus actually was the Messiah?

____ Why do you think the Lord allowed Paul to go to prison?

____ Are there any "prisons" in your life right now?

____ What needs to change in your attitude toward your "prisons" so that they can become your "pulpits"?

Main Objective in Day Two: In Day Two, we learn some of the specifics of how finding our identity in Christ affects our attitude. In fact, as we see in Paul, when Christ is the essence of our lives, His attitude becomes our attitude. Check which discussion questions you will use from Day Two.

____ What do you see reflected in the fact that we are commanded to have the attitude of Christ?

____ What came across your mind as you identified the characteristics of the attitude of Christ?

____ Is the attitude of Christ what you usually see in other Christians you know?

____ Is the attitude of Christ what others usually see in you?

Main Objective in Day Three: Day Three introduces us to how Paul's goals changed when he met Christ. When we find our identity in Christ, He becomes our goal. What discussion questions do you like from the list below?

____ What were Paul's intentions for contrasting true and false circumcision?

____ What do you think it means to "put no confidence in the flesh"?

____ Are there any areas where you struggle with putting confidence in the flesh?

____ What does it say to you that after twenty-five or thirty years as a Christian, Paul didn't consider himself to have arrived?

____ Were there any other questions raised by your study in Day Three?

Main Objective in Day Four: In Day Four, our study of Paul takes us to the reality that when we are walking in right relationship to Christ, He gives us the strength and supply for whatever path of life He calls us. Where God guides, He provides. Possible discussion questions from Day Four are . . .

____ What does it say to you that there were things Paul had to "learn"?

____ How did Paul learn the lessons he speaks of in Philippians 4?

____ What does the promise of Philippians 4:19 mean in your life?

_____ Do you see any prerequisites in Philippians 4 to Paul offering this promise to the Philippians?

Day Five—Key Points in Application: The most important application point out of Day Five is that we must find our identity in Christ. Make sure your group members understand that there is no room in Christianity for a "self-made man." Examine the list of questions below, and choose one or two for your group session.

_____ Is there a "prison" that God has allowed in your life—something unpleasant that you cannot change?

_____ What does your attitude say about where your identity is being found?

_____ What are some ways you are tempted to put confidence in your flesh?

_____ To whom do you tend to look to meet your needs?

⏳ CLOSING: 5–10 MINUTES

❑ **Summarize**—Restate the key points. You may want to read the statement called "The Main Point" at the beginning of these leader notes for this first lesson on Paul

❑ **Preview**—If time allows, preview next week's lesson on **"Paul: Walking in the Will of God"** (Paul 2). Encourage the group to be sure to do their homework.

❑ **Pray**—Close in prayer.

 ## TOOLS FOR GOOD DISCUSSION

From time to time, each of us can say stupid things. Some of us, however, are better at it than others. The apostle Peter certainly had his share of embarrassing moments. One minute, he was on the pinnacle of success, saying, _"Thou art the Christ, the Son of the Living God"_ (Matthew 16:16), and the next minute, he was putting his foot in his mouth, trying to talk Jesus out of going to the cross. Proverbs 10:19 states, _"When there are many words, transgression is unavoidable. . . ."_ What do you do when someone in the group says something that is obviously wrong? First of all, remember that how you deal with a situation like this not only affects the present, but the future. In the "Helpful Hints" section of **How to Lead a Small Group** (p. 9), you'll find some practical ideas on managing the obviously wrong comments that show up in your group.

9

WALKING IN THE WILL OF GOD

MEMORY **Romans 15:30–32** VERSES

"Now I urge you, brethren, by our Lord Jesus Christ and by the love of the Spirit, to strive together with me in your prayer s to God for me, . . . so that I may come to you in joy by the will of God and find refreshing rest in your company."

BEFORE THE SESSION

❏ Pray each day for the members of your group—that they spend time in the Word, grasp the message God wants to bring to their lives, and that they surrender to what God is saying.

❏ Be sure you have searched the Scriptures carefully for each day's lesson.

❏ Familiarize yourself with the chart, "An Outline of the Life and Ministry of the Apostle Paul" at the end of this lesson (Workbook pp. 135-39).

❏ Study through the suggested discussion questions in these leader's notes, and select which questions you will use.

❏ To better understand the life of Paul, review the last couple of weeks' lessons (Lessons 7 and 8), first on Barnabas and then on the heart of Paul. The next two lessons (Lessons 10 and 11) look at **Paul's Companions** and at **Timothy**. You can find several articles in Bible dictionaries on Paul and his missionary journeys as well as on all the letters (epistles) he wrote.

❏ Remain ever teachable. Look first for what God is saying to you. This will help you in relating to some of the situations your group members may be facing as they are seeking to make an impact on those around them.

WHAT TO EXPECT

Studying the life of Paul can be an encouragement, and can sometimes leave us out of breath. So much happened to Paul, and he wrote so much that we can get lost in the many details. We have seen in Lessons 7 and 8 some of the background and heart of Paul. He knew Christ as his life and always wanted to walk in the will of God. All that God had planned for him to know and do, he wanted to experience! This lesson will take us from AD 56, through the last ten chapters of **Acts** and into several of the epistles, ending with Paul's release from his first Roman imprisonment around AD 62. (See the workbook chart.) The important thing in this lesson is not so much the **events** of Paul's journey as much as the **ways of God** in and through those events. Seeing Paul walk through many delays, detours, and dark days can look discouraging at first. However, seeing the fulfillment of the mission for which he prayed and the evident work of God in and through the detours and delays can give strong encouragement to the members of your group as they too pray to know and do God's will. The key is in trusting God with the big picture, knowing that as He orchestrates **the ends** to which He is taking us, He is also orchestrating (in some way) **the means** to get us to that end. He continually led Paul and encouraged him along the way, and He will be faithful to do the same for you and the members of your group.

> ### THE MAIN POINT
> God led Paul through the delays, detours, and dark days. We can be confident that He will do the same for us.

DURING THE SESSION

 OPENING: 5–10 MINUTES

Opening Prayer—Remember to ask the Lord for His wisdom. He promised to guide us into the truth.

Opening Illustration—On September 15, 1999, a lone, deranged gunman entered the Wedgwood Baptist Church in Fort Worth, Texas, during a Wednesday night service and shot several adults and youth, killing 7 of them. It was a great tragedy, yet in the midst of it there were many miracles. He had enough ammunition to kill dozens but didn't. Many letters, cards, calls, and e-mails made their way to the church in the days afterward. One of those cards attached to some flowers made the statement "No one can explain the tragedies, just as no one can explain the miracles." At the memorial service held at Texas Christian University stadium, a pastor concluded his remarks stating, "God wastes nothing." Summed up in those two statements is the mystery of God's will—of what He authors and what He allows. We do not understand the tragedies, the evil plots and wicked schemes, the detours our lives take. Nor do we understand all the miraculous ways God protects us or the ways He moves kings and kingdoms to clear the way before us. We often must wait to clearly see how He has ordered events and their consequences with a timing and a time that is nothing short of miraculous. He fills us with wonder and awe as we see His will worked out. That is the case with the detours, delays, and dark days Paul faced in the journeys in which God led him. As you walk through these journeys with Paul, ask the Lord to make the connections to your own life and the lives of those in your group. This can be a time of great discovery for everyone as you and your group see the wondrous ways of God in unfolding His will.

 DISCUSSION: 30–40 MINUTES

Select one or two specific questions to get the group started. Keep the group directed along the main highway of Paul. By this point in the course (Week 9) you know the talkative and the quiet. Continue to encourage each member in the importance of his or her input. Some of the greatest life lessons we will ever learn may come from someone who has said very little up to this point.

Main Objective in Day One: In Day One, the main objective is to see the reality of surrender to God's will in the heart of the apostle Paul. Using some of the questions below or your own ideas, decide upon some discussion starters for Day One.

_____ God's will is a moment-by-moment reality, not reserved just for the big events (college, marriage, family, career, etc.). How important is the Holy Spirit in **knowing** God's will?

_____ How important is the Holy Spirit's power in **doing** God's will?

_____ Plans are a part of everyday life. How do plans fit into our **walking** in the will of God?

_____ Where does prayer fit in surrender to and walking in the will of God?

Main Objective in Day Two: Day Two focuses on the adventures on which God takes us as we walk in His will. Check which discussion questions you will use from Day Two.

_____ Paul certainly faced some adventurous times. We may not face those same types of adventure, but God does have a place for us in His will. How would you describe some of the adventures on which the Lord has led you?

_____ Sometimes we will walk in the ordinary (even mundane) things of everyday life. How can that be in God's will?

_____ Can you think of some detours or delays in your life that could have been (or perhaps were) used to get the message of Jesus Christ to someone?

Main Objective in Day Three: In Day Three, we see the goal of God's will—a right relationship with Him and with others. Check which discussion questions you will use from Day Three.

_____ Paul's change in circumstances and location was a protection for him. Have you ever seen changes in location or in circumstance provide some sort of protection for you or someone close to you?

_____ What are some ways we can more effectively share the message of Christ when faced with a detour or delay?

_____ God uses **time** and **timing** to accomplish His will. How does that help you in seeking to walk in God's will?

Main Objective in Day Four: Day Four looks at seeing life from God's point of view—seeing the detours and delays His way. What are some discussion ideas that you are considering? Below are some suggestions.

_____ Can you look back at a detour or delay in life that was really a blessing to you or to someone you knew?

_____ How does this lesson speak to you about prayer and how God answers prayer?

_____ Paul's testimony of rejoicing in Philippians 1:12–20 reveals that he was confident in the way God led Him in fulfilling His will. What does this say to you about God's will in your life?

_____ In light of all you have seen this week, read Romans 12:1–2. What applications do you see?

Day Five—Key Points in Application: The most important application point in the lesson on Paul is to see how clearly the Word of God describes the will of God and leads us with wise counsel for the areas we are uncertain about. Good application-based questions from Day Five include . . .

_____ The psalms of David reveal much about daily life including the struggles. What applications have you seen in some of David's psalms?

_____ How can we help one another with what looks like delays—the **time** and the **timing** issues we each face?

_____ From looking at the Workbook chart in Day Five, how much of the will of God for daily life is very clear? Fifty Percent? Seventy-Five percent? Ninety-Eight percent?

_____ What has this lesson taught you about prayer for yourself and for others?

⏳ CLOSING: 5–10 MINUTES

❑ **Summarize**—Restate the key points the group shared. Review the objectives for each of the days found in these leader notes.

❑ **Focus**—Using the memory verse (Romans 15:30–33), focus the group on the importance of knowing and doing the will of God and how God uses prayer in accomplishing His will. We can trust the ways of God and the power of God at work through our prayers. Encourage each one to prayerfully seek the Lord with hearts totally surrendered to His will.

❑ **Ask** your group members to share their thoughts about the key applications from Day Five.

❑ **Encourage**—We have finished nine lessons, but this is no time to slack off! Encourage your group to keep up the pace. We have three more lessons full of life-changing truths. Take a few moments to preview next week's lesson on **"Paul's Companions: Following God Together."** Encourage your group members to do their homework in proper fashion by spacing it out over the week.

❑ **Pray**—Close in prayer.

TOOLS FOR GOOD DISCUSSION

The Scriptures are full of examples of people who struggled with the problem of pride. Unfortunately, pride isn't a problem reserved for the history books. It shows up just as often today as it did in the days the Scriptures were written. In your group discussions, you may see traces of pride manifested in a "know-it-all" group member. **"Know-It-All Ned"** may have shown up in your group by this point. He may be an intellectual giant, or he may be a legend only in his own mind. He can be very prideful and argumentative. If you want some helpful hints on how to deal with "Know-It-All Ned," look in the "Helpful Hints" section of **How to Lead a Small Group Bible Study** (p. 7).

10

Paul's Companions

MEMORY · I Peter 4:10–11 · VERSES

"As each one has received a special gift, employ it in serving one another, as good stewards of the manifold grace of God.... so that in all things God may be glorified through Jesus Christ, to whom belongs the glory and dominion forever and ever. Amen."

BEFORE THE SESSION

❑ Never underestimate the importance of prayer for yourself and for the members of your group. Ask God to give your group members understanding in their time in the Word and bring them to a new level of knowing Him.

❑ Spread your study time over the week.

❑ Remember to highlight those ideas and questions you want to discuss or ask as you go through the study.

❑ To see the many companions associated with Paul throughout his illustrious years of ministry, you may want to familiarize yourself with the chart, "The Companions of the Apostle Paul" at the end of this lesson (Workbook p. 155).

❑ To better understand the ministries of Paul and the place of his companions in ministry you may want to read **Acts** and the epistles of Paul as well as some of the articles in a good Bible dictionary on "Paul's Missionary Journeys," or "Paul the Apostle." You may also want to review last week's lesson on Paul and the chart on Paul's life at the end of Lesson 9 (Workbook pp. 135–38). The lesson on Barnabas (Lesson 7) and next week's lesson on Timothy (Lesson 11) will also give added information.

WHAT TO EXPECT

When most people think of the companions of Paul, they think of one of the "big three," Barnabas, Silas, or Timothy. However, on careful observation, we find the names of at least seventy people who were involved with Paul in ministry over the years. That is an eye-opening fact, especially for those who tend to think of the apostle Paul as a kind of "Lone Ranger" or "Superman" apostle. Each one of us is **a member**—note, an **individual** member—of the body of Christ. No one person can function as the whole body, and Christ is the Head of this many-membered body. Paul understood that and proclaimed that in several passages (Romans 12, 1 Corinthians 12, etc.) We need to understand and apply that as well. There is kingdom work for each of God's children, and hopefully this lesson will make that clear. Let your group be encouraged and challenged by the example of Paul and his companions.

THE MAIN POINT
We as the body of Christ should all follow the Lord and work together to fulfill the Father's will.

DURING THE SESSION

 OPENING: 5–10 MINUTES

Opening Prayer—Have one of the group members open the time with prayer.

Opening Illustration—In any major military operation, there are several jobs that must be done. There are companies of soldiers who are assigned to artillery, to tank movement, or to troop ground movements. There are aircraft assignments—for fighter jets, large bombers, and helicopters. Then, equally important are those assigned to communications (radio, radar, satellite communications), or to fuel distribution, food distribution (or meal preparation), to laundry, to medical needs (on the front lines, in a field hospital, or in evacuating extreme cases), and even to correspondence and media concerns. It is more than the plans of a four or five-star general at headquarters or simply a group of soldiers with a few backpacks full of ammo.

The same is true in the Body of Christ. We each need one another. No one is useless; everyone is essential. No one has all the gifts, but every Christian has at least one gift. The ministry and the journeys of the apostle Paul have chronicled this truth. From around AD 35 (when Paul was converted on the Road to Damascus), we find others involved in his life, such as Ananias, who immediately helped him in Damascus. This loving support for Paul by others lasted to his dying day in Rome around the year AD 68. Paul's execution occurred about six months after he had penned his final letter to Timothy, a letter in which he mentions almost 20 fellow workers. This lesson can help the members of your group see that no one is insignificant and no ministry given by God is without value both now and in eternity. May this be an encouragement to you and to the members of your group.

 DISCUSSION: 30–40 MINUTES

Select one or two specific questions to get the group started in discussion. This lesson on Paul's companions covers over 30 years of Paul's life and ministry. Whether in a home or in a synagogue, on board a ship or walking one of the many Roman highways, each man or woman involved in ministry played a significant part in what God was doing through the apostle Paul **even after** Paul had left that particular place. Continue to encourage each member in the impor-

tance of his or her place in the body of Christ, including his or her insights and input in the discussion time.

Main Objective in Day One: Day One looks at the ministry of John Mark and of Silas alongside the apostle Paul. Check which discussion questions you will use from Day One.

_____ Name one or two principles that you have learned from the life and ministry of John Mark.

_____ How does all that happened to John Mark encourage you in your part in the body of Christ?

_____ What are some principles you have gleaned from the ministry of Silas?

_____ What applications about following God as part of the body of Christ do you see for your life in Day One?

Main Objective in Day Two: In Day Two, we look at the life and work of Titus and Epaphras, two noteworthy companions of Paul. Examine the discussion question list below, and choose one or two that are applicable to your group session.

_____ What are your thoughts concerning the life and ministry of Titus?

_____ We see both struggles and triumphs in the lives and ministries of Paul and Titus. What encouragement can we gain from their testimonies?

_____ What do you learn from Epaphras that can apply to your life?

_____ Seeing the faithfulness of these men in working alongside Paul and on assignment away from him, what practical applications do you see for your own life?

Main Objective in Day Three: In Day Three, we look at the faithful ministry of Aquila and Priscilla. Choose a discussion starter or two from the list below.

_____ We find Aquila and Priscilla in at least three cities, and in each one they were involved in ministering the Word of God. What does this say about where we are or how long we stay in a place?

_____ Aquila and Priscilla had to move from Rome to Corinth because of the decree of Emperor

Claudius. How does this speak to us today about job transfers or "circumstantial" moves?

____ Where has God placed you? What can you learn from Aquila and Priscilla?

____ We know that ministry is received from the Lord, but what are the essential elements in ministry? In other words, what does it take to have a ministry to others? What do you see in the case of Aquila and Priscilla?

Main Objective in Day Four: Day Four looks at Luke, *"the beloved physician"* (Colossians 4:14), and his part in ministry alongside the apostle Paul. Good Day Four discussion questions include . . .

____ Acts 16:10 notes that *"we"* concluded *"that God had called* **us** *to preach the gospel"* in Macedonia (emphasis added). What does this tell you about Luke's part in this ministry team?

____ Knowing what you know about Luke, what does this say to you about your witness or ministry in your field of work?

____ Luke was faithful in service to the Lord where God placed him. How can we encourage one another in the body of Christ to be faithful where God has placed us?

____ Paul considered Luke to be a *"fellow worker"* (Philemon 24). What picture does this give you about Paul and about Luke?

Day Five—Key Points in Application: The most important application point seen in this lesson on Paul's Companions is the part each one can play regardless of his or her place in the body of Christ. Each of us is a servant and can serve where God has placed us. Onesiphorus and Epaphroditus are good examples of those who served God in their place. Check which questions you will use to help focus the applications from Day Five.

____ What are the marks of a servant? What does it mean to have a servant's heart?

____ What does it mean to you when someone **serves you** in some way?

____ What does it mean to you when **you serve** someone else in some way?

____ How important is the mind or attitude of Christ (Philippians 2:5) in fitting where God wants you to fit in the body of Christ?

⌛ CLOSING: 5–10 MINUTES

❑ **Summarize**—Restate the key points the group shared. You may want to reread the "Main Point" statement at the beginning of these leader notes for **Paul's Companions**. Also, ask your group members to share their thoughts about the key applications from Day Five.

❑ **Focus**—Use the memory verse (1 Peter 4:10–11) to focus the group on the fact that each one is gifted to speak or serve in some way and can do so by the power that God supplies. It is His will that all Christians possess at least one spiritual gift. God is pleased and glorified when we use our gifts that he gave to us.

❑ **Remind** your group that the companions of Paul discovered where they fit in the body of Christ and began fulfilling the ministries they received from God.

❑ **Preview**—Take a few moments to preview next week's lesson on **"Timothy: Following Those Who Follow Christ."** Encourage them to do their homework.

❑ **Pray**—Close in prayer.

✂ TOOLS FOR GOOD DISCUSSION 🔨

So, group leaders, how have the first nine weeks of this study been for you? Have you dealt with anyone in your group called **"Agenda Alice"**? She is the type that is focused on a Christian "hot-button" issue instead of the Bible study. If not managed properly, she (or he) will either sidetrack the group from its main study objective, or create a hostile environment in the group if she fails to bring people to her way of thinking. For help with "Agenda Alice," see the "Helpful Hints" section of **How to Lead a Small Group Bible Study** (pp. 7–8).

MEMORY **2 Timothy 2:2** VERSE

"And the things which you have heard from me in the presence of many witnesses, these entrust to faithful men, who will be able to teach others also."

BEFORE THE SESSION

❑ Pray for your group as they walk through this week's lesson.

❑ Spread your study time over the week. Think of this lesson as if it were a large meal. You need time to chew each truth and digest it fully.

❑ Remember to mark those ideas and questions you want to discuss or ask as you go.

❑ To better understand Timothy, you may want to consult a good Bible dictionary.

WHAT TO EXPECT

Probably everyone in your group has heard of Timothy before, yet they may be unfamiliar with many of the details in his life. Recognize that some in your group will be encouraged and challenged by Timothy's humanness. They will be able to identify better with him, perhaps, than with most of the characters we have studied. Be patient. Study diligently in your preparation time. As you progress through the lesson seek to keep the main point the main point. Emphasize what you clearly know and understand. Then you can move on to the things that are not as clear as the Lord gives you time and insight.

> ### THE MAIN POINT
> Everyone needs a mentor, and everyone should become one as well.

DURING THE SESSION

⧗ **OPENING: 5–10 MINUTES**

Opening Prayer—Have one of the group members open the time with prayer.

Opening Illustration—You probably have heard of the ministries of such significant twentieth century leaders as Billy Graham (evangelist), Bill and Vonette Bright (founders of Campus Crusade for Christ), Jim Rayburn (Founder of Young Life), Dawson Trotman (Founder of the Navigators), and Richard Halverson (former chaplain of the U.S. Senate). Each of these, in their own way, has significantly impacted the body of Christ in America and around the world. Their ministries have led countless men and women into the kingdom and have raised up scores of laborers for the fields of the Lord's harvest. But you may not know that the ministry of one woman significantly influenced all these leaders. The teaching ministry of Dr. Henrietta Mears, inspiration and genius of the Sunday school ministry at Hollywood Presbyterian Church during the late

1940's and early '50's, impacted each. Bill Bright credits her for giving him a vision for college students. Billy Graham says, "I doubt if any other woman outside of my wife has had such a marked influence [on my life]." The things she had seen and heard, she entrusted to faithful men and women who in turn taught others. We see this same witness flowing out of Timothy.

⧗ DISCUSSION: 30–40 MINUTES

Once your group gets talking, you will find that all you need to do is keep the group directed and flowing with a question or two or a pointed observation. You are the gatekeeper of discussion. Don't be afraid to ask someone to elaborate further or to ask a quiet member of the group what they think of someone else's comments. Time will not allow you to discuss every single question in the lesson, but you can make it your goal to cover the main ideas of each day and help the group to share what they learned personally. You don't have to use all the discussion questions. They are there for your choosing.

Main Objective in Day One: The main point here is to gain a feel for Timothy's conversion and early faith. We see in him the power of family in shaping values, but we also see the impact of a mentor. Check which discussion questions you will use from Day One.

_____ What kind of impact did Timothy's family have on his faith?

_____ What do you think attracted Paul to Timothy as a potential disciple?

_____ Certainly Timothy had a need to be mentored, but what needs can you see that Timothy met in Paul?

Main Objective in Day Two: In Day Two, we focus on what the Scriptures reveal and suggest of Timothy's character. Decide now which discussion starters you will use for your Day Two study.

_____ What affect do you think being half-Jewish and half-Gentile had on Timothy growing up?

_____ From what you saw in the passages you studied in Day Two, what weaknesses do you see suggested in Timothy?

_____ What stands out to you from the way God chose to use Timothy as a youth?

_____ Can you think of any situations in your own walk with God where you can identify with Timothy?

Main Objective in Day Three: Day Three focuses on God's calling and the sense of purpose in Timothy's life. Check which discussion questions you will use from Day Three.

_____ What do you think is the significance of the "laying on of hands" in Timothy's gifts and calling?

_____ How does that relate to us today?

_____ Can you think of some ways that God can use spiritual leaders today to help us determine our gifts and calling?

Main Objective in Day Four: Day Four looks at how the Lord equipped Timothy to fulfill the calling He had given him. Make sure your group sees the necessity of preparation to fulfill his ministry. Select a discussion question or two from the list below.

_____ What do you think Timothy was learning of ministry in the early days of his travels with Paul?

_____ What does Paul's mentoring of Timothy say about the importance of observing an excellent example?

_____ What kind of feedback do you think Paul gave to Timothy when he sent him on ministry assignments?

_____ What are some other aspects of Paul's training of Timothy?

_____ Did this week's lesson raise any questions for you that weren't answered?

Day Five—Key Points in Application: The most important application point seen in this lesson on Timothy is the difference between just ministering "to" people, and actually having a ministry "through" people. In addition to any discussion ideas that you may have, the following suggested questions may prove useful to your group session.

_____ As you reflect on your own spiritual growth, who have been the "Pauls" in your life who have had the greatest impact on your walk and ministry?

_____ What sort of things did they do with and for you?

_____ Who are the "Timothys" in your life – the people in whom God is calling you to "entrust" what you have "seen and heard" from those who have ministered to you?

_____ How are you going to personally apply this lesson?

⏳ CLOSING: 5–10 MINUTES

❑ **Summarize**—Restate the key points the group shared.

❑ **Ask** those in your group to express their thoughts about the key applications from Day Five.

❑ **Preview**—Take a few moments to preview next week's lesson on **"The Son of Man: Following His Father."**

❑ **Pray**—Close in prayer.

⚒ TOOLS FOR GOOD DISCUSSION ⚒

Well, it is evaluation time again! You may be saying to yourself, "Why bother evaluating at the end? If I did a bad job, it is too late to do anything about it now!" Well, it may be too late to change how you did on this course, but it is never too late to learn from this course what will help you on the next. Howard Hendricks, that peerless communicator from Dallas Theological Seminary, puts it this way: "The good teacher's greatest threat is satisfaction— the failure to keep asking, 'How can I improve?' The greatest threat to your ministry is **your ministry.**" Any self-examination should be an accounting of your own strengths and weaknesses. As you consider your strengths and weaknesses, take some time to read through the evaluation questions listed in the **How to Lead a Small Group Bible Study** section on pages 11–12 of this leader's guide. Make it your aim to continue growing as a discussion leader. Jot down below two or three action points for you to implement in future classes.

ACTION POINTS:

1. _____

_____

2. _____

_____

3. _____

_____

The Son of Man

MEMORY **Matthew 16:24, 27** VERSES

Then Jesus said to His disciples, "If anyone wishes to come after Me, let him deny himself, and take up his cross, and follow Me. . . . for the Son of Man is going to come in the glory of His Father with His angels; and WILL THEN RECOMPENSE EVERY MAN ACCORDING TO HIS DEEDS."

BEFORE THE SESSION

❑ You will certainly need to pray for your group as they walk through this last lesson in *Following God: Life Principles from the New Testament Men of Faith.* Ask the Lord to give clear insight into what the Scripture teaches about the Son of Man. Never underestimate the place of Prayer for yourself and for the members of your group. Pray for each group member by name.

❑ To better see the Son of Man, you may want to look at the lessons that refer to Christ in other Following God studies: **"Adam: Following God's Design"** (Lesson 1) in *Following God: Life Principles from the Old Testament,* **"The True King in Israel: Following the King of Kings"** (Lesson 12) in *Following God: Life Principles from the Kings of the Old Testament,* and **"Christ the Prophet: Worshiping in Spirit and Truth"** (Lesson 12) in *Following God: Life Principles from Prophets of the Old Testament.* You may also want to look in a Bible dictionary for articles on Jesus Christ or on "The Son of Man."

❑ Remember to mark those ideas and questions you want to discuss or ask as you go through the study. Add to those some of the questions listed below.

❑ As an added tool for discussion, you may want to familiarize yourself with the small chart, "Jesus Christ: The Son of Man," at the beginning of Lesson 12 (Workbook p. 171).

❑ Be sensitive to the working of the Spirit in your group meeting, ever watching for ways to help one another truly follow God.

WHAT TO EXPECT

Some in your group will have heard the title "Son of Man" either from studying the Old Testament, particularly Daniel, or from a survey of the Gospels in which Jesus often refers to Himself as "the Son of Man." For others, this will be a new journey into the Scriptures that will lead to a new understanding of Jesus as the Son of Man. Seeing Jesus as the Son of Man and the Son of God, watching Him follow His Father in every detail of life, hearing Him call us to take up our cross and follow Him, and experiencing the reality of Him being a man who can identify with us at every level, will bring each member of your group to a more personal walk with the Lord. Understanding that Jesus is the God-Man, will help your group relate more readily to Jesus in their everyday lives. As you progress through the lesson, seek to keep the main point the main point. You will not be able to answer all the questions about Jesus as the Son of Man. Emphasize what you clearly know and understand. Then you can move on to the things that are not as clear as the Lord gives you time and insight.

> ### THE MAIN POINT
> Studying the "Son of Man" shows us the importance of knowing and following Christ as Lord and Savior.

During the Session

 ### OPENING: 5–10 MINUTES

Opening Prayer—Psalm 119:18 says, *"Open my eyes, that I may behold wonderful things from Thy law."* Ask the Lord to open your eyes as you meet together. Have one of the group members open the time with prayer.

Opening Illustration—"Coming to a theater near you" or "Coming next week" is what we hear when movie and TV producers want to give us a taste of what's coming up. The "trailers" and promotional previews give you just enough of a glimpse to make you want to see the entire movie or show. Of course, the shows are not real life. They are mere stories produced in a Hollywood set—just make-believe. We are living in what is real, and the Scriptures tell us what is real—past, present, and future. The Bible gives us a preview of what will happen when the Son of Man returns in His glory. He wants us to get in on all He is doing now as preparation for all He will do in the future.

He is now preparing us like He prepared the building stones for the Temple. In 1 Kings 6:7 we read, "And the house, while it was being built, was built of stone prepared at the quarry, and there was neither hammer nor axe nor any iron tool heard in the house while it was being built." Now, we are in the quarry, and He is chiseling our lives to fit His future plan. Then, in His Kingdom, we won't hear the sound of His tools. We will be seeing by sight all that we await by faith. What a privilege!!! As you walk through this lesson on the Son of Man, you and the members of your group have a great opportunity to move to a new level of readiness for His return and a new measure of reward when He does return.

Allow this lesson to be something of a training manual as you look for and follow the Son of Man and help others follow Him as well

 ### DISCUSSION: 30–40 MINUTES

Select one or two specific questions to get the group started. This lesson on the Son of Man focuses on His life from Old Testament prophecy, through His birth and earthly ministry, and into His glorious reign. Remember to look for those "velcro" points where members can see something that applies to their own lives. The admonition of Hebrews 12:1-2 cries out to all of us, *". . . let us run with endurance the race that is set before us,* **fixing our eyes on Jesus,** *the author and perfecter of faith. . . ."* As you and your group set your eyes on Christ, looking to Him as the Son of Man, you can experience a greater endurance in the race and a deeper joy in looking forward to His return and His eternal reign.

Main Objective in Day One: In Day One, the main objective is to see Jesus as the prophesied Son of Man who walked about declaring Himself to be the Son of Man and calling men and women to follow Him. Check which discussion questions you will use from Day One.

_____ Nathaniel and some of the other disciples saw Jesus as the Son of Man, the Messiah, the King who would rule Israel, and their perception gave them great hope for the future. What hope does Jesus, the Son of Man, give you?

_____ How have you found Jesus to be a ladder (staircase) or bridge connecting heaven to earth?

_____ Seeing Jesus as Lord and Savior comes by the revelation and conviction of His Spirit. How does this apply as we witness to others about Jesus as the Way to Heaven?

Main Objective in Day Two: In Day Two, the main objective is to see how the Son of Man came to die in our place. Place a checkmark next to the discussion questions that are appealing to you. Or you may want to rank each suggested question in preferential order.

_____ Jesus came as the Son of Man to seek and save the lost (you and me). What does this tell you about His heart toward you?

_____ Think of the picture of Moses lifting up the serpent in the wilderness for the healing of the people and how it portrays the Son of Man. What insights do you see in this picture?

_____ What does it mean to you that Jesus as the Son of Man fully understands everything you have ever been through, ever done, ever thought, or ever will do or think or go through?

Main Objective in Day Three: Day Three focuses on Jesus' call to us to take up our crosses daily and follow Him. Below are some discussion question ideas that may enhance your group session.

_____ What significant truth do you see in the picture of the grain of wheat falling into the ground and dying? Why does it matter what happens to the grain of wheat?

_____ What are some of the things we gain in giving our lives to Jesus—now and eternally?

_____ Thinking of what Jesus said about serving or _"lording it over"_ others (Mark 10:42; Luke 22:25), what reasons do you see for becoming a servant to others?

Main Objective in Day Four: Day Four looks at the glory of the Son of Man both during His walk with the disciples and the glory that is to be revealed at His coming. Check which discussion questions you will use from Day Four.

_____ What do you think it would have been like to have been on the Mount and seen Jesus' transfiguration and all that went on that day?

_____ Having a preview of what is to come and knowing something about the rewards that await those who faithfully follow Jesus, what applications do you see for your life?

_____ How can you help others to prepare for the return of the Son of Man? How should you encourage them to get ready?

Day Five—Key Points in Application: The most important application point seen in our study of The Son of Man is that we should now live in light of eternity and the imminent return of the Son of Man. Check which discussion questions you will use to help focus the applications from Day Five.

_____ What has this lesson on the Son of Man said to you about your walk now? How is your relationship with the Lord?

_____ How can you help others in their walk and better prepare them for the return of the Son of Man?

_____ As was mentioned in the opening illustration, the Lord is building us (as at the Temple—1 Kings 6:7) and we are joining in the building process (1 Corinthians 3:9–15). How can your daily surrender to the Son of Man and His Word help in this building process?

 **CLOSING: 5–10 MINUTES**

❑ **Summarize**—Restate the key points the group shared. Review the Main Objectives for each of the days found in these leader notes).

❑ **Ask** your group members to share their thoughts about the key applications from Day Five.

❑ **Pray**—Close your time in prayer thanking the Lord for the journey in which He has led you over the past 12 weeks.

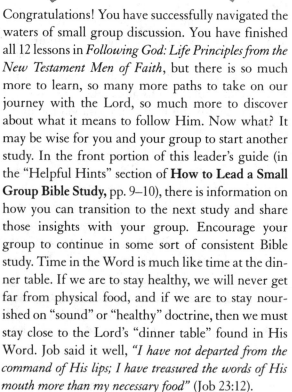

Tools for Good Discussion

Congratulations! You have successfully navigated the waters of small group discussion. You have finished all 12 lessons in _Following God: Life Principles from the New Testament Men of Faith_, but there is so much more to learn, so many more paths to take on our journey with the Lord, so much more to discover about what it means to follow Him. Now what? It may be wise for you and your group to start another study. In the front portion of this leader's guide (in the "Helpful Hints" section of **How to Lead a Small Group Bible Study,** pp. 9–10), there is information on how you can transition to the next study and share those insights with your group. Encourage your group to continue in some sort of consistent Bible study. Time in the Word is much like time at the dinner table. If we are to stay healthy, we will never get far from physical food, and if we are to stay nourished on "sound" or "healthy" doctrine, then we must stay close to the Lord's "dinner table" found in His Word. Job said it well, _"I have not departed from the command of His lips; I have treasured the words of His mouth more than my necessary food"_ (Job 23:12).